Land Bargains and Chinese Capitalism

The Politics of Property Rights under Reform

Land reforms have been critical to the development of Chinese capitalism over the last several decades, yet land in China remains publicly owned. This book explores the political logic of reforms to landownership and control, accounting for how land development and real estate have become synonymous with economic growth and prosperity in China. Drawing on extensive fieldwork and archival research, the book tracks land reforms and urban development at the national level and in three cities in a single Chinese region. The study reveals that the initial liberalization of land was reversed after China's first contemporary real estate bubble in the early 1990s and that property rights arrangements at the local level varied widely according to different local strategies for economic prosperity and political stability. In particular, the author links fiscal relations and economic bases to property rights regimes, finding that more "open" cities are subject to greater state control over land.

MEG E. RITHMIRE earned her Ph.D. in Government from Harvard in 2011 and joined the faculty of Harvard Business School as an Assistant Professor in the Business, Government, and International Economy Unit, where she primarily teaches political economy. She was a Fulbright Scholar in China in 2007–8.

Advance Praise for *Land Bargains and Chinese Capitalism*

"China's remarkable development in the last two decades has taken place in ways that notoriously confound many Western assumptions about the way that states, markets, and intermediate institutions should relate to one another to produce growth. As Meg Rithmire shows in this fascinating and remarkably well-researched book, an especially important yet utterly counterintuitive area in the political economy of Chinese development has been the problem of property rights, where, despite the fact that the state officially owns all land, enormous, vital, and innovative markets for its use have grown up all over the country. Rithmire's book lays out the historical peculiarity and broad political and economic significance of landed property governance in China's transformation since the 1980s. Her general argument for the whole of China is then contextually fleshed out with three detailed studies of property politics in the northern cities of Dalian, Harbin, and Changchun. Anyone wanting to understand the dynamics of growth in contemporary China, or, indeed, anyone interested in shaking up their deepest assumptions about what is possible in the development process, will benefit greatly by consulting this rich and informative book."

Gary Herrigel,
University of Chicago

"Rithmire's work tackles the most important socioeconomic–political phenomenon in contemporary China: urban transformation. She combines careful conceptualization and detailed case studies to explain patterns of urban changes that have impacted the lives of hundreds of millions of people. Through a mix of careful documentary research and in-depth interviews, Rithmire offers convincing and engrossing historical institutional accounts of urban transformation in some of China's most important cities. For any student of contemporary China, this is a must-read."

Victor Shih,
School of International Relations and Pacific Studies,
University of California, San Diego

Land Bargains and Chinese Capitalism

The Politics of Property Rights under Reform

MEG E. RITHMIRE
Harvard Business School

CAMBRIDGE
UNIVERSITY PRESS

CAMBRIDGE
UNIVERSITY PRESS

Shaftesbury Road, Cambridge CB2 8EA, United Kingdom

One Liberty Plaza, 20th Floor, New York, NY 10006, USA

477 Williamstown Road, Port Melbourne, VIC 3207, Australia

314–321, 3rd Floor, Plot 3, Splendor Forum, Jasola District Centre, New Delhi – 110025, India

103 Penang Road, #05–06/07, Visioncrest Commercial, Singapore 238467

Cambridge University Press is part of Cambridge University Press & Assessment, a department of the University of Cambridge.

We share the University's mission to contribute to society through the pursuit of education, learning and research at the highest international levels of excellence.

www.cambridge.org
Information on this title: www.cambridge.org/9781107539877

© Meg E. Rithmire 2015

First published 2015

A catalogue record for this publication is available from the British Library

Library of Congress Cataloging-in-Publication data
Rithmire, Meg E., 1982–
Land bargains and Chinese capitalism : the politics of property rights under reform / Meg E. Rithmire.
     pages   cm
Includes bibliographical references and index.
ISBN 978-1-107-11730-3 (Hardback) – ISBN 978-1-107-53987-7 (Paperback)
 1. Land reform–China.   2. Land use, Rural–China.   3. Right of property–China.   I. Title.
HD1333.C6R58 2015
333.3´151–dc23   2015014003

ISBN   978-1-107-11730-3   Hardback
ISBN   978-1-107-53987-7   Paperback

For my parents, Maxine Rithmire and Jack Bertram

Contents

Tables

Figures

Acknowledgments

I – and certainly the readers of this book – have benefited from a tremendous amount of help and support in the process of research, writing, and rewriting. The book began as my Ph.D. dissertation at the Harvard Department of Government in 2007. First and foremost, I would like to express thanks and admiration for my thesis committee. Elizabeth Perry is the kind of mentor that young scholars dream of working with. Her sharp eye and tireless logistical and intellectual support are behind almost every good idea and good piece of research in this book. I hope that the work I do throughout a career can serve as an appropriate testament to the training I received under her direction. Tim Colton has been a kind and honest mentor, available to answer questions large and likely irritatingly small. Alan Altshuler contributed to this project and to my growth in measures that far exceeded his duty. All three of these teachers, scholars, and mentors were incredibly available to me and critical without being discouraging. I have been fortunate to enjoy their support also as the thesis became this book. My interest in politics and political science was kindled during my time as an undergraduate at Emory University. Rick Doner, Dani Reiter, Tom Remington, Paul Talcott, and Carrie Rosefsky Wickham were and continue to be generous mentors and inspiring scholars.

Twenty-two months of fieldwork in Northern China and Beijing between 2007 and 2009 were supported by the Fulbright Fellowship, the Harvard Real Estate Academic Initiative, the Chinese Ministry of Education, the Weatherhead Center for International Affairs, and the Harvard Project on Justice, Welfare, and Economics. I am grateful to CET Harbin for logistical help in the field and including me in their *danwei*. I could not possibly thank everyone in China who helped with the research. I appreciate institutional support from the Harbin Institute of Technology and especially the Urban Planning Institute, Dalian Ligong University, Jilin University, and the Chinese Academic of Social Sciences, specifically the Center for Urban and Environmental Studies under the direction of Pan Jiahua. I am incredibly grateful to Xu Suning, Yu Dabo, Liu Shengjun, and Du Lizhi in Harbin; Kong Yuhang and Lü Yi in Dalian; Ma Xin in Changchun; and Zhu Shouxian, Wang Mou, and Tao Ran in Beijing. Alex Tian Yu and "Happier" Hai Peng provided helpful research assistance in Harbin and Beijing. Harvard Business School made return trips in 2012 and 2013 possible.

I am grateful to many graduate school peers, including Masha Hedberg, Elina Treyger, Lili Sussman, Didi Kuo, Alex Liebman, Jason Lakin, Allison Post, Brad Holland, and the others who took time to read and comment on my work. Andy Harris, Phil Jones, and Sean McGraw continue to be inspiring colleagues and friends. Also in graduate school, I appreciated the intellectual guidance and professional development advice of Nara Dillon, Steve Levitsky, Daniel Ziblatt, Rod MacFarquhar, Nahomi Ichino, Susan Pharr, Prerna Singh, Marty Whyte, Nancy Rosenblum, and especially Jorge Dominguez. Special credit is due to my "comrades," fellow travelers in the journey to understand the world of China. Nick Smith, Miriam Kingsberg, and Chris Ross kept me sane and curious during field research; Li Hou, Kyle Jaros, Jennifer Pan, and Rachel Stern have read my work and generously shared the joys and frustration of studying China; Kristen Looney and Jonas Nahm have been supportive through the production of this book and many other things.

A great many scholars commented on the ideas and research in the book as it evolved from thesis through various manuscript drafts: Michael Bernhard, Rafael DiTella, Rick Doner, Catherine Duggan, Amy Glasmeier, Sebastian Heilmann, Yu-hung Hong, You-Tien Hsing, Lakshmi Iyer, Peter Katzenstein, Akshay Mangla, Kelly McMann, Sophus Reinert, Elizabeth Remick, Tom Remington, Julio Rotemberg, Tony Saich, Jeffrey Sellers, Victor Shih, Vivienne Shue, Terry Sicular, Richard Stren, Fubing Su, Gunnar Trumbull, Matt Weinzierl, Eric Werker, and Weiping Wu. Several brave and patient people read the entire manuscript and provided feedback. Susan Whiting, Peter Hall, Gary Herrigel, Rawi Abdelal, Yoi Herrera, Kristen Looney, and Jonas Nahm attended a book workshop supported by Harvard's Weatherhead Center for International Affairs. The workshop was among the most difficult and rewarding experiences of my career. Dorothy Solinger read the entire manuscript several times, and the final result is much improved because of it. I am especially indebted to Rawi Abdelal, who has read more than his fair share of my work and, more than anyone, helped me come into my own voice, and also to Veronica Herrera, who came along right when I needed her most and supported me in ways far exceeding her duties. Nancy Hearst lent her considerable skills as a librarian, editor, and friend over the years. I was incredibly fortunate to find Kait Szydlowski, who provided valuable research assistance in the production of the book. Anonymous reviewers for both Cambridge and Oxford University Presses immeasurably improved the manuscript by providing careful and constructive criticism. Many of these people prevented me from making an untold number of mistakes and errors in judgment but certainly are not responsible for ones that remain.

Figures

Tables

My family has been patient and supportive in ways that reach far beyond what those adjectives can convey. My husband and best friend, Dave Hampton, has a sharp mind and a wonderful heart. Thank you for our life, your love, and our beautiful son, whose arrival was an excellent deadline. My sister, Jill Bolduc, has shared a life with me in a different way and has been supportive all along. My father, Jack Bertram, has always believed in me and follows my pursuits with the zeal of a sports fan. My mother, Maxine Rithmire, gave me everything I have and everything I need. My greatest fortune is to have been raised by a strong, independent woman; I know many more books will be required to make it all worth her while.

Meg E. Rithmire
Boston, Massachusetts

Abbreviations

BLPM	Bureau of Land Planning Management
CCP	Chinese Communist Party
CNR	China National Rail Corporation Ltd.
DDA	Dalian Development Area
DRC	Development Research Center of the State Council
ETDZ	Economic and Technology Development Zone
FAI	fixed-asset investment
FAW	First Automobile Works
FIE	foreign-invested enterprise
FDI	foreign direct investment
FYP	five-year plan
GRP	regional GDP
GVIO	GDP and industrial output
HMA	Heilongjiang Municipal Archives
KMT	Guomindang
LMB	Land Management Bureau
MBIC	Municipal Bureau of Industry and Commerce
MLR	Ministry of Land Resources
MoC	Ministry of Construction
NBS	National Bureau of Statistics
NDRC	National Development and Reform Commission
NIE	new institutional economics
PBoC	People's Bank of China
PLA	People's Liberation Army
PRC	People's Republic of China
PSB	Public Security Bureau
REB	Real Estate Bureau
SEZ	special economic zone

SOE	state-owned enterprise
SPC	State Planning Commission
TVE	township and village enterprise
UPB	Urban Planning Bureau

Glossary

banqian 搬迁	relocation
baoshuiqu 保税区	tax-free zone
beifang Xianggang 北方香港	make Dalian the "Hong Kong of the North"
chai 拆	demolition
chaiqian banqian 拆迁搬迁	demolition and relocation
Chengshi guihuaju, 城市规;划局	Urban Planning Bureau
churang 出让	paid transfer, land conveyance
difangzhi 地方志	gazetteer
dingzihu 钉子户	"nail house"
dongbei 东北	the Northeast
gaige kaifang 改革开放	reform and opening
gao xinqu 高新区	high-tech new zone
gaokaiqu 高开区	high-tech park
geti 个体	private
geti hu 个体户	individual laborers
guihua 规划	land-use plan
huafa 划发	administrative allocation
hukou 户口	urban citizenship
jiedao 街道	neighborhood
jiedao banshichu 街道办事处	street office
jihua 计划	[economic] plan
jihua danlie chengshi 计划单列城市	central economic city
jingji tequ 经济特区	special economic zone
jingji zhufang 经济住房	economic housing
kaifaqu 开发区	smaller development zone within a city
lao gongye jidi 老工业基地	"old industrial base"

xvi

liudong renkou 流动人口	floating population
nianjian 年检	yearbook
paimai 拍卖	auction
penghu 棚户	slum
penghuqu 棚户区	shanty town
shangpinhua 商品化	commodification
shiqu 市区	urban district
suoyouquan 所有权	ownership
tudi caizheng 土地财政	fiscalization
xiaoqu 小区	residential neighborhood, apartment community
xieyi 协议	negotiation
xinfang shangfang 信访上访	letters and visits
weifang 危房	slum
yanhai kaifang chengshi 沿海开放城市	coastal open city
yi digai cu qigai 以地改促企改	use land reform to encourage enterprise reforms
yitu shengcai 以土生财	make money by developing land
yiqi 一汽	First Automobile Works
youxian gongsi 有限公司	limited liability company
yusuannei shouru 预算内收入	budgetary revenues
yusuanwai shouru 预算外收入	extrabudgetary revenues
zhaobiao 招标	bid invitation
zhengyong 征用	state acquisition
zhenxing Ha'erbin 振兴哈尔滨	"rejuvenate Harbin"
zhuada fangxiao 抓大放小	grasp the large and release the small

I

Property and Politics in China

If the land problem can be solved, one half of the problem of livelihood will be solved.

Sun Yatsen (1924)[1]

Whoever wins the peasants will win China. Whoever solves the land problem will win the peasants.

Mao Zedong (1936)[2]

INTRODUCTION

The vast majority of political and economic change in China during the past century can be understood as a series of land reforms. As the preceding epigraphs from two of the most recognizable twentieth-century political figures indicate, power to make rules about who controls land is at the heart of political contestation in China. Mao Zedong and the Chinese Communist Party (CCP) assumed their positions at the helm in 1949 after decades of rural insurgence, occupying parts of the countryside and then carrying out land reforms that redistributed land to peasants in an effort to win political support and to foment class struggle as the primary axis of conflict in Chinese society. Largely for the same reasons, national implementation of land reform was the paramount task of the new regime once in power.[3] Thirty years later, approval of another land reform – decollectivization – once again signaled a sea change in Chinese politics. The land reform that generated the resumption of family

[1] Sun Yatsen, *Three Principles of the People* (Taipei: China Publishing Company, 1964), 179.
[2] Quoted in Edgar Snow, *Red Star over China* (New York: Grove Press, 1961), 70.
[3] Vivienne Shue, *Peasant China in Transition: The Dynamics of Development toward Socialism, 1949–1956* (Berkeley: University of California Press, 1980).

farming in the 1970s and early 1980s introduced markets in goods and labor in rural China, setting the stage for reforms that would transform the country from a planned economy to an economy characterized by "socialism with market characteristics."

This book is about another land reform, and one that is currently far less understood: the commodification of land that began in the 1980s. According to Article 10 of the Constitution of the People's Republic of China (PRC), all urban land is owned by the state *guoyou*, (国有) and all rural land is owned by the collective (*jiti*, 集体).[4] Prior to 1986, land-use rights were allocated by urban or village governments to state units or farmers essentially free of charge. In 1988, however, a revision to the Land Management Law separated ownership rights from use rights, permitting landowners to lease land-use rights for fixed terms in exchange for capital in the form of land-use fees.[5] For the first time in PRC history land markets of some kind were legal in both rural and urban China.

Land and real-estate investment and development have become indispensable to Chinese economic growth in the years since 1988, yet Chinese property rights institutions bear no resemblance to the types of institutions lauded by Western social scientists and policy-makers as requisite for growth. Though capital and labor have mostly been privatized, land in urban China is still owned by the state and land in rural China is owned by the collectives. Despite the seeming stasis of national-level formal property rights institutions, the informal rules governing property and land development have been subject to intense political negotiation both at the lower levels of the Chinese state and at the center. In this book I examine property rights practices as they emerged during the process of the economic reforms undertaken since the 1980s in urban China.

In political science and related fields, most studies of the emergence of property rights examine the national level over the *longue durée*. As such, these studies focus primarily on how changes in property rights institutions produce changes in economic and political behavior at the very macrolevels. Typically, these studies are narratives about the centrality of property rights institutions in the emergence of "modern" forms of economic and political organization,

[4] The "collective" generally refers to the unit of organization in Chinese villages during the Maoist era. Decision making in rural China was concentrated in village teams, which were generally based on "natural villages" as they existed prior to 1949, and on "administrative villages," a group of teams united in a production brigade during the Maoist era. In general, since the 1990s the administrative village, typically referred to as the "village," makes decisions about land allocations. See You-tien Hsing, *The Great Urban Transformation: Politics of Land and Property in China* (Oxford: Oxford University Press, 2010), 134, 148n26, n27; Qin Hui, *Nongmin Zhongguo: Lishi fansi yu xianshi xuanze* (Peasant China: Historical Reflections and Practical Choices) (Zhengzhou: Henan renmin chubanshe, 2003).
[5] On the mechanics of land allocations and transfers before and after the 1986 law, see Samuel P. S. Ho and George C. S. Lin, "Emerging Land Markets in Rural and Urban China: Policies and Practices," *The China Quarterly* no. 175 (2003): 681–707.

that is, capitalism and democracy, or the lack thereof.[6] Yet, in China, and indeed in much of the developing and postsocialist world, the politics of property rights are intensely local and vary within the same nation-state and, at times, even within the same city or region.[7] How do we explain the emergence of different subnational rules and practices of property rights even within the same institutional system? Similarly, how are these practices sustained in the face of national efforts to unify the rules governing property rights?

In explaining the emergence of land politics in urban China since the 1980s, this book offers a new perspective on the politics of property rights during times of transition – one that sees property rights as political bargains struck between local state actors and groups in society under conditions of uncertainty. Even in an authoritarian regime with state ownership of urban land, state actors distribute property rights as political resources to ensure compliance with economic reforms and to maintain social stability.[8] In cities in China where reforms were comparatively easy to implement, local governments designed property rights regimes to maximize their own accumulation of capital. However, where reforms were difficult and other resources were limited, local governments designed property rights regimes to placate potential losers from the reforms and to provide capital accumulation opportunities for groups outside the state. Such political bargains were struck early during the reform

---

[6] Douglass C. North and Robert Paul Thomas, *The Rise of the Western World: A New Economic History* (Cambridge: Cambridge University Press, 1973); Douglass C. North, John Joseph Wallis, and Barry R. Weingast, *Violence and Social Orders: A Conceptual Framework for Interpreting Recorded Human History* (Cambridge: Cambridge University Press, 2009); Douglass C. North and Barry R. Weingast, "Constitutions and Commitment: The Evolution of Institutions Governing Public Choice in 17th-Century England," *Journal of Economic History* 49, no. 4 (1989): 803–32. Barrington Moore Jr., *Social Origins of Dictatorship and Democracy: Lord and Peasant in the Making of the Modern World* (Boston: Beacon Press, 1966). Exceptions include Tomas Larsson, *Land and Loyalty: Security and the Development of Property Rights in Thailand* (Ithaca, NY: Cornell University Press, 2012); Susan H. Whiting, *Power and Wealth in Rural China: The Political Economy of Institutional Change* (Cambridge: Cambridge University Press, 2001); Stephen H. Haber, Noel Maurer, and Armando Razo, *The Politics of Property Rights: Political Instability, Credible Commitments, and Economic Growth in Mexico, 1876–1929* (Cambridge: Cambridge University Press, 2003): Gary D. Libecap, *Contracting for Property Rights* (Cambridge: Cambridge University Press, 1989).

[7] For example, on variations in African land rights, see Catherine Boone, *Property and Political Order in Africa: Land Rights and the Structure of Politics* (Cambridge: Cambridge University Press, 2014).

[8] Political scientists have made similar arguments about the strategic use of land and property rights in other contexts. Catherine Boone argues that land is deployed as a patronage resource in electoral strategies in sub-Saharan democracies. David Collier and, more recently, Alisha Holland make similar arguments about the use of land and informal property rights as a form of redistribution in Latin America. Catherine Boone, "Electoral Populism Where Property Rights Are Weak: Land Politics in Contemporary Sub-Saharan Africa," *Comparative Politics* 41, no. 2 (January 2009): 183–201; Alisha C. Holland, "The Distributive Politics of Enforcement," *American Journal of Political Science*, 59, no. 2 (April 2015): 357–371. David Collier, *Squatters and Oligarchs: Authoritarian Rule and Policy Change in Peru* (Baltimore: Johns Hopkins University Press, 1976).

era as urban officials sought to dismantle socialism and build capitalism, and they were accompanied by moral narratives that attempted to generate legitimacy for the new property rights arrangements. Later in the reform era, as land became central to local government revenue, local officials attempted to override the bargains, but they were constrained by these "moral entitlements." Understanding property rights as bargains with both political and moral content explains why property rights regimes vary subnationally and why specific regimes endure despite concerted pressures for change.

The empirical contribution of the book concerns the centrality of property rights to China's economic development strategy at both the national and local levels. The control of land – at every level of the administrative hierarchy – has been fundamental to the construction and execution of strategies for reform and development. The argument I make, however, is very different from the classic social science idea that the forms of property rights determine investment and growth outcomes. In China land control did not determine the pursuit of wealth or vice versa. Rather, urban governments, as well as the national government in Beijing, experimented with land markets and systems of property rights at the same time that they were fashioning plans to dismantle socialism and to build markets.

At the local level, cities were home to different constellations of political power as they navigated both property markets and development and reform agendas. Property rights were deployed as political and economic resources, figuring prominently in various groups' efforts to accumulate capital as well as local governments' strategies for political inclusion and appeasement. Specifically, the staging and sequencing of reforms to the public sector and the opening to foreign capital – undertaken early in some cities and later in others – afforded local governments different incentives and constraints with regard to urban land and property markets. In cities that opened to foreign capital before or while they were undertaking state-sector reforms – essentially building capitalism before dismantling socialism – local governments were able to extend authority over urban land as part of their reform strategies. But in cities that built capitalism at the same time they dismantled socialism (undertaking state-sector reforms before they had access to global capital), urban land control was ceded to non- and semistate actors, such as state firms, laid-off workers, and the emerging private sector, thus eroding the power of local governments over land. The sequencing of the reform efforts, combined with the structure of the local economy and the mediating role of socialist legacies, led to different systems for managing property rights over land, which I call "property rights regimes." These regimes, and reform efforts more generally, emerged in tandem with new moral narratives to justify them. Property rights became both moral and material entitlements, setting the stage for the intractable political conflicts that ensued when entitlements were threatened.

At the national level, the creation of land and property markets required a dramatic change in how land was considered a resource in China. During the

1980s and 1990s, land changed from being a resource whose primary value was in its use for production to a resource with exchange value – in other words, one that could become capital. National institutions governing land control and property rights changed drastically as central officials experimented with policies and made judgments about the risks and rewards that would accompany land markets and the real estate sector. I find that the direction of this reform has not been the one that many assumed or predicted, that is, that land markets would gradually liberalize and property rights would become more secure, thereby becoming private over time. On the contrary, land markets were far more liberal and subject to far less state dominance and interference during their first decade than they have been ever since.[9] In addition to explaining the variation in land control regimes at the subnational level, I examine how and why the nature and importance of land control have been reconsidered and dramatically reorganized by the central government in the course of the reforms. Property rights institutions at the national level have also been the products of political bargains made under conditions of uncertainty.

Later in this chapter, I more fully conceptualize property rights regimes, the dependent variable in this study, and elaborate on the book's explanation of the emergence of and variation in these regimes. The chapter also introduces the empirical context: the puzzle of subnational variations within a single region of China. But first, I situate the problem of land politics and property rights in the context of Chinese politics since the onset of the market reforms.

LAND, PROPERTY RIGHTS, AND CHINA

Land control has emerged as the most contentious and important economic and political issue in contemporary China. In urban China, the demolition and relocation of urban residents have constituted an incendiary flash point for state–society conflict. International media and scholarly attention have increasingly focused on the dislocations that have resulted from grand projects of urban renewal and transformation.[10] The phenomenon of "nail houses" (*dingzihu*, 钉子户), residences in the middle of vast construction projects whose occupants refuse to leave, is endemic in almost every Chinese city.[11] The

---

[9] This finding accords with Huang Yasheng's arguments about the direction of reforms in the private sector in the 1980s versus those in the 1990s. See Yasheng Huang, *Capitalism with Chinese Characteristics: Entrepreneurship and the State* (Cambridge: Cambridge University Press, 2008).

[10] On Beijing, see Yue Zhang, "Steering towards Growth: Symbolic Urban Preservation in Beijing, 1990–2005," *Town Planning Review* 79, nos. 2–3 (2008): 187–208. On Shanghai, see Qin Shao, "Waving the Red Flag: Cultural Memory and Grassroots Protest in Housing Disputes in China," *Modern Chinese Literature and Culture* 22, no. 1 (Spring 2010): 197–232.

[11] The most famous "nail house" is that of Yang Wu and Wu Ping, in Chongqing City. See Howard French, "In China, Fight over Development Creates a Star," *New York Times*, March 26, 2007,

scramble for rural land has constituted an equally visible flash point for antag-
onism between peasants and local governments. China's preeminent sociolo-
gist, Yu Jianrong, has argued that contestation over land rights has replaced
that over rural taxes and fees as the primary axis of state–society conflict in
rural China.[12] Chinese academics estimate that as many as sixty million peasants have lost their land since the early 1990s. Scholars have argued that if the
trends persist at present speeds, China will be home to 110 million landless
peasants as a result of the conversion of land from agriculture to construction
by 2030.[13] Sixty percent of peasants who file complaints (*shangfang*, 上访)
with higher-level governments do so over lost land, most of which is lost as a
result of state acquisition (*zhengyong*, 征用).[14] The process of land conversion
is extraordinarily contentious, and often violent. Chinese journals frequently
report beatings, assaults, incinerations, and mass brawls among peasants and
local leaders over land disputes.[15] In December 2011, villagers in the town of
Wukan, in southeastern Guangdong province, mounted an extraordinarily

at www.nytimes.com/2007/03/26/world/asia/26cnd-china.html, accessed January 26, 2015. See
also Kent Ewing, "The Coolest Nail House in History," *Asia Times*, March 31, 2007, and
Andrew C. Mertha, "From 'Rustless Screws' to 'Nail Houses': The Evolution of Property Rights
in China," *Orbis* 53, no. 2 (2009): 233–49.

[12] Yu Jianrong, "Dangqian Zhongguo quntixing shijian de zhuyao leixing jiqi jiben tezheng"
(Major Types and Basic Characteristics of Mass Incidents in Today's China), *Zhongguo zhengfa
daxue xuebao* (Journal of China University of Political Science and Law) no. 6 (2009): 114–20.
One of the reasons that land conflicts displaced tax conflicts is the abolition of the agricultural
tax in 2006, which I discuss later and in Chapter 6.

[13] Song Binwen et al., cited in Sally Sargeson, "Villains, Victims and Aspiring Proprietors: Framing
'Land-Losing Villagers' in China's Strategies of Accumulation," *Journal of Contemporary China*
21, no. 77 (2012): 764. On the number of landless peasants, see also Liu Shouying and Ulich
Schmitt, "China's Urbanization and Land: A Framework for Reform," in *Urban China: Toward
Efficient, Inclusive, and Sustainable Urbanization*, ed. World Bank and Development Research
Center of the State Council of the PRC (Washington, DC: World Bank Group, 2014), 163–336.

[14] Lu Ying, "Chengshihua zuizhong shenghuo anzhi wenti de kaolü" (Reflections on the Problem
of Allocating Support to Peasants Rendered Landless During Urbanization), *Nongye jingji*
(Agricultural Economics), no. 6 (2006): 56–7.

[15] Examples of the dramatic escalation of these disputes abound in the Chinese press. One of the
most famous is the Longnan incident, during which petitions to the local government from thirty
people whose homes had been demolished evolved into riots involving thousands of people and
at least seventy casualties. See Ma Jiuqi, "Gansu Longnan shijian: Baoli xu qianze, siwei xu
geming," *Nanfang baowang*, November 19, 2008, at www.nfdaily.cn/opinion/opinionlist/con
tent/2008-11/19/content_4714177.htm, accessed January 26, 2015. In 2004, villagers in Hunan,
led by farmer Tang Fei, opened fire on local authorities after protesting against land seizures and
being beaten by cadres. Some reports state there were more than twenty deaths. In June 2005, a
cadre in Yuhuazhaimoujia village, under the administration of Xi'an city, sold land without the
villagers' permission, culminating in a massive brawl that resulted in eleven serious injuries.
These are but a few examples. Reportedly, in 2004, of the 130 collective actions organized by
villagers, 87 (66.9 percent) involved land seizures. Yang Liu, "Jingti tudi jiufen baolihua
miaotou" (Guarding against a Trend of Land Dispute Violence), *Liaowang xinwen zhoukan*
(*Outlook News Weekly*) no. 29 (July 2005): 32–33.

dramatic protest over the sale of collective land to a real-estate developer. Angered over their meager compensation and their loss of farmland, the villagers eventually took physical control of the village and forced the dismissal of the party leadership. The protests culminated in a siege of the village that lasted ten days, ending only when the provincial leaders acknowledged corruption and promised the fair redistribution of land.[16]

According to the PRC Constitution, land is legally owned by the state in urban areas and by the collective in rural areas. However, a determination of the actors in each category is problematic. From 1949 to 1980, most urban citizens were organized in work units associated with public enterprises, and the business of collective production and consumption was governed by a centralized command economy. As a result, specifying who exactly speaks for the "state" in any given urban center was not a simple task. During the early period of land commodification, described in the empirical chapters that follow, ambiguity about who represents the "state" as the owner of urban land opened space for local political battles over land control.

As detailed in Chapter 2, in the 1990s local governments emerged as the most powerful claimants to landownership, meaning that local governments (municipal- or district-level governments) typically had the right to lease use rights for land and to claim the revenues (see Figure 1.1 for an outline of China's land rights system). Land-lease revenues, for lease terms that varied depending on the type of land use, were paid in lump sums at the beginning of the term of the lease. Since the mid-1990s, local governments have become increasingly dependent on land lease revenues to meet budgetary obligations, leading the Ministry of Land Resources (MLR), which oversees land policy, to impose limits on the conversion of farmland and to attempt to slow real-estate development within cities.[17] In 2007, galvanized by fears of food insecurity and diminishing land for cultivation, the MLR adopted what it called its "toughest" policy to preserve farmland: a strict quota program by which each subnational jurisdiction is assigned an amount of arable land that cannot be decreased and an annual amount of rural land that may be converted for urban construction. The quota program has spawned a cottage industry of programs to maximize available land for lease and construction while preserving the required amount of farmland. Innovations run the gamut from establishing land exchanges by which rural dwellers exchange their homestead land for urban citizenship (*hukou*, 户口) to trading or exchanging land development rights between jurisdictions to move peasants forcibly into concentrated, high-rise housing so

---

[16] Michael Wines, "A Village in Revolt Could Be a Harbinger for China," *New York Times*, December 26, 2011, at www.nytimes.com/2011/12/26/world/asia/in-china-the-wukan-revolt-could-be-a-harbinger.html?pagewanted=all&_r=0, accessed January 26, 2015.

[17] See Susan H. Whiting, "Fiscal Reform and Land Public Finance: Zouping County in National Context," in *China's Local Public Finance in Transition*, ed. Joyce Yanyun Man and Yu-Hung Hong (Cambridge, MA: Lincoln Institute of Land Policy, 2011), 125–44.

Land-Use Rights Leasehold System:

- - 40-year term for commercial land
- - 50-year term for industrial land
- - 70-year term for residential land

Land-lease revenues paid for the entire term at the beginning of the lease

Methods of Transferring Land-Use Rights:

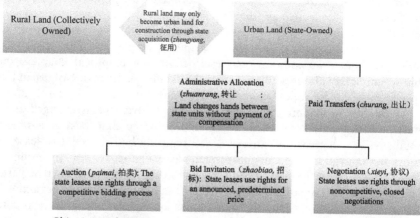

FIGURE 1.1. China's Land System

as to maximize the amount of arable land.[18] Nonetheless, survey and land cadastral satellite data suggest that local governments and villagers both continue to encroach on the land for cultivation.[19]

Social scientists have long considered clear and enforceable property rights to be a necessary condition for sound economic growth and development.[20]

---

[18] Hui Wang et al., "Farmland Preservation and Land Development Rights Trading in Zhejiang, China," *Habitat International* 34, no. 4 (2010): 454–63; Meina Cai, "Land-Locked Development: The Local Political Economy of Institutional Change in China" (PhD diss., University of Wisconsin, Madison, 2012); Kristen E. Looney, "The Rural Developmental State: Modernization Campaigns and Peasant Politics in China, Taiwan and South Korea" (PhD diss., Harvard University, 2012).

[19] Hui Wang et al., "Rural Residential Properties in China: Land Use Patterns, Efficiency and Prospects for Reform," *Habitat International* 36, no. 2 (2012): 201–9.

[20] North and Thomas state this most famously and forcefully in their explanation of the economic rise of the Western world: "Efficient economic organization is the key to growth; the development of an efficient economic organization in Western Europe accounts for the rise of the West. Efficient organization entails the establishment of institutional arrangements and property rights." North and Thomas, *The Rise of the Western World*, 1. See also North and Weingast, "Constitutions and Commitment," 803–32.

The protection of property rights through established laws and contracts is said to be a major function of the modern state; states that are unwilling to or incapable of protecting property rights are viewed as predatory, weak, or ineffective.[21]

The institutions that determine and enforce property rights in China are often ambiguous and the rules are often arbitrarily enforced. This narrative has been applied to property rights in a number of arenas, including intellectual property, firms, and natural resources such as land and water.[22] The 1988 Land Management Law sanctioned the creation of markets for land use, but it did not – especially at the outset – establish clear regulations about rights of control, income, and transfer in the context of public ownership over land. Although many may agree that property rights institutions are ambiguous, scholars disagree about whether that ambiguity has led inexorably to negative incentives and externalities. The conventional view interprets the extraordinary amount of conflict over land in China as the inevitable result of ambiguous property rights, meaning both unclear laws on the books and the lack of effective enforcement institutions, chiefly the absence of an independent judiciary to arbitrate claims and to enforce findings. According to this view, land markets not only are mired in political and social conflict, but also produce inefficiencies and distortions in land use. Until property rights are clarified by law and enforced through an independent judiciary or some other autonomous bureaucracy, distortions, inefficiencies, conflicts, and injustices will continue to plague land relations in China.[23]

Yet this conventional explanation has gained little traction among scholars who work on property rights practices in China. Instead, research on land property rights in China has challenged the dominant view that private property rights defended by an independent judiciary are a necessary precondition for efficient investment and sustainable growth. In rural China, survey and fieldwork data have indicated that farmers are accepting and even supportive of impermanent rights over plots of land and periodic reallocations if such policies function in ways to enhance fairness and agricultural production.[24]

---

[21] Margaret Levi, *Of Rule and Revenue* (Berkeley: University of California Press, 1988).

[22] Martin K. Dimitrov, *Piracy and the State: The Politics of Intellectual Property Rights in China* (Cambridge: Cambridge University Press, 2009); William P. Alford, *To Steal a Book Is an Elegant Offense: Intellectual Property Law in Chinese Civilization* (Stanford, CA: Stanford University Press, 1995); Andrew C. Mertha, *China's Water Warriors: Citizen Action and Policy Change* (Ithaca, NY: Cornell University Press, 2008); Andrew Mertha, *The Politics of Piracy: Intellectual Property in Contemporary China* (Ithaca, NY: Cornell University Press, 2005).

[23] Wang et al., "Farmland Preservation and Land Development Rights Trading in Zhejiang, China"; Wang et al., "Rural Residential Properties in China"; Xiaolin Guo, "Land Expropriation and Rural Conflicts in China," *China Quarterly* no. 166 (2001): 422–39.

[24] Loren Brandt et al., "Land Rights in Rural China: Facts, Fictions and Issues," *China Journal* no. 47 (January 2002): 67–97; Guo Li, Scott Rozelle, and Loren Brandt, "Tenure, Land Rights, and Farmer Investment Incentives in China," *Agricultural Economics* 19, nos. 1–2 (September 1998): 63–71; Xiao-Yuan Dong, "Two-Tier Land Tenure System and Sustained Economic Growth in post-1978 Rural China," *World Development* 24, no. 5 (1996): 915–28; Qian Forrest Zhang, "Retreat from

Comprehensive studies of Chinese land development patterns challenge the idea that property rights are simply bestowed from above and seek to demonstrate that in China property relations are "evolving" apace with social and economic change from the bottom up. Peter Ho has examined institutional change in property rights systems across land types, concluding that "the central state's choice to allow local, informal institutions a certain space for existence rather than formalizing them through national laws is the fundamental explanation of such institutions' credibility and successful functioning."[25] In contrast, top-down attempts to change institutions that govern grasslands, wasteland, and forests have ignored local socioeconomic circumstances, with results ranging from complete disregard for "empty institutions" to violent conflict. George C. S. Lin, on the basis of the 1996 national cadastral survey, examines regional differences in urban expansion and concludes that there is no single model of land development in China and that the conventional view of property rights bestowed from the top down is overly simplistic.[26] Scholars of China with a variety of disciplinary perspectives have carefully documented patterns of state–society conflict over land, variations in justice claims in disputes over land rights, and different patterns of urbanization in China.[27]

Although scholars of contemporary China recognize the heterogeneity in patterns of urbanization and the politics of social "resistance," the majority of work on urbanization and land in China implicitly imagines local governments to be pursuing similar if not identical projects of state building and capital

Equality or Advance towards Efficiency? Land Markets and Inequality in Rural Zhejiang," *China Quarterly* no. 195 (2008): 535–57; Q. Forrest Zhang and John A. Donaldson, "From Peasants to Farmers: Peasant Differentiation, Labor Regimes, and Land-Rights Institutions in China's Agrarian Transition," *Politics & Society* 38, no. 4 (2010): 458–89.

[25] Peter Ho, *Institutions in Transition: Land Ownership, Property Rights, and Social Conflict in China* (Oxford: Oxford University Press, 2005), 18. Ho's arguments are similar in spirit to those in an edited volume by Oi and Walder on property rights in China more generally, i.e., not only with respect to land. They conclude that "ownership has evolved decisively, if gradually, away from traditional forms of state and collective ownership toward a mixed economy pervaded by contracting, lease-holding, and various forms of private enterprise – the family firm, the elite industrial empire, and the private companies owned by government agencies and enterprises." Jean C. Oi and Andrew G. Walder, eds., *Property Rights and Economic Reform in China* (Stanford, CA: Stanford University Press, 1999), 12.

[26] George C. S. Lin, *Developing China: Land, Politics and Social Conditions* (London: Routledge, 2009). Lin's book examines variations in patterns of urbanization in China. He distinguishes between two such patterns: outward expansion of existing cities (what he calls "city-based urbanization") and the transition of rural-to-urban settlements in the countryside ("region-based urbanization"). A geographer, Lin is explaining different patterns of land use rather than who controls the land and how property rights are distributed. That said, some of his findings about the relative importance of global and domestic capital are consistent with my study of the politics of land control.

[27] Hsing, *The Great Urban Transformation*; Susan Whiting, "Values in Land: Fiscal Pressures, Land Disputes and Justice Claims in Rural and Peri-Urban China," *Urban Studies* 48, no. 3 (March 2011): 569–87.

accumulation through land development.[28] I find this image of local governments to be inaccurate both temporally and spatially; local governments have not always pursued land development this way, and local state strategies of land management vary in politically important ways. Many local governments have been at times quite eager to establish and protect systems that very much resemble private property rights, and local government predation is of relatively recent vintage. This book aims to provide a systematic explanation of subnational variation in property rights and land politics, systematically linking urban political economies with different subnational systems for managing property rights over land.

PROPERTY RIGHTS REGIMES

The goal of this book is to explain the emergence and staying power of property rights regimes, or the system of rules that governs who assigns what kinds of property rights to which parties. The book does not explain the efficiency of the outcomes; nor does it attempt to ascertain which systems of property rights are "better" for any number of outcomes, but rather "why and how people create property rights and for what purposes, why and how they choose the types of property institutions they do, and how and why they change property rights over time."[29]

A dominant approach to thinking about resource distribution is to distinguish between market-based and authority-based (or hierarchy-based) systems of allocation.[30] Yet, as Boone and others have acknowledged, "in the real world, all national economic systems and property regimes are hybrids of these two," and therefore the question is the relative influence of states and markets in various property regimes.[31] Other conceptualizations aim to capture variations in rights holders or kinds of rights, for example, examining how regimes vary from individually held, private property rights to public ownership or

---

[28] Hsing writes that "local politics centers on the politics of urban development projects, which define the dynamics of the local state and its relations with the market and society." Hsing, *Great Urban Transformation*, 7. She compares urban development and the politics of "civic territoriality," or social resistance, at the urban core, the urban periphery, and the rural fringe. She does not, however, offer a framework for understanding how the politics of urban development plays out differently within these geographical ideal types, i.e., in different urban cores. Implicit in her argument about urban politics is the premise that all local governments in China seek the same sort of state-building through land conquest. I have not found this to be the case.

[29] William Blomquist, "A Political Analysis of Property Rights," in *Property in Land and Other Resources*, ed. Daniel H. Cole and Elinor Ostrom (Cambridge, MA: Lincoln Institute of Land Policy, 2012), 370.

[30] Charles E. Lindblom, *Politics and Markets: The World's Political Economic Systems* (New York: Basic Books, 1977). In the Chinese context, urban scholars have long posited that urbanization in China is "state-led," as opposed to "market-led," a contention that would not surprise anyone. For a discussion, see Hsing, *The Great Urban Transformation*, 7.

[31] Boone, *Property and Political Order in Africa*, 21.

national domain. Typically, these studies ask how regimes vary in terms of the security of property rights, presumably from state expropriation. Most of such studies examine the national level, often looking at differences in property rights regimes, as laid out in national constitutions, and inquire how these various regimes affect a host of other outcomes: such as economic growth, electoral politics, democratic stability, and so forth.[32]

In the Chinese context, however, and in other places undergoing rapid and uncertain economic and political transitions in which local practice is not determined by a national legal framework, the nature of the property rights regime is a question of fact.[33] In any given local area, what kinds of actors – individuals or groups, private or public – can conceivably defend property rights over land? How are these rights granted? When conflicts emerge, who decides or adjudicates? It is not possible to identify a property rights regime simply by looking at a local or national legal framework. Instead, we must ascertain how property rights are extended and held in practice.

To this end, property rights regimes can be conceptualized as differing in the distribution of regulatory authority and the scope of legitimate claimants. Regulatory authority refers to those who can extend or grant legitimacy to property rights claims. Almost always, this authority rests with "the state," but, especially in the postsocialist context, the question is what part of the state and whether there exists an exclusive arbiter. The scope of legitimate claimants includes which actors are allocated rights over land. In some regimes, the state is the only legitimate claimant to land rights, whereas elsewhere restrictions take a number of forms, such as ethnic requirements or limits to the scope of politically acceptable economic actors, such as in the case of gradually reformed socialism.[34] In the Chinese case, the permissibility of various forms of ownership has changed over time. For example, Huang Yasheng documents how private enterprises masqueraded as collectively owned township and village enterprises (TVEs) in the 1980s because private enterprise was politically suspect at the time.[35] As private enterprise became politically acceptable in China, we may think of this as a change in the scope of the legitimate claimants.

---

[32] In addition to Boone, see Stanley L. Engerman and Jacob Metzer, eds., *Land Rights, Ethno-Nationality, and Sovereignty in History* (London: Routledge, 2004). Linking differences in the security of property rights is at the heart of the neoclassical approach, typically associated with the work of Barry Weingast and Douglass North, which I discuss later in this chapter.

[33] Huang Yasheng makes this point quite well: "In studies of American economy[sic], scholars may debate about the effects of, say, 'Reagan tax cuts.' In studies of the Chinese economy, the more relevant question would be, Did the government cut taxes in the first place?" Huang, *Capitalism with Chinese Characteristics*, xi.

[34] On exclusive regimes and ethnicity, see Engerman and Metzer, eds., *Land Rights, Ethno-Nationality, and Sovereignty in History*. On citizenship and land access in contemporary Africa, see Boone, *Property and Political Order in Africa*.

[35] Huang, *Capitalism with Chinese Characteristics*.

		Legitimate Claimants	
		Restrictive	Expansive
Regulatory Authority	Concentrated	*Oligopoly or Monopoly* *Statist*	*Pluralistic* *Regulated Market*
	Dispersed	*Oligarchy* *Neocustomary**	*Fragmented* *Unregulated Market*

FIGURE 1.2. Conceptualizing Property Rights Regimes
Note: In which traditional or customary authority structures distribute and assign land property rights. See Boone, *Property and Political Order in Africa*, 27–38.

Regulatory authority can be concentrated in a clearly designated state agency, such as the judiciary or a bureaucracy such as the MLR, or it can be dispersed, with multiple agencies and arms of the state competing for authority. The scope of legitimate claimants can be expansive, when a wide range of actors effectively claim to be rights holders, or restrictive when the reverse is the case. Figure 1.2 elaborates on the conceptualization of property rights regimes along these dimensions, suggesting how different kinds of property rights regimes fall. This conceptualization on its own says nothing about the sources of variation on either dimension. For example, regulatory authority may be dispersed because there is a lack of state capacity or because state actors strategically choose to cede control over land and property rights allocations to other groups, as is the case in the neocustomary land tenure regimes that Boone examines. The goal of conceptualizing property rights regimes in this way is to identify subnational variation and to categorize cases systematically so as to generate explanations for their divergence.

EMPIRICAL CONTEXT

The following chapters examine the process of land commodification from the late 1980s to the present in three cities that entered the reform period with similar political economic legacies as part of a single Chinese region – the northeastern rust belt (see Figure 1.3). Thirty years after the introduction of the economic reforms, however, these cities belong to fundamentally different

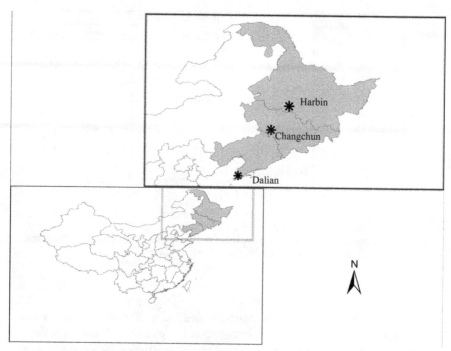

FIGURE 1.3. China, the Northeast, and the Research Sites

political economic orders. Without an understanding of how the post-1978 economic reforms altered the urban hierarchy and established cities with different political economies, it is difficult to make sense of the varying experiences of land politics in these northeastern cities.

The growth rates of Heilongjiang, Jilin, and Liaoning provinces were among the highest in the country between 1952 and 1978.[36] Beyond growth and state investment, it was in the Northeast where the socialist model of urban organization was most thoroughly developed because of the region's heavy share of state-owned enterprises (SOEs) and formal sector workers.

During the decades since the initiation of the reforms in 1978, these northeastern cities that began the reform period at a similar socioeconomic base have fared very differently. The substantive chapters that follow will trace

---

[36] Zeng Juxin and Liang Bin, "Zhongguo quyu jingji zengzhang bijiao yanjiu" (Comparative Research on Regional Economic Growth in China), *Jingji dili* (Economic Geography), no.1 (1994): 16–20. Unfortunately for scholars of the Chinese political economy, comprehensive data on economic growth and its composition for the years between 1957 and 1978 are rarely available at the provincial level, much less at the municipal level. See Thomas P. Lyons, *Economic Integration and Planning in Maoist China* (New York: Columbia University Press, 1987), 18–22.

each city's growth trajectory from the early 1980s through the mid-2000s, and Chapter 3 will provide more detailed comparative data. But a brief comparison here underscores the radical differences among these cities in the contemporary period. Table 1.1 displays basic data on each city's population, physical size, and economic performance in 1985, 1990, 2000, and 2010.

From 1985 to 2010, all three cities grew in size (urban built-up area, *jianshequ*, 建设区), but it is clear that Dalian expanded substantially in the 1990s and earlier, whereas Harbin and Changchun grew significantly later in the period. As is abundantly clear, Dalian became substantially richer than the other cities over the course of the 1990s and 2000s. Dalian's earlier and wider opening to global capital is on dramatic display in the foreign direct investment (FDI) data; Dalian was receiving orders of magnitude of more FDI than the other two cities in 1990, and more than ten times as much in 2010. The workforces of all three cities, however, suffered in the late 1990s and 2000s, as public-sector enterprises were restructured or forced to enter bankruptcy. The number of employed persons was reduced by more than one-half in each city between 1990 and 2000. Chapter 3 contains more granular data on job losses and changes in the capital structure in each city.

Looking more deeply into the experiences of these cities during the reform era, I find that not only economic outcomes, such as levels of FDI and wealth, but also the very rules of economic reform, investment, and organization differ as well. Following scholars who have identified subnational variation in political economic organization in Italy and Germany, we may think of these different sets of rules of economic engagement as completely different "economic orders."[37] Participants in these cities' different political economic orders – from local officials to private entrepreneurs to publicly owned firms and urban citizens and workers – shared different expectations about the rules of economic activity, in particular about the extent and nature of the role of local government in the economy. These expectations were central to the rules of engagement in the local economy, such as how much and what kinds of local firms could depend on the local government for protection and promotion, how secure property rights were and for whom, and how much and what kind of protection or support

[37] Gary Herrigel, *Industrial Constructions: The Sources of German Industrial Power* (Cambridge: Cambridge University Press, 1996); Richard M. Locke, *Remaking the Italian Economy* (Ithaca, NY: Cornell University Press, 1995). Herrigel deploys the term "economic order" precisely because it is more encompassing than "industrial structure" or "industrial organization" (pp. 22–3). Both Herrigel and Locke seek to characterize variation in a broader array of economic activities than interfirm relations: for example, Locke examines the structure of intergroup relations, patterns of associationalism, and links to the national center.

TABLE I.I. *Selected Data on Harbin, Dalian, and Changchun*

	1985(*1987)	1990	2000	2010
Population (million)				
Harbin	3.8	4.07	9.35	9.92
Dalian	4.85	5.18	5.51	5.86
Changchun	5.89	6.38	6.99	7.59
Urban built-up area (km²)				
Harbin	156	156	165	359
Dalian	84	101	234	406
Changchun	105	108	154	388
GDP* (RMB billion)				
Harbin	6.37	11.2	100.27	366.49
Dalian	10.09	17.86	111.08	515.82
Changchun	6.31	10.54	81.1	332.9
GDP per capita* (RMB)				
Harbin	1,317	2,762	10,563	36,951
Dalian	2,022	3,464	19,366	77,704
Changchun	1,055	1,667	11,550	43,936
FDI* (US$ million)				
Harbin	–	.224	203.14	700.10
Dalian	49.9	201.29	1,305.97	10,030.25
Changchun	–	.66	143.83	698.79
Employed persons (million)				
Harbin	2.02	2.36	1.72	1.35
Dalian	2.37	2.65	.929	.942
Changchun	2.96*	2.46	.982	.928

Sources: Population and Urban Size: 1985 data are from *Zhongguo chengshi tongji nianjian, 1985* (China Urban Statistical Yearbook, 1985) (Beijing: Xin shijie chubanshe, 1985), 26, 44; 1990, 2000, and 2010 data are from EPS Net.com, China City Data, accessed September 2013; 1990 Harbin population figure is confirmed in *Heilongjiang jingji tongji nianjian, 1991* (Heilongjiang Economic Statistical Yearbook, 1991) (Harbin: Zhongguo tongji chubanshe, 1991), 178; 1990 Harbin city size is confirmed in *Zhongguo chengshi tongji nianjian, 1990* (China Urban Statistical Yearbook, 1990) (Beijing: Zhongguo tongji chubanshe, 1990), 55. Population figures for Dalian and Harbin are reported slightly differently in local yearbooks (9.41 million for Harbin, 5.45 million for Dalian); see *Ha'erbin tongji nianjian, 2001* (Harbin Statistical Yearbook, 2001) (Ha'erbin: Ha'erbin nianjianshe, 2001) and *Dalian shi nianjian, 2001* (Dalian City Yearbook, 2001) (Beijing: Zhongguo tongji nianjian, 2001). Harbin 2010 city size data are from the National Bureau of Statistics via CEIC, China Premium Database, accessed September 2013. *GDP:* 1987 data are from the city yearbooks, various years; Dalian GDP per capita, author's calculation; 1990 GDP and per capita data are from *Xin Zhongguo chengshi wushinian, 1949–98* (Fifty Years of Chinese Cities, 1949–1999) (Beijing: Xinhua chubanshe, 1999), 317–23, 353–4; 2000 GDP and per capita and 2010 GDP data are from China Data Online (China Data Center, University of Michigan), accessed September 2013, except for the 2000 Harbin GDP per capita data, which are from *Ha'erbin tongji nianjian, 2001*, 460. 2010 GDP per capita data are from EPS Net.com, China City Data, accessed September 2013. Note that the 1990 Harbin data are confirmed in *Ha'erbin nianjian, 1990* (Harbin Yearbook, 1990) (Ha'erbin: Heilongjiang renmin chubanshe, 1991), 529; *Heilongjiang jingji tongji nianjian, 1991*, 69. Changchun 1990 per capita figure is from *Changchun nianjian, 1991* (Changchun Yearbook, 1991) (Changchun: Jilin renmin chubanshe, 1991). *FDI:* Dalian FDI data for 1987 are from *Dalian shi zhi: Waijing waimao zhi* (Dalian City Gazetteer: Foreign Economy and Foreign Trade) (Beijing: Fangzhi chubanshe, 2004), 268. 1990 data are from *Xin Zhongguo chengshi wushinian, 1949–1998*, 401–2; 2000 and 2010 data are from EPSnet.com, accessed September 2013. *Employment:* 1985 and 1990 data are from *Xin Zhongguo chengshi wushinian, 1949–1998*; 2000 and 2010 data are from China Data Online, accessed September 2013; Changchun 1990 data are from *Changchun tongji nianjian, 1991*, 8; Changchun 1987 data are from *Changchun nianjian, 1988* (Changchun Yearbook, 1988) (Changchun: Jilin renmin chubanshe, 1988). Note that the Harbin 1990 figure is confirmed in *Heilongjiang jingji tongji nianjian, 1991*, 2.

local citizens, especially those facing hardships as a result of the economic reforms, would receive, and so forth.

The shared expectations and understandings that underlay the local economic orders were forged during the reform era as local governments attempted to pursue economic growth and political survival in the face of differing constraints. Inherited economic and social bases matter tremendously but do not, especially in the cities I examine, explain the most fundamental differences in the local rules of economic engagement. Instead, the distribution of preferential policies from Beijing and the differential sequencing of economic reform and opening to global capital empowered and constrained local governments in ways fundamental to their exercise of power in the local economy.

Beginning with the declaration of the special economic zones (SEZs) along the southeastern coast of China in 1979, market reforms in China were introduced unevenly across regions, with some areas along the east coast accessing foreign capital and local autonomy well in advance of the inland areas. The spatial sequencing of economic liberalization had economic, political, and public-policy rationales. The economic argument focused on turning the east coast cities, which were said to have natural advantages in terms of geography, historical legacies of international trade, and denser populations with better-trained workforces, into "growth poles" that would allow higher returns on concentrated investments and then would "trickle out" to the wider national economy. Politically, spatial sequencing allowed reformers to introduce liberalization incrementally rather than engaging in disagreements with conservatives at the level of national policy. From a public-policy standpoint, the preferential policies allowed the CCP to examine and contain the effects of the reform policies to specific cities and regions and to experiment with policy alternatives before scaling up. Deng Xiaoping's famous adage about allowing "some people to become rich before others" refers to the inevitability of individual inequalities, but it also expresses the promise that although the reforms would introduce prosperity to the areas in the east first, it would eventually expand westward. I discuss the progress and sources of regional divergence in more detail in Chapter 3.

The differential sequencing of the reform and opening policies, even in a single region with a shared political economy heritage, had clear and observable effects on the political and economic resources and constraints experienced by local governments as well as on the various groups in urban society. Even though the cities in the Northeast all eventually came to enjoy the same privileges and access to foreign capital, the differential timing of these policies meant that some groups in certain cities were empowered, whereas the same groups in other cities were disempowered, and the property rights regimes that emerged in the different cities were reflections of these different power distributions. Importantly, these power distributions contravene dominant social-science theoretical expectations that greater market power and economic

		Legitimate Claimants	
		Restrictive	Expansive
Regulatory Authority	Concentrated	*Statist: Dalian*	*Pluralistic: Changchun*
	Dispersed	*(No cases)*	*Fragmented: Harbin*

FIGURE 1.4. Typology of the Cases

liberalization "erode" the power of the state. Counterintuitively, it is in the cities that opened widely and early to global capital and markets that local governments exercised the greatest power over the economy, and in the cities that identify themselves as "latecomers" that we observe greater pluralism in the distribution of local economic power.[38]

The sequencing of global opening and economic reform provides the context in which both city officials and local residents sought to fashion strategies for survival and prosperity after socialism. Figure 1.4 summarizes how the cases fit within the conceptualization laid out earlier in this chapter. The emergence of land markets and property rights practices figured prominently in all of these strategies, but local land markets differed in terms of the impetus for their emergence, the nature of the political bargaining that produced them, and the content of the moral entitlement that accompanied local property rights practices.

Dalian, which enjoyed preferential policies to open to global capital nearly a decade earlier than the rest of the region, typifies what I call a statist property rights regime, in which the local government enjoys a monopoly on the power to regulate and allocate property rights over land and the scope of legitimate claimants to land rights is restricted to the local state. Land markets emerged in Dalian at the initiation of and under the monopolistic control of the local government; local officials consciously and publicly endeavored to use land and land commodification as a state asset that would generate revenues for and

---

[38] This finding is similar to others who acknowledge that neoliberal reforms and globalization do not reduce the power of the state, but rather redirect state power into new realms of regulation and social and economic management. The argument here, however, is slightly different: Early openness to capital did not simply redirect the local state's regulatory activities. Rather, it allowed the local state to capture the gains of economic growth and to assert greater political power vis-à-vis society. In essence, the state became stronger in degree as well as different in kind. Many in the China field have argued that strengthening the state has been the point of the reforms all along; Peter Evans, "The Eclipse of the State? Reflections on Stateness in an Era of Globalization," *World Politics* 50, no. 1 (1997): 62–87.

allow the local government to direct investment and economic development. In many ways, Dalian's experience with land markets in the late 1980s and early 1990s was a precursor to the national land regime that emerged in the late 1990s and 2000s, as cities elsewhere progressed from commodifying land to fiscalizing land.

Dalian, like many cities that benefited from early access to foreign capital as a result of the preferential policies bestowed by Beijing in 1984, designated a development zone outside the urban core to rebalance the concentration of economic power in favor of proreform coalitions, while leaving the downtown, prereform power base undisturbed during the early period of reform and opening. By introducing dual pressures for downtown enterprises to restructure and relocate later during an "enterprise relocation campaign" that began in 1992, the city government established itself as the sole claimant to urban land as well as the critical link between foreign investors and local firms. These roles confirmed the local government as the arbiter, rather than the target, of political conflict. The role of the state in the land and real estate markets – establishing the markets and acting as participant and coordinator – paralleled other areas of economic activity. The Dalian Municipal Government was the autonomous coordinator of FDI, enterprise reforms, economic and urban planning, and so forth.

Because Dalian was able to carry out politically difficult reforms, such as layoffs, bankruptcies, and relocations later in the 1990s, with the support of foreign capital, the local government was not forced to engage in the sort of particularistic bargaining that was endemic in Harbin and Changchun. Instead of deploying land control and property-rights rules as political resources, the city of Dalian articulated a unified vision about the role and use of land in the city's economic strategy. Under the leadership of Bo Xilai, the city's well-connected and ambitious leader during the 1980s and 1990s (sentenced to life in prison in 2013 after a stunning turn to populism and subsequent conflict with other CCP elites), the municipal government was successful in disciplining lower-level state agents and situating the municipal government at the apex of urban politics and the urban economy. The dependence of local residents and firms on the local government for a place (i.e., capital, employment, and a physical location) in Dalian's postsocialist economy and coordinated ideological campaigns about land stunted the development of alternative narratives of land and property rights practices. Ironically, for a city supposedly embracing markets and capitalism early during the reform period, the moral content of the campaigns that accompanied land politics in Dalian emphasized the role of land as a state asset – one to be deployed by the local government in its pursuit of collective prosperity for the region. Individual claims were regarded as self-interested obstacles to progress and reform.

In contrast, the city of Harbin, which did not enjoy open privileges until the mid-1990s, instead pursued a decentralization of authority over policies, such as housing, enterprise reform, and the growth of private entrepreneurship, distributing urban land control to assuage the losers from the economic reforms and to spur growth. Unlike in Dalian, Harbin authorities articulated no over-arching strategy for economic modernization; instead they experimented with some policies and changed course to adopt others. Harbin's experiences under reform typify what I call a "fragmented property rights regime," in which the various parts of the local state focused on dispensing resources to groups (such as firms or workers), with each decision more or less individualized and improvised rather than connected to an overarching economic strategy dictated by the local state. In Harbin, land became a resource for distribution, and informal property rights became a political strategy. Over time, as multiple claimants to urban land became increasingly embedded both socially and physically, de facto land claims became powerful constraints on the govern-ment's ability to regulate urban land and to execute its own projects for spatial restructuring. Rules about land markets and property rights were the products of particularistic bargaining, as local government actors negotiated with other state agents and groups in society for their political acquiescence to the dismantling of state socialism. The lowest levels of local government were frequently the agents that negotiated with the various groups and that distrib-uted informal, and sometimes formal, claims to land and property.

Land markets were informally initiated in Harbin early during the reform period, even prior to implementation of the 1988 Land Law, as enterprises underwent stages of reform and used the land they occupied and controlled either to pursue market ventures or to distribute to their workers. A primary impetus for land commodification was to create value for firms and individuals rather than exclusively for the state. As the economic reforms proceeded in the late 1980s and 1990s under conditions of capital scarcity and high unemploy-ment, control over land rivaled employment and wages as the main axis of political conflict in the city. Residents, workers, and enterprise managers cam-paigned successfully that they were morally entitled to property ownership, convincing local officials not only that their claims were legitimate, but also that a decentralized approach to land control and property rights would be best for the city's economic growth. Over the course of the 1990s, Harbin's urban planning policies emphasized the commodification of worker housing at pref-erential rates for the residents, the formalization of incipient private business claims to physical space, and a dynamic process of planning in which the local government learned from social practices and drafted land policies to legitimate and formalize emerging economic activity.

Although these distributive policies benefited many residents, the private sector, and the entrepreneurial activities of public enterprises, these policies did not have universally positive results. Harbin's efforts at urban expansion – the declaration of a high-tech development zone and a new administrative zone – fell prey to similar distributive conflicts. The projects were largely perceived as corrupt and wasteful, and they mostly failed to generate economic growth, employment, political prestige, or fiscal revenues for the city.

The local government of Changchun, in Jilin province, neither articulated an overarching economic strategy as Dalian did, nor simply muddled through as Harbin did. Changchun's economy was dominated by a single sector – the automobile industry. Moreover, its largest employer and main contributor to local GDP was a large, centrally owned SOE, over whose choices and performance the city government had little control. Changchun's local government explored the postsocialist prospects of the automobile industry but also sought to take advantage of the advent of land markets and real estate as an additional source of economic dynamism. As did Harbin, Changchun experimented with different approaches to reform and growth. But unlike in Harbin, the administrative power of the local government, buttressed by a sense of vulnerability as a result of single-sector and single-firm dominance, was better able to manage internal discipline and establish policies that regularized relations among workers, firms, and arms of the state. Changchun's property rights regime became pluralistic; The local government enjoys concentrated regulatory authority, but it does not hold a monopoly over property rights. Instead, we see a range of economic actors who successfully stake land claims.

Property rights and land markets were central to Changchun's trajectory after 1978. Similar to Harbin, Changchun underwent economic reforms in a climate of high unemployment and capital scarcity in the 1980s and the early 1990s. Additionally, control over homes and space for informal economic activities were political resources over which social and economic groups bargained with the state. Changchun adopted particularistic rules about the control of property that would apply differently to various groups. But regulatory authority over property rights – the registration of deeds, the collection of taxes on exchanges, and so forth – was established as the exclusive jurisdiction of the municipal government (specifically, the Urban Planning Bureau and the Real Estate Bureau). Land commodification offered an opportunity for the Changchun Municipal Government to establish power independently of the auto sector, but the government did not regard land as the exclusive asset of the state.

Urban planning and land policies in the 1980s and early 1990s in Changchun sought to assuage the losers from the early economic reforms while encouraging the growth of the private sector as well as the city's traditional industrial base. In the early 1990s as land markets became widespread, Changchun established a new development zone and sought to promote local revenue and economic growth through real estate. All the while, local actors conformed to a moral narrative about the city's economic specialization and vulnerability and the need for regulation of real estate and property rights. In the late 1990s and 2000s, Changchun authorities, having solidified regulatory authority over land politics and real estate, used that power to direct industrial investment and to engineer the city's partial economic recovery.

THEORETICAL APPROACH

The following chapters make sense of property rights change in China by applying a theoretical approach that sees property rights as outcomes of political debates and interactions. This approach contrasts with both the classical approach that views property rights as outcomes of efficiency pursuits and more recent approaches that view property rights as bargained contracts among self-interested parties.

Both of these existing approaches are rooted intellectually in new institutional economics (NIE) and typically take the evolution of Western property rights institutions as their subjects. What I call the classical approach, as typified by Demsetz and North, envisions the emergence and change in property rights as an almost inevitable part of the pursuit of greater efficiency. As the value of some heretofore common resource – be it land, water, fish, or furs – changes, actors seek to internalize costs, exclude some actors, and reduce transaction costs by creating or changing property rights arrangements. In Demsetz's classic example, the advent of the fur trade and the accompanying incentives to overhunt the local fox population gave rise to private hunting and land rights in Quebec.[39] This "efficiency view" fails to account for why some societies adopt efficient property rights institutions (typically defined as private-property rights) and others do not.[40] Although efficient property rights institutions may be beneficial for aggregate growth and social gains, we require an understanding of distributional politics – which groups stand to gain or lose as property rights institutions change – to understand why actual arrangements fall short of what would be socially optimal.

A more recent strain of scholarship takes up where the classical NIE framework leaves off, theorizing from the rational choice perspective about how property rights emerge from a political process. Libecap has proposed a view of property rights change as a process of political bargaining that he calls "contracting." The impetus for property rights change arises from changes in relative prices or technology, but proposals for institutional change are then mediated through the political process, in which self-interested parties argue over the distributional gains. Ultimately, Libecap concludes that it is the degree of potential and actual distributional conflicts that impedes property rights modifications that would benefit society at large.[41] Another

---

[39] Harold Demsetz, "Toward a Theory of Property Rights," *American Economic Review* 57, no. 2 (May 1967): 347–59.

[40] Douglass North, in later publications, abandons the "efficiency view of institutions" in favor of a more nuanced approach whereby rulers devise property rights systems according to their own (rather than society's) interests, and social organizations interact with institutions both to preclude and to create institutional change. See Douglass C. North, *Structure and Change in Economic History* (New York: Norton, 1981); Douglass C. North, *Institutions, Institutional Change, and Economic Performance* (Cambridge: Cambridge University Press, 1990), 7–8.

[41] Libecap, *Contracting for Property Rights*, 120–1.

more consciously political approach to property rights sees them as selectively enforced private goods rather than as public goods. Haber et al. begin by observing that investment and economic growth take place under conditions of political instability, when we can assume that investors would be wary because political actors either would not enforce their property rights or would violate them. They argue that "investors, first and foremost, care about the sanctity of their property rights; they do not require governments to protect property rights as a public good in order for investment to take place."[42]

The framework in this book adopts some elements of these approaches, namely, the ideas of political bargaining and that property rights arrangements are fundamentally private goods, but it departs from these approaches in significant ways. Specifically, I propose a different perspective on the impetus to change property rights, an alternative approach to political bargaining, and a view of property rights that regards them as moral as well as material entitlements.

The Endogeneity of Property Rights Change

The impetus to change property rights institutions is more frequently endogenous rather than exogenous to the political process. By this I mean that the phenomenon of relative price change – assigning value to that which previously had no value or less value – is a result of political decisions. Questions about property rights arrangements – whose claims to property are legitimate, what a property claim entitles the claimant to do with the property, and so forth – often involve ideas and debates about how property should be valued and what kinds of arrangements should be adopted to ensure price stability, changes, and so forth. To be sure, we can imagine examples of exogenous price changes, such as the advent of the fur trade in Quebec or the sudden discovery of gold in northern California, but just as many, if not more, property rights changes come about because of political debates over the need for changes in values and prices.[43]

For example, consider what is among the most highly scrutinized modern property rights changes in social science: the Urban Property Rights Program in Peru, by which the World Bank and others implemented a large-scale

---

[42] Haber, Maurer, and Razo, *The Politics of Property Rights*, 10. They propose a specific property rights arrangement as an alternative to limited government and stationary banditry, that is, "vertical political integration," by which the lines between asset holders (i.e., industrialists) and the government are sufficiently blurred that asset holders can influence government decisions to uphold their own property rights and government actors can gain from the rents generated by these arrangements (pp. 29–36).

[43] For an argument about neoliberalism and the global push for privatization, see Katherine Verdery and Caroline Humphrey, eds., *Property in Question: Value Transformation in the Global Economy* (Oxford: Berg, 2004).

formalization (or "titling") program to formalize property claims and to enable mortgages for settlement dwellers in urban Peru in the early 2000s. Though this institutional change serves as the subject of landmark studies in economics and related disciplines on the effects of property rights on economic behavior, the change itself was the result of political debates and expectations about what value should be extractable from what sorts of property rights.[44] Formalization and property rights manipulation in other settings have similarly been the results of political, rather than economic, imperatives.[45]

The chapters in this book analyze political debates occurring within the state and between state and society about what property rights arrangements will best optimize land values. For the decision-makers and participants in these debates and according to the political, social, and economic rationales that I analyze, optimizing the value of land for political goals was not the same as maximizing value, that is, ensuring its exchange for the highest value. Actors within the CCP as well as outside it saw fit to arrange property rights in ways that suited very different political, economic, and social objectives. At different points during (and before) the Chinese reforms and in different cities in China, we observe variations in whether land held value, relative value, and who was entitled to that value not on the basis of technological or exogenous factors but rather on how the actors regarded the role of land in their political and economic strategies.

In the Chinese cities under study, early access to preferential policies and global capital aided early movers to establish local government control over land. Early experiences in establishing development zones outside the traditional urban core enabled these local governments to initiate land markets to generate capital for the local government. As we will see, this was certainly the case in Dalian in the 1980s, but also in other coastal cities in the early 1990s. Cities facing greater constraints, however, initiated land markets to generate value for groups mostly outside the state, such as firms, residents, and, especially, those facing economic obsolescence due to the dismantling of state socialism. Land markets and property rights changes had different origins in different cities owing to their status in the post-Mao national political economy.

---

[44] Erica Field, "Entitled to Work: Urban Tenure Security and Labor Supply in Peru," *Quarterly Journal of Economics* 122, no. 4 (2007): 1561–1602; Erica Field and Maximo Torero, "Do Property Titles Increase Credit Access among the Urban Poor? Evidence from a Nationwide Titling Program," unpublished paper, 2010. Hernando Soto, in collaboration with the Instituto Libertad y Democracia, *The Other Path: The Invisible Revolution in the Third World* (New York: Harper & Row, 1989). For this idea in more detail, see Timothy Mitchell, "The Work of Economics: How a Discipline Makes Its World," *European Journal of Sociology* 46, no. 2 (2005): 297–320.

[45] Larsson, *Land and Loyalty*.

Political Bargaining

Property rights change tends to occur not in isolation, but rather accompanying substantial economic and social change in the wider political environment. This is especially true, as we shall see, in the Chinese case, in which property rights arrangements changed during a long period of gradual market transition. But it also describes environments outside China. In the former Soviet Union and Eastern Europe, property rights changes were frequently the centerpiece of dramatic programs of democratization and of the transition to markets from planned economies.[46] Tomas Larsson describes how the formalization of property rights in Thailand in the twentieth century was primarily the result of security concerns and the need to recruit the political allegiance of poor farmers in the face of the Communist threat.[47] Because property rights changes rarely occur under conditions in which other political and economic parameters are held constant, property rights arrangements are but one political resource over which groups form interests and preferences and negotiate for status and recognition as well as for distributional gains. Property rights decisions are often made in the aftermath of other more seismic political fights, and property arrangements are more likely to reflect constellations of power and preferences formed outside the realm of property rights decisions.

Without an understanding of how property rights debates fit into the larger political context of change and transition, it is difficult, or impossible, to make sense of the various actors' positions.[48] More pointedly, if we assume that the preferences of the parties are based primarily on their expectations of distributional gains and losses, it is impossible to understand why parties support arrangements that are not beneficial either to them or in aggregate social terms.

[46] For an example of an argument about how transition complicates our understanding of formal and informal institutional change, see Anna Grzymala-Busse, "The Best Laid Plans: The Impact of Informal Rules on Formal Institutions in Transitional Regimes," *Studies in Comparative and International Development* 45, no. 3 (2010): 311–33. On property rights in the post-Communist world, see Stanislav Markus, "Secure Property as a Bottom-Up Process: Firms, Stakeholders, and Predators in Weak States," *World Politics* 64, no. 2 (2012): 242–77; Timothy Frye, "Credible Commitment and Property Rights: Evidence from Russia," *American Political Science Review* 98, no. 3 (2004): 453–66; and Timothy Frye, "Original Sin, Good Works, and Property Rights in Russia," *World Politics* 58, no. 4 (2006): 479–504; David L. Weimer, ed., *The Political Economy of Property Rights: Institutional Change and Credibility in the Reform of Centrally Planned Economies* (Cambridge: Cambridge University Press, 1997); Jessica Allina-Pisano, *The Post-Soviet Potemkin Village: Politics and Property Rights in the Black Earth* (Cambridge: Cambridge University Press, 2008); Jessica Allina-Pisano, "Sub Rosa Resistance and the Politics of Economic Reform: Land Redistribution in Post-Soviet Ukraine," *World Politics* 56, no. 4 (2004): 554–81; Katherine Verdery, *The Vanishing Hectare: Property and Value in Postsocialist Transylvania* (Ithaca: Cornell University Press, 2003).

[47] Larsson, *Land and Loyalty*.

[48] Tulia G. Falleti and Julia F. Lynch, "Context and Causal Mechanisms in Political Analysis," *Comparative Political Studies* 42, no. 9 (2009): 1143–66.

I will argue that the parties adopt such positions somewhat strategically as a part of their expectations regarding the outcomes of a much wider program of reform and transition.[49]

Last, the strategic bargaining approach assumes that the participating parties understand their expected interests (or at least they have clear ideas about their expected interests) and they negotiate accordingly. In contrast, I find that bargaining occurs under conditions of "genuine uncertainty," in which "past events are not necessarily a reliable guide to future probabilities."[50] As the next chapter demonstrates, the path of land reform and commodification in China was highly contingent, and actors faced extreme uncertainty: uncertainty about what to expect and prefer in terms of property rights change but also uncertainty about the direction of economic and political reform, the statuses of groups and individuals, and, especially for policy-makers, which property arrangements were most beneficial for their own interests as well as for those of society. The approach to bargaining in this book, in contrast to strategic bargaining, includes attention to experimentation, when actors briefly adopt some arrangements to examine the consequences and then sometimes discontinue them, as well as to transformation, when actors change in their preferences and desires in the process of negotiation. Bargaining, in this approach, is the interaction among various social and political actors and their ideas, during which both power and preferences may change.

In all of the case study cities, groups inside and outside the local state bargained over the organization of property rights and the rules governing land markets. Land and property rights also figured prominently in other political bargains, such as over employment, enterprise reforms, and the retreat of socialist welfare provisions. But land figured differently in urban distributive politics as the cities undertook reforms at different times; constrained and capital-scarce urban governments used informal, and sometimes formal, property rights as forms of redistribution and political appeasement, whereas stronger and more resource-rich governments consolidated their own control

---

[49] Jessica Allino-Pisano makes a similar argument about land privatization in rural Ukraine. Because local officials objected to the dissolution of the large conglomerates that had guaranteed economic and social security to their constituent populations, instead of blocking reforms in order to enrich themselves in formerly collectivized areas they engaged in "sub rosa" resistance against privatization programs that would have turned the countryside over to individual farmers. Allina-Pisano, "Sub Rosa Resistance and the Politics of Economic Reform."

[50] Here, I intend to invoke an idea of uncertainty associated with constructivist thought. That is, instead of envisioning a "materially unambiguous world ... populated by agents with clear interests whose realization rests on available resources, barriers to collective action, and further information restrictions," the Chinese political context was one in which many outcomes in question would have been perceived as unique, and therefore impossible to calculate or strategize exclusively on the basis of material interests. Rawi Abdelal, Mark Blythe, and Craig Parsons, "Introduction," in *Constructing the International Economy*, ed. Rawi Abdelal, Mark Blyth, and Craig Parsons (Ithaca, NY: Cornell University Press, 2010), 12.

over the land by rendering firms and residents dependent on the state for economic survival. The irony is that the state became the major landlord in the most "market-exposed" cities, whereas socialist decline (the dismantling of state ownership) actually presaged the emergence of land markets and nonstate property rights in the more "unexposed" cities. Put differently, the cities that housed global capitalism appeared to be the least capitalist in their land arrangements, whereas the cities long thought to be in a postsocialist stupor were quietly and unintentionally adopting capitalist forms of property arrangements.

Moral Entitlements

Finally, the approach in this book devotes as much attention to moral arguments and claims as it does to material or distributional conflicts. Other approaches acknowledge that legal precedents and distributional norms affect the negotiation environment, but the focus is primarily on power resources and material gains and losses in the process of institutional change.[51] Yet, under conditions of general social and political change and when actors are uncertain about potential distributional outcomes, moral arguments and claims to moral legitimacy are fundamental to debates about what kinds of property rights arrangements are just or optimal. Property rights debates of all kinds involve competing narratives about what arrangements are normatively best. Arguing that one arrangement is more efficient than another is simply one example of a normative argument – one that holds a great deal of persuasive power in some environments but very little in others.

Because national-level expectations about land markets were ambiguous and local policy was set by experimentation and according to local needs, the moral content and persuasive power of claims to land and space were of particular importance. Rather than responding exclusively to efficiency motivations, local governments and social groups articulated different political and moral views on the use of land and property, and on the rights and entitlements of various groups, as the economic reforms reshaped urban built environments. Property rights regimes are molded not only by the coercive power of the state and the competing economic interests of various state and social groups, but also by ideological debates in which different approaches to property rights acquire or lose legitimacy.

Although it is easy to imagine, as many have, conflict over property rights in urban and periurban China as one of social resistance against a powerful and coercive local government, such a view does not accurately describe the ways in which different property rights regimes were generated and experienced. In cities where the local state established itself as an exclusive urban landlord,

---

[51] Libecap, *Contracting for Property Rights*, 18.

government actions were accompanied by ideological campaigns to recast evictions and dislocations as necessary elements of local efforts to compete and prosper. In other cities, social groups lodged successful "moral economy" claims only after they received messages from local governments that they were entitled to land and urban property. The negotiations and struggles over property rights were less about defending and specifying a "right" bestowed from above by some third party and more about establishing the local rules of political and economic engagement.[52] Local economic and political orders were hardened and reproduced as agents of both state and society repeatedly drew on the ideological, moral, and persuasive content of claims to urban land and property.

ORGANIZATION OF THE BOOK

In Chapter 2, I offer a genealogy of land in contemporary China, tracing how political authorities envisioned land as a resource from before 1949 to commodification in the 1980s to "fiscalization" in the 1990s and 2000s. By examining critical moments in the organization of land control and property rights in China, I make the case that political imperatives motivated decisions to change property rights arrangements over land, and the kind and degree of value in land – and to whom that value would accrue – were the results, rather than the causes, of formal and informal institutional change. For a large sweep of recent Chinese history, land was chiefly imagined as an input for production, and land property policies aimed to maximize the production value of land. Only in the 1980s did the idea of land's "exchange value," or land as capital, become widespread among Chinese elites.

The chapter also analyzes China's first reform era real-estate boom and bubble from 1992 through 1994 and the policy reactions. Drawing on official and popular sources from the period, I show that real estate and land investment and exchange in China in the early 1990s bore a much stronger resemblance to open markets than anything thereafter. Analysis of the causes of the bubble led the CCP to adopt a number of changes to property rights over land as well as other fundamental political economic institutions. Most frequently omitted from accounts of the Chinese political economy in the 1990s, the politics of land control were at the center of the seismic changes to fiscal and

---

[52] This approach to urban politics is not novel, but it draws on a foundational understanding of political power – particularly the local variety of political power – that has been lost in contemporary comparative and China-specific debates about subnational politics. This perspective privileges the autonomy of urban politics, envisions power as dispersed and contingent, and conceptualizes political outcomes – policies, economic growth strategies, property rights, and so forth – as products of political interactions among groups and individuals. For a similar approach, see Norton E. Long, "The Local Community as an Ecology of Games," *American Journal of Sociology* 64, no. 3 (1958): 251–61.

financial institutions. The structure of contemporary Chinese capitalism – the institutional arrangements that determine political and economic incentives and investment – was indeed forged by reforms to these systems. Ultimately, I find in the real-estate bubble and its aftermath the story of how land in China went from being a state resource to a commodity to "fiscalization" – "the management of land resources by political authorities for the purpose of generating fiscal revenue" – that has generated the tremendous political and economic challenges outlined at the beginning of this chapter.[53]

Chapters 3 through 6 turn to the city cases. Chapter 3 provides an overview of the cases and comparative data. I show how the three cities diverged during the process of opening to global capital and reforming the state sector during the 1980s and 1990s. The chapters are organized to show the utility of the theoretical framework – viewing property rights regimes as products of political bargaining and moral entitlements – by describing the initiation of, negotiation over, and moral language that accompanied land markets in the context of each city's experience with economic reforms. Because the individual case chapters are relatively self-contained, Chapter 3 does much of the comparative work and puts each city into the regional context.

The sources in these chapters include primarily local documentary materials and some interview and ethnographic data. When possible – for the vast majority of claims – I cite documentary sources rather than interviews. Many of these materials are publicly available, for example, local yearbooks (*nianjian*, 年检), gazetteers (*difangzhi*, 地方志), or nationally circulated magazines or journals in which local planners or bureaucrats publicized their ideas. In Harbin and Changchun, I enjoyed access to local municipal archives, where I was able to view materials internal to agencies of the local government, such as the Urban Planning, Land Use, and Housing Bureaus. In all three cities, I benefited greatly from the generosity of local bureaucrats, officials, and academics, who granted me access to local documents, such as urban and land use plans, statements of policy direction, and local memos and directions about granular neighborhood-level plans. As much as possible, I endeavored to use materials from similar sources in each city, for example, comparing ten- and twenty-year urban plans and land use plans. In addition to providing an overall narrative about the cities' reform efforts and the role of land markets and property rights, the chapters on Harbin and Changchun track the experiences of neighborhoods within the city to illustrate the argument at a lower level.

The concluding chapter explores the meaning of China's national and sub-national systems of property rights over land in terms of China's past, present, and futures models of urbanization. I argue that by pursuing land-driven, state-controlled urbanization, the CCP is proceeding on an unprecedented path of economic transformation and human migration. I also examine prospects for

---

[53] Definition from Whiting, "Values in Land," 570.

reform in China's land institutions and central-local relations. Ultimately, I conclude that state ownership of land was indispensable to both economic growth strategies and urbanization in the past, and it is likely to remain so in the future.

I also explore the larger implications of the political theory of property rights developed in this volume. Dominant approaches to the origins of property rights focus either on efficiency motivations or on how property rights, once clarified and enforced, empower some groups or generate incentives for certain types of behavior. Drawing on a tradition that emphasizes – to the point of preoccupation – the function of rights as a limit to the power of the state, these approaches fail to establish an understanding of why state actors pursue predatory behavior for any reason other than because they can. We are left to assume that, without limits to the form of legally enforceable claims to rights, state power expands infinitely throughout society, just as gas will expand to fill whatever volume is available to it.

Instead, I have made the case for viewing property rights change as endogenous to the political process and in the context of larger political changes. In this view, the more fundamental question becomes the level of mutual dependence between state and society that induces governments to refrain from predatory behavior, whether there are limits in place or not. In the Chinese case, that mutual dependence has been forged and destroyed as fiscal relations between local governments and the economic agents in society have changed. In Latin America and India, this mutual dependence is political as well as economic because political parties depend on alliances with property rights claimants for electoral success. Ultimately, I propose a research agenda that centers on the core bonds between governments and societies as an alternative to isolating, and frequently decontextualizing, the effects of specific institutions.

2

The Making of the Real Estate Economy

Urban Reform and the Origins of the Party's Land Dilemma

If "all politics is local," then most of Chinese politics is about land. By the mid-2000s, as a result of the dual dependence on land revenue as a key source of finance and on the real estate sector for economic growth, the pursuit of land control and development became the primary activity undertaken by local (city and county) governments in China. The ratio of land leasing and property – or land-related taxes to local government budgetary revenues – grew from 25 percent in 2000 to more than 90 percent in 2010.[1] Real estate investment – funds invested in the development of land and property – grew from 2 percent of GDP in 1992 to 13 percent in 2011.[2]

The extent of China's political and economic dependence on land and real estate was likely surprising even to the land-reform architects who made them possible. Zhao Ziyang, premier from 1980 to 1987 and general secretary of the Chinese Communist Party (CCP) from 1987 until his purge during the Tiananmen protests in 1989, writes in his memoir: "It was perhaps 1985 or 1986 when I talked to Huo Yingdong [a Hong Kong tycoon, better known as Henry Fok] and mentioned that we didn't have funds for urban development. He asked me, 'If you have land, how can you not have money?' I thought this was a strange comment. Having land was one issue; a lack of funds was another.

---

[1] See data compiled in Tables 2.2 and 2.3. There are two categories of government revenues and expenditures: budgetary and extrabudgetary. Budgetary revenues (*yusuannei shouru*) consist primarily of tax revenues, whereas extrabudgetary revenues (*yusuanwai shouru*) are made up of various fees and charges. Land revenues fall into the latter category. See Christine P. Wong, "Paying for Urbanization in China: Challenges of Municipal Finance in the Twenty-First Century," in *Financing Metropolitan Governments in Developing Countries*, ed. Roy W. Bahl, Johannes F. Linn, and Deborah Wetzel (Cambridge, MA: Lincoln Institute of Land Policy, 2013), 273–308.

[2] "Guding touzi: Fangdichan" (Fixed Investment: Real Estate), National Bureau of Statistics (NBS), via CEIC. See Figure 2.1.

What did the two have to do with one another?"[3] Zhao goes on to describe how, presumably after he made the connection between landownership and capital accumulation, he presided over the initial experiments to separate ownership and use rights of land, and leasing the latter in return for capita – essentially, commodifying urban land.

This discovery of the "exchange value" of land – its ability to serve as a means of capital accumulation independent of its productive or use value – has resulted in a dramatic reorganization of intergovernmental and political economic relations in China during the last three decades.[4] This chapter narrates the CCP's relationship to land, tracing how land evolved from a national resource to be distributed in the service of socialist production and consumption to a form of capital to an instrument of fiscal and financial policy. Although distributing and redistributing land in order to maximize production – essentially, regulating the use of land as a means of production– is a familiar theme in the history of the Chinese political economy, the deployment of land as a vehicle for capital accumulation or as an instrument through which the state manipulates the economy is not. Indeed, these two roles for land emerged through a process of experimentation, crisis, and, ultimately, political choice that unfolded from the late 1980s through the first decade of the twenty-first century. The various political and economic roles assigned to land and property rights – and the changes in the ways that land was valued and to whom that value would accrue – emerged as a part of the political process of the economic reforms in China.

Several scholars have written about national policy with regard to land development and land markets in China, but because these studies focus chiefly on social contestation over property rights or on changing policy over rural land, none of them links these developments to more fundamental developments in the Chinese political economy.[5] Furthermore, scholarly debates about how the CCP manages internal discipline and governs the economy for the most part neglect land issues.[6] Only very recently, since the global financial crisis in 2008 and the stimulus program that made the centrality of land and

---

[3] Zhao Ziyang, *Prisoner of the State: The Secret Journal of Zhao Ziyang*, ed. Bao Pu, Renee Chiang, and Adi Ignatius (New York: Simon & Schuster, 2009), 108.

[4] See the later discussion of these terms.

[5] You-tien Hsing, *The Great Urban Transformation: Politics of Land and Property in China* (Oxford: Oxford University Press, 2010); Peter Ho, *Institutions in Transition: Land Ownership, Property Rights, and Social Conflict in China* (Oxford: Oxford University Press, 2005); George C. S. Lin, "Reproducing Spaces of Chinese Urbanisation: New City-Based and Land-Centred Urban Transformation," *Urban Studies* 44, no. 9 (2007): 1827–55; George C. S. Lin, *Developing China: Land, Politics and Social Conditions* (London: Routledge, 2009).

[6] Yasheng Huang, *Inflation and Investment Controls in China: The Political Economy of Central–Local Relations during the Reform Era* (Cambridge: Cambridge University Press, 1996): Victor C. Shih, *Factions and Finance in China: Elite Conflict and Inflation* (Cambridge: Cambridge University Press, 2008).

real estate to the Chinese economy painfully obvious, have land issues featured prominently in popular commentary.[7] In general, this analysis, based primarily on developments after 2004, conveys a narrative that the land dilemma – local governments' dependence on land revenue versus the central government's desire to rein in real estate investment and land conversions – is an unfortunate and unintended consequence of changes in China's fiscal and political institutions.

Yet, an examination of the conceptual thinking and political decisions that led to changes in property rights upends this logic, revealing that all along land control was at the heart of these institutional changes. Far from an accidental or unrelated consequence, the discovery of land as a vehicle for capital accumulation under state ownership made possible a dramatic reconfiguration of Chinese central–local relations in the 1990s and presented the central government with a new tool with which it could indirectly manage the macroeconomy. The emergence of land financing and the recentralization of the fiscal and monetary systems should be understood together as mutually reinforcing institutional developments that have determined the CCP's stewardship of the economy since 1992.

A major argument in this chapter – and in this book – is that land markets and property-rights practices have become less rather than more liberal over time. In the early period of land commodification, a greater number of actors outside the state were identified as property rights holders and markets were subject to less state intervention. During the turn toward fiscalization in the mid-1990s, the state (in the form of local governments) reasserted its sole ownership over land. This change had profound consequences at the local level. Whereas urban governments had adopted various property-rights regimes during the early period – including quite liberal ones with incipient systems of private property rights – almost all urban governments pursued land development and urban expansion in the late 1990s and 2000s. This finding runs counter to general expectations of gradual reform. It accords, however, with Yasheng Huang's argument about the status of entrepreneurship in China in the 1980s and 1990s, which he described as "directionally liberal" until a reversal in the 1990s on the heels of the Tiananmen uprising. In the case of property rights and land markets, the turning point was not Tiananmen, but

---

[7] Patrick Chovanec, "China's Real Estate Bubble May Have Just Popped," *Foreign Affairs*, December 18, 2011, at www.foreignaffairs.com/articles/136963/patrick-chovanec/chinas-real-estate-bubble-may-have-just-popped, accessed January 27, 2015; Lynette H. Ong, "Indebted Dragon: The Risky Strategy Behind China's Construction Economy," *Foreign Affairs*, November 27, 2012, at www.foreignaffairs.com/articles/138449/lynette-h-ong/indebted-dragon, accessed January 27, 2015. For a more scholarly (and earlier) take, see Victor C. Shih, "Local Government Debt: Big Rock-Candy Mountain." *China Economic Quarterly.* Vol. 14, no. 2. (June 2010): 26–32. Christine Wong, "The Fiscal Stimulus Programme and Public Governance Issues in China," *OECD Journal on Budgeting* 11, no. 3 (2011): 1–22.

rather the experience of unmanageable economic activity in the post-Tiananmen recovery that precipitated a reversal.[8]

A word about terms is in order before I proceed. This chapter narrates how Chinese property-rights policy moved from a policy to maximize the value of the use of land to a policy that permitted growth in the exchange value of land – what I call "commodification" to "fiscalization." The concepts of "use" and "exchange" value have their origins in Marx, but they have a wider use in urban politics and land politics.[9] Within the Marxist tradition, David Harvey theorized that urban political conflict is manifested as battles over the use (for the working class) versus the exchange (for capital) value of the built environment.[10] Logan and Molotch, writing about cities as "growth machines," use these concepts to argue that urban politics in the United States can be viewed as competition over exchange values; every urban landowner seeks to use the political process to maximize the exchange value of her land relative to that of others.[11] Commodification is simply the process by which something (e.g., land) previously not for sale gains a sale value or an exchange value.[12] Fiscalization (*tudi caizheng,* 土地财政, or "land finance"), a term widely used in both the Chinese- and English-literature on contemporary land politics, refers to "the management of land resources by political authorities for the purpose of generating fiscal revenue."[13] Commodification assigns land an economic exchange value, and fiscalization is the process by which land values accrue directly to the state for revenue purposes.

I do not intend to signal any particular intellectual affinity or theory of the world in the use of these terms. Rather, I use them strictly as defined previously and simply in reference to the processes and values they describe. In addition to their descriptive simplicity, "commodification" and "fiscalization" are the terms used in Chinese to discuss these processes; when talking about assigning economic values to land, Chinese official sources describe the process as *shangpinhua* (商品化), literally commodification or commercialization. The primary argument presented in the chapter is that the kinds and degrees of land values

[8] Yasheng Huang, *Capitalism with Chinese Characteristics: Entrepreneurship and the State* (Cambridge: Cambridge University Press, 2008), p. 41. Huang only tenuously identifies Tiananmen as a turning point.

[9] The distinction is from Karl Marx, *Selected Writings,* ed. David McLellan (2nd ed., Oxford: Oxford University Press, 2000), 458–72.

[10] David Harvey, "Labor, Capital, and Class Struggle around the Built Environment in Advanced Capitalist Societies," *Politics & Society* 6, no. 3 (1976): 265–95.

[11] John R. Logan and Harvey Luskin Molotch, *Urban Fortunes: The Political Economy of Place* (Berkeley: University of California Press, 1987); Harvey Molotch, "The City as a Growth Machine: Toward a Political Economy of Place," *American Journal of Sociology* 82, no. 2 (1976): 309–32.

[12] Karl Polanyi, *The Great Transformation* (Boston: Beacon Press, 1957).

[13] Susan Whiting, "Values in Land: Fiscal Pressures, Land Disputes and Justice Claims in Rural and Peri-Urban China," *Urban Studies* 48, no. 3 (March 2011): 507.

are the outcomes of political debates and political choices, so I aim to describe these debates and choices in the most literal terms possible.

LAND IN CHINESE HISTORY: THE LONG VIEW

The "land problem" to which Mao Zedong refers in the epigraph to Chapter 1 was unique neither to Mao nor to China. Almost any official or peasant in contemporary China would state the problem in much the same way: Land in China is relatively scarce given how many people depend on it as a source of livelihood and subsistence. This basic condition – the abundance of labor and the scarcity of arable land – has been at the center of efforts to govern China and to manage the lives of Chinese people from imperial to modern times. An understanding of the novelty of the land reforms in the 1980s that gave rise to land as a commodity instead of as a means of production requires some understanding of the political history of land and land reforms in China.

The claim that the quality or quantity of land resources is related to the long-term development of various kinds of economic and political institutions will not strike any reader as radical. Debates about the programs of economic and institutional change within many societies have typically revolved around how societies have managed to extract value from the land resources that they have inherited.[14] Scholarship on the "great divergence" or the "Needham question" – essentially why scientific and industrial revolutions developed in Europe after 1500 but not in China, which previously had been more advanced in science and technology – has more often than not focused on the question of how Europe made the transition to capitalist agriculture, whereas agricultural production in most of Asia remained labor-intensive and primarily for subsistence.

Although an exhaustive discussion of the puzzle of "divergence" is neither necessary nor possible here, thinking about changes in land policy over the long term is useful for understanding the land revolution that came about during the last quarter of the twentieth century.[15] There is much disagreement among

[14] Kenneth L. Sokoloff and Stanley L. Engerman, "History Lessons: Institutions, Factors Endowments, and Paths of Development in the New World," *Journal of Economic Perspectives* 14, no. 3 (2000): 217–32; Ross Levine, "Law, Endowments and Property Rights," *Journal of Economic Perspectives* 19, no. 3 (2005): 61–88.

[15] In thinking about the use of land, labor, and capital in China in comparison to their use in Europe, scholars have proffered explanations of the "agrarian traditionalism" in China that run the gamut from "hydraulic" or "oriental despotism," to Europe's discovery of colonialism and access to distant lands and resources, to the simple but elegant idea that farming technologies in China never necessitated a change to capital-intensity. Karl August Wittfogel, *Oriental Despotism: A Comparative Study of Total Power* (New Haven, CT: Yale University Press, 1957); Karl A. Wittfogel, "The Marxist View of China (Part 1)," *China Quarterly*, no. 11 (1962): 1–22; Karl A. Wittfogel, "The Marxist View of China (Part 2)," *The China Quarterly* no. 12 (1962): 154–69; Barrington Moore Jr., *Social Origins of Dictatorship and Democracy: Lord and*

analysts of divergence, including about whether land in China was privately held and whether property rights even mattered for production. But they tend to agree that the ultimate goal of land policy in China was to maximize the food production value of land given the extant technology. No matter whether land schemes established and encouraged large farms, allowed the state to confiscate privately held lands, or targeted population movement and reclamation of wastelands, the goal of political land reforms, that is, those reforms initiated by both local and imperial political authorities, was consistently to maximize agricultural output given the abundance of labor and the scarcity of land.

I do not mean to imply that the concept of the exchange value of land was completely nonexistent in China prior to the late 1980s. Rather, it was far from the dominant way of thinking about land and wealth, and certainly it was not the goal of state policy toward land.[16] As George Lin has written, "The established Chinese tradition to take land as a basic source of living has been a fundamental social condition upon which land use and land development are pursued by Chinese peasants and regulated by the state."[17] Indeed, this approach to land held firm even against the winds of revolution that swept through China in the twentieth century.

LAND UNDER MAO: THE FIRST LAND REFORM

Land redistribution was the primary goal of the CCP as it "liberated" swaths of the countryside prior to assuming power and establishing the PRC. Thereafter,

---

Peasant in the Making of the Modern World (Boston: Beacon Press, 1966); Francesca Bray, *The Rice Economies: Technology and Development in Asian Societies* (Oxford: Blackwell, 1986); E. L. Jones, *The European Miracle: Environments, Economies, and Geopolitics in the History of Europe and Asia* (Cambridge: Cambridge University Press, 1981). Perhaps the most dominant approach, if not the most convincing, looks at the structure of political institutions, examining how Europe developed institutions (such as private-property rights and contracts) that protected individual economic interests and political voice, whereas Asia did not develop such institutions. Douglass C. North, John Joseph Wallis, and Barry R. Weingast, *Violence and Social Orders: A Conceptual Framework for Interpreting Recorded Human History* (Cambridge: Cambridge University Press, 2009). More recent scholarship has questioned the geographic scope of the comparison, instead comparing parts of China and Europe and showing that China was by no means stagnant and wholly lacking in market-oriented institutions. Kenneth Pomeranz, *The Great Divergence: China, Europe, and the Making of the Modern World Economy* (Princeton, NJ: Princeton University Press, 2000); Jean-Laurent Rosenthal and R. Bin Wong, *Before and Beyond Divergence: The Politics of Economic Change in China and Europe* (Cambridge, MA: Harvard University Press, 2011).

[16] Exceptions include, for example, a never-implemented Guomindang scheme to issue land-backed national bonds. Huang Xianjin, "1940–1948 nian de tudi zijinhua: Jianlun woguo tudi zheng-juanhua celüe" (Land Designated Funds: China's Land Securities Strategy), in *Zhongguo fangdi chanye yu jinrong fazhan wenti yanjiu* (Reseach on Problems Related to China's Real estate Industry and Financial Development), ed. Yu Yongshun (Beijing: Jingji guanli chubanshe, 1995), 143–60.

[17] Lin, *Developing China*, 2.

land reform became the paramount mechanism of state building and the manifestation of revolution throughout the PRC during the first five years after 1949. The land reforms carried out in the base areas of the People's Liberation Army (PLA) and during the First Five-Year Plan (FYP) entailed organizing rural Chinese into class categories (landlord, rich peasant, middle peasant, and landless peasant) based on the amount of land they owned, the number of cultivators they hired, and the amount of land they rented out. The revolutionary aspects of these reforms have been well documented; the class struggle element of social change was accomplished through the rural reforms, and the machinery used to implement these reforms was local-level agitation and political force.[18] However, the CCP was not willing to sacrifice economic modernization and production goals for its political objectives. From the outset, the land reforms were about maximizing economic production as well as making revolution.

The dual logics of production maximization and political change were apparent in the language of the Land Law, which was circulated on June 30, 1950: "The land ownership system of feudal exploitation by the landlord class shall be abolished and the system of peasant land ownership shall be introduced in order to set free the rural productive forces, develop agricultural production and thus pave the way for New China's industrialization."[19] Although the land reform campaign was violent, it was also not unrelentingly radical, since the CCP leadership explicitly curbed the political impetus to eliminate the rich peasant class in favor of its production goals. In a speech in June 1950, Mao stated, "there should be a change in our policy toward the rich peasants, a change from the policy of requisitioning their surplus land and property to one of maintaining the rich peasant economy in order to facilitate the early rehabilitation of rural production."[20] Although data for the period are unreliable and it is difficult to establish how much of the boost in rural production in the early 1950s was a direct result of the land reforms, most economists and historians view the early 1950s as a success in terms of rehabilitating agricultural production.[21] It is more difficult to understand the economic logic of the agrarian radicalism that would follow in the 1950s and the early 1960s during creation of the people's communes and implementation of the Great Leap Forward. I will not wade into the details of the origins and course of the Great Leap Forward and the famine it produced, except to note that there were many

[18] Vivienne Shue, *Peasant China in Transition: The Dynamics of Development toward Socialism, 1949–1956* (Berkeley: University of California Press, 1980).
[19] *Agrarian Reform Law of the People's Republic of China: Together with Other Relevant Documents* (Peking: Foreign Languages Press, 1950), 1.
[20] "Speech at the Third Plenum of the Seventh Central Committee," quoted in Chris Bramall, "Chinese Land Reform in Long-Run Perspective and in the Wider East Asian Context," *Journal of Agrarian Change* 4, nos. 1–2 (2004): 112.
[21] Ibid., 115. For an entirely different perspective, see Frank Dikötter, *The Tragedy of Liberation: A History of the Chinese Revolution, 1945–1957* (New York: Bloomsbury, 2013).

mistakes and miscalculations, the idea that communalization and mass mobilization would enhance agricultural output among them.[22]

Land was nationalized in urban China during the transition to socialism in 1956. Surprisingly, and especially in comparison to the rural land reforms, nationalization of urban land was not particularly contentious. There are several reasons for this. First, much of the most highly valued land in the coastal cities was owned and occupied by Guomindang (KMT) bureaucrats or foreigners, most of whom had fled before or shortly after 1949.[23] Second, most privately owned housing stock was dilapidated and crowded and would require more investment for renovation than most owners or occupants considered worth fighting for. The massive construction projects of the 1950s to establish state- and collectively owned enterprises organized for collective production and consumption promised employment, housing, and social welfare for the vast majority of urban Chinese, and for most they represented a far better alternative to the pre-1949 urban housing.[24]

Ironically, perhaps, land was deployed in urban China during the Maoist period with another logic, but one equally far from realizing the exchange value of land as a vehicle for capital accumulation. Land was distributed through bureaucratic allocations to enterprises and institutions – factories, schools, government offices, and so forth – essentially free of charge and in the service of socialist production. Many commentators have focused on how land allocations during the period of state socialism were inefficient: Enterprises could acquire land at essentially no cost, producing patterns of urban land use and physical expansion that seemed to be unlimited and to entail little consideration of long-term infrastructure needs. This pattern of overconsumption but underutilization of land reached its height during the Great Leap Forward, as urban authorities indulged in a construction binge on a monumental scale, most frequently according to a mobilizational rather than a productive logic. For example, urban planners and construction authorities were instructed to expand the size of major roads on the basis of the size of their respective cities: eighty to one hundred meters for Beijing, Shanghai, and Tianjin; sixty to eighty

[22] See Dali L. Yang, *Calamity and Reform in China: State, Rural Society, and Institutional Change since the Great Leap Famine* (Stanford, CA: Stanford University Press, 1996); Jisheng Yang, *Tombstone: The Great Chinese Famine, 1958–1962*, ed. Edward Friedman, Guo Jian, and Stacy Mosher (New York: Farrar, Straus & Giroux, 2012); Roderick MacFarquhar, *The Origins of the Cultural Revolution: 2. The Great Leap Forward 1958–1960* (New York: Columbia University Press, 1983).

[23] Kenneth G. Lieberthal, *Revolution and Tradition in Tientsin, 1949–1952* (Stanford, CA: Stanford University Press, 1980); Ezra F. Vogel, *Canton under Communism: Programs and Politics in a Provincial Capital, 1949–1968* (Cambridge, MA: Harvard University Press, 1969); Hua Lanhong, *Chongjian Zhongguo: Chengshi guihua sanshinian, 1949–1979* (Reconstructing China: Thirty Years of Urban Planning, 1949–1979) (Beijing: Shenghuo dushu, xinzhi, Sanlian shudian, 2009), 40–69.

[24] Hua Lanhong, *Chongjian Zhongguo*, 40–69.

meters for large-sized cities; forty to fifty meters for medium-sized cities; and so forth.[25] Within a single year, Beijing undertook construction of a major train station, an eighty-thousand-person sports arena, the Cultural Palace of Nationalities, the National Museum of Chinese History, and the Great Hall of the People, and cities all over China embarked on a residential construction frenzy to create urban communes that provided libraries, kindergartens, mess halls, and performance areas but that lacked within-unit kitchens and bathrooms.[26]

Urban land was envisioned as an input to maximize production, although not a scarce one. Both rural and urban land during the Maoist period was commonly imagined to have little intrinsic economic value beyond its role as a space in which to place factories and to raise crops. Land held political value only insofar as it could be distributed – to peasants, firms, urban workers, and so forth – in exchange for support or acquiescence. The idea of land as a commodity for exchange, and therefore the idea of a market for land, would not emerge until the late 1980s as an innovation that would dramatically reconfigure the relationship between local governments and the territories under their purview.

THE SECOND LAND REFORM: DECOLLECTIVIZATION

The second major land reform in the PRC was the restoration of family farming in the late 1970s and 1980s. This "most massive single act of privatization in history," as Daniel Kelliher has called the dismantling of the communes in rural China, was achieved through the household responsibility system, whereby households contracted with collectives to farm individual plots and were permitted to sell in those markets products that exceeded the quotas assigned to the collectives.[27] The results of this land reform, accompanied by price reforms and technological changes, are well known: Agricultural output grew dramatically between 1978 and 1984, lifting nearly 140 million rural Chinese out of poverty.[28]

The decollectivization of agricultural production was not, however, accompanied by the decollectivization of landownership in rural China. Rather, the

---

[25] Zheng Guo, *Chengshi fazhan yu guihua* (Urban Development and Planning) (Beijing: Zhongguo renmin daxue chubanshe, 2009), 158.

[26] Hua Lanhong, *Chongjian Zhongguo*, 91.

[27] Daniel R. Kelliher, *Peasant Power in China: The Era of Rural Reform, 1979–1989* (New Haven, CT: Yale University Press, 1992): 5. See also David Zweig, *Freeing China's Farmers: Rural Restructuring in the Reform Era* (Armonk, NY: M. E. Sharpe, 1997); Joseph Fewsmith, *Dilemmas of Reform in China: Political Conflict and Economic Debate* (Armonk, NY: M. E. Sharpe, 1994), 1–55. To be sure, land was not actually privatized, but land-use rights and income rights were somewhat privatized.

[28] Bramall, "Chinese Land Reform in Long-Run Perspective," 115; Justin Yifu Lin, "Rural Reforms and Agricultural Growth in China," *American Economic Review* 82, no. 1 (1992): 34–51.

institutional change was the separation of use rights from ownership rights: Farmland continued to be owned by the collective, but the rights to use the land were leased to individual households for a fixed term, with the understanding that tenure would be periodically renegotiated on the basis of the needs of the village. The separation of use and ownership rights in the countryside prompted the creation of markets for labor and for crops, but it did not create land markets. The "two-tiered" tenure system permitted households to rent and to farm the land, but it did not permit the trading or transferring of land-use rights on open markets.[29] Rural Chinese could benefit from the use value of rural land, but not from its exchange value.

LAND AS CAPITAL

As the rural reforms were scaled up nationally in the early 1980s, the urban reforms were for the most part restricted to the southeastern special economic zones (SEZs), which, beginning in 1979, enjoyed a number of special privileges regarding capital and labor mobility and markets. In 1984, these privileges were extended to fourteen coastal "open" cities, including Dalian, the subject of Chapter 4. Nonetheless, the increased mobility put pressures on all urban environments to expand, both to accommodate returnees from the countryside after the end of the Cultural Revolution and to relieve neighborhoods that for years had been suffering from low or no investment.

Yet, unlike in rural China, where agricultural surpluses were sufficient to fund rural industrialization, urban China lacked capital to invest in urban construction and expansion. The vast majority of urban land was controlled by industrial or commercial enterprises that enjoyed land-use privileges essentially free of charge, leaving city governments to face the dual problems of inefficient land use and the lack of stable funds to invest in infrastructure. As early as 1980, urban planners began to float the idea of charging land-use fees to address these problems by generating funds for the cities and by erecting cost barriers for inefficient land use. In preparation for the National Urban Work Conference that would take place in October 1980, the director of the National Construction Committee, arguing that cities had "no formal, stable sources of investment for infrastructure," drafted a proposal that would force urban work units that used and benefited from urban public works to pay for them through a set of taxes and fees. The proposal did not win approval at the conference,

---

[29] Survey data results from Brandt et al. report that as of 1995 households could rent use rights, but rental markets were not at all widespread, and in fact most rentals were to other family members. Loren Brandt et al., "Land Rights in Rural China: Facts, Fictions and Issues," *China Journal* no. 47 (Januay 2002): 67–97; Guo Li, Scott Rozelle, and Loren Brandt, "Tenure, Land Rights, and Farmer Investment Incentives in China," *Agricultural Economics* 19, nos. 1–2 (September 1998): 63–71.

primarily because the State Council feared that it would alienate the powerful enterprise leaders in key urban centers.[30]

Instead, land-use fees began the way that most policies in China begin: with local experimentation that is then replicated on a national scale.[31] In 1984, Fushun city, a heavy industry base outside Shenyang in Liaoning province, began assessing a per-square-meter usage fee for land at different rates depending on the long-term impact of the land use (i.e., commercial versus residential versus industrial occupancy). By 1985, the city had collected more than 10 million RMB (70 percent of which was recycled back into a city preservation and construction fund), thus providing an incentive for enterprises to scale down land use, indeed forcing enterprises that had been allocated vast swaths of land to cede areas that they could not afford to put to productive use.[32] By the mid-1980s, on the heels of these successes, cities nationwide began imposing land-use fees, leading to debates about how to value and price land. What had been a means of production allocated or distributed by the plan began to be considered a commodity that could be priced and acquired through market means.[33]

EXPERIMENTING WITH COMMODIFICATION

Though taxes and fees on land use set the stage, the separation of use rights and ownership rights and the commodification of the former were truly the beginning of China's third major land reform. The Land Law of 1986, drafted and promulgated in reaction to illegal farmland transfers, conservatively reified the lack of land markets: "No individual or organization may seize, sell or buy, rent or otherwise illegally transfer land." A mere two years later, a 1988 revision added the following sentence: "Land-use rights may be transferred according to law."[34] During the intervening two years, reformers promoted experiments in coastal cities that would mollify concerns about relinquishing state ownership

[30] Han Guang's proposal was called "A Suggestion for Collecting Fees for Urban Land Use" (Guanyu zhengshou chengzhen tudi shiyongfei de yijian). Song Qilin, "Chengshi tudi changyong de qianhouhou" (The Ins and Outs of Urban Land Use Experimentation), in *Wushinian huimou: Xin Zhongguo de chengshi guihua*, ed. Zhongguo chengshi guihua xuehui (China Urban Planning Society) (Beijing: Shangwu yinshuguan, 1999), 152–61.

[31] Sebastian Heilmann, "Policy Experimentation in China's Economic Rise," *Studies in Comparative International Development* 43, no. 1 (2008): 1–26.

[32] This was approximately one-fourth of the city's budgetary revenue. *Dangdai Zhongguo de chengshi jianshe* (Contemporary China's Urban Construction) (Beijing: Zhongguo shehui kexue chubanshe, 1990), 132. Guangzhou and Shenzhen were experimenting with land-use fees for new occupants as early as 1981.

[33] Indeed, real estate handbooks and histories published in the early 1990s universally consider the introduction of land-use fees to be the first necessary step en route to land leasing. Wang Yanju and Yang Xiaoze, eds., *Fangdi chanye jingying guanli shouce* (Real Estate Industry Management and Operations Handbook) (Shanghai: Shanghai renmin chubanshe, 1990), 22.

[34] Ibid., 22.

over China's most limited factor of production and would demonstrate the potential of real estate to generate much-needed capital for urban development.

The first proposal to create a market in land-use rights was by Gu Mu, a vice premier of the State Council and a prominent reformer. On March 31, 1987, he presented a novel idea to the foreign capital working group of the State Council: Coastal cities are starving for capital for urban construction and infrastructure development, so why not allow them to transfer land-use rights for payments? His language was careful: Such actions would not transfer the ownership (*suoyouquan*, 所有权) of land, but only the use rights, allowing the economic activities of firms to generate capital for the state.[35] Gu Mu is said to have proposed: "Let's find a small plot of land in a SEZ and experiment.... The people of Shenzhen may get to eat the first crab leg."[36] They did just that. On September 9, 1987, after great excitement and support from Hong Kong, Macau, and reformers in the mainland, the Shenzhen government leased land-use rights for a fifty-year term over a five-square-kilometer plot to the Shenzhen branch of China Aerospace Technology Company at the price of 200 RMB per square meter. By November 1987, Hainan Island was permitted to transfer use rights in return for currency payments, and officials in the Land Office had delivered to the State Council a proposal to permit land leasing in Shanghai, Tianjin, and Guangzhou, as well as Shenzhen.[37]

Novel though the Shenzhen experiments were, leasing land-use rights to state-owned firms nonetheless did not stoke political fears of privatization. In the following year, however, Shanghai experimented with leasing land-use rights to foreign and private firms, heralding a new era for a Communist Party that previously had been preoccupied with struggling against foreign encroachment on Chinese land. A fierce ideological debate preceded the Shanghai experiment, detailed in Zhao Ziyang's memoirs, from which I quote at the beginning of this chapter. According to Zhao, the idea of "renting" land in the developing areas of Shanghai was initially circulated by overseas Chinese businessmen, but it met opposition from conservatives, especially Chen Yun, a party elder and by the late 1980s a major critic of the market reforms. Zhao reports that Chen said that "in dealing with regions such as Shanghai and Zhejiang, one must proceed with caution, because people in these areas were especially skilled and familiar with capitalist behavior."[38] Zhao credits Chen's objections and a general lack of consensus among party elders for the delay in land experiments in Shanghai, despite Deng Xiaoping's approval, until 1988.

---

[35] Bai Xiaodong, ed., *Xin Zhongguo tudi guanli dashiji, 1949–2008* (Chronology of Land Management in New China, 1949–2008) (Beijing: Zhongguo dadi chubanshe, 2009), 75.

[36] Wang Yanju and Yang Xiaoze, eds., *Fangdi chanye jingying guanli shouce*, 13.

[37] Bai Xiaodong, ed., *Xin Zhongguo tudi guanli dashiji*, 80. The Land Office (*tudiju*, 土地局) was established in 1988.

[38] Zhao, *Prisoner of the State*, 109–10.

On August 8, 1988, a day chosen for its auspiciousness,[39] the Shanghai Municipal Government for the first time accepted international bids at a public auction. A contract for plot number 26 in the Hongqiao Development Zone was awarded to a firm owned by Sun Zhongli, an overseas Chinese business-man. This was the first time since 1949 that a foreign business had secured independent control over a plot of land in China.[40] The Shanghai experiments alerted urban governments on the east coast to the potential of land leasing to generate funds,[41] and foreign investors were eager to encourage them. Over the next few years, Chen Yun's suspicions about the capitalist tendencies of the eastern regions would be vindicated, as the pursuits of local governments, land occupants, and foreign investors coalesced into contemporary China's first real estate bubble.

THE BUBBLE

In 1991, the third year of land-use commodification, local governments col-lected a total of 3.17 billion RMB in land-use taxes, 3.72 billion in real estate taxes, and more than 2 billion RMB in firm taxes collected from real estate enterprises; together, these taxes constituted 2.3 percent of the annual revenue. In the coastal cities with more active real estate markets, the contribution to local budgets was even higher – around 4.5 percent in Guangzhou and more than 10 percent in Shenzhen.[42] But it was not until 1992 that the industry took off. The June 1989 crackdown, which ended six weeks of protests by students and workers, generated uncertainty about the future of the economic reforms and the fate of China's opening to global capital. Deng Xiaoping's Southern Tour, during which, in Shenzhen, he proclaimed, "To get rich is glorious," signaled a commitment to reform and reinvigorated market activity throughout the country.

On the heels of the successes and renewed political support for coastal SEZs and open cities, development zones were established all over China. Local governments looked to the examples of Pudong and Shenzhen, seeking to lease land in exchange for capital to develop infrastructure. Moreover, explicit support from Beijing for developing the sector ignited a national real estate frenzy. A 1992 State Council document stated: "The real estate industry is

[39] The number 8 is considered auspicious in China. The 2008 Olympic opening ceremonies, for example, began at 8 pm on August 8, 2008.
[40] For a firsthand account of the auction and the "cultural change" required within the land and the urban planning bureaucracies, see Geng Yaxin, "Tudi pizu cujinle guihua guanli gongzuo de gaige" (The Reform of Urban Planning Work after the Introduction of Land Leasing), in *Wushinian huimou*, ed. Zhongguo chengshi guihua xuehui, 162–5.
[41] Note that, at this stage, local governments were eager to generate funds primarily indirectly through taxes on land transactions rather than directly through lease fees.
[42] Cheng Hu and Zhang Lu, eds., *Zhongguo fangdichan redian datexie* (Collection of Special Writings on China's Real-Estaste Craze) (Beijing: Zhongguo shenji chubanshe, 1993).

one of China's new burgeoning industries. It is a large part of the growth of the service/tertiary sector, and with the leasing of use rights for state land and privatization of the housing sector, it will become a pillar industry in China."[43]

During this period – the first nationwide venture into land leasing, property development, and real estate commercialization – the rules governing land-ownership, and who could lease or rent land, were exceptionally vague, more so than during any other period under study here. The 1988 revision of the Land Law clearly permitted the transfer of land-use rights in return for capital, but it did not elucidate much more. The original 1986 Land Law had indicated that the state was the owner of Chinese urban land, but it did not set out clear provisions to determine who would represent the state and, therefore, to whom the land-lease fees would accrue. National laws set no uniform regulations governing ownership, pricing, land-use planning, administration of land leasing, and so forth. A lack of a national legal or regulatory infrastructure did not preclude the emergence of land markets in urban China, but it did ensure that – similar to liberalization in other arenas such as entrepreneurship or rural industrialization – land markets were subject to local interpretations under conditions of uncertainty.[44] Between 1987 and 1990, more than two hundred laws and regulations were issued by various national and local governments and departments.[45] By the time the sector took off in 1992, the rules and norms governing who could enter the industry, who could represent the "state" as owner of the land, and to whom capital would accrue from land leasing varied subnationally and were especially poorly efined.

The period from 1992 through the middle of 1994 is described – by local and national officials, scholars, and the media – as a "real estate craze" (*fangdichan re*, 房地产热) and a "bubble" (*paomo*, 泡沫). The growth in real estate activity was rapid (see Figure 2.1). There were 117 development zones in the country at the end of 1991, and 1,993 such zones at the end of 1992.[46] There are no official figures about how many development zones existed by the end of the bubble in the second half of 1993, since many were concealed from higher levels, but some estimates note as many as 8,700 zones that occupied more land

[43] State Council Document [1992] 62, "Guoyuyuan guanyu fazhan fangdi chanye ruogan wenti de tongzhi" (State Council Communiqué Regarding Issues in Developing the Real Estate Sector), November 4, 1992, at www.kj2100.com/Html/1992/11/04/201110334737.html, accessed January 28, 2015.

[44] Adam Segal, *Digital Dragon: High-Technology Enterprises in China* (Ithaca, NY: Cornell University Press, 2003); Susan H. Whiting, *Power and Wealth in Rural China: The Political Economy of Institutional Change* (Cambridge: Cambridge University Press, 2001).

[45] Wang Yanju and Yang Xiaoze, eds., *Fangdi chanye jingying guanli shouce*, 26. The authors insist that even these numbers are incomplete.

[46] Yu Yongshun, ed., *Zhongguo fangdi chanye yu jinrong fazhan wenti yanjiu* (Research on Issues Related to China's Real Estate Industry and Financial Development) (Beijing: Jingji guanli chubanshe, 1995).

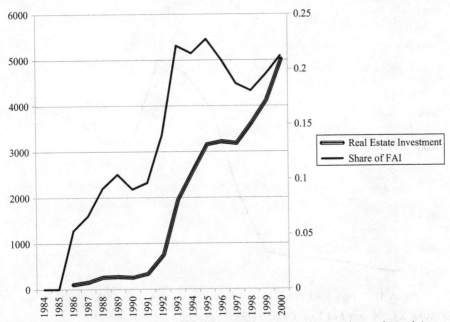

FIGURE 2.1. Gross Real-Estate Investment (Billion RMB) and as a Share of Fixed-Asset Investments (FAIs), 1986–2000
Source: National Bureau of Statistics, via CEIC.

area than the total actual built-up area of five hundred cities.[47] The city of Beihai in Guangxi province illustrates the extreme: Between 1992 and 1995, eighty-five square kilometers were leased, but the actual built-up area of the city was only seventeen square kilometers.[48]

Even more revealingly, the number of registered real estate development companies increased from 5,128 in 1991 to 13,566 in 1992 (see Figure 2.2). Critically, the frenzy of real estate investment was arising not only from local governments. In fact, nearly everyone seemed to be in the business of real estate development. Initially, this was an optimistic sign: Reports issued by the Ministry of Construction in 1992 promoted real estate as a special industry because "even non–real estate firms can set foot in real estate," and, very optimistically, "all places in the country will see prices rise and not fall."[49] Universities, hospitals, enterprises, and government departments at all levels

---

[47] A "built-up area" (*jianchengqu*) is a measure of the land area controlled by a city that is actually developed urban construction. This estimate is from Huang Xiaohu, ed., *Xinshiqi Zhongguo tudi guanli yanjiu* (A New Era in China Land Management Research) (2 vols., Beijing: Dangdai Zhongguo chubanshe, 2006), 18.

[48] Ibid.

[49] Quoted in Cheng Hu and Zhang Lu, eds., *Zhongguo fangdichan redian datexie*, 207.

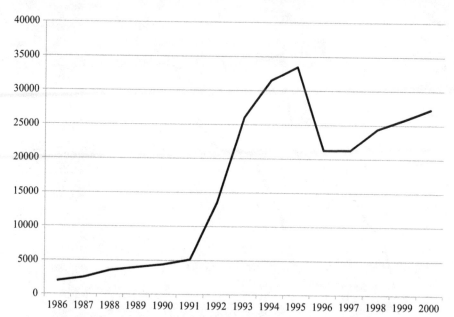

FIGURE 2.2. Number of Real-Estate Firms, 1985–2000
Source: Zhongguo guding zichan touzi shudian, 1950–2000 (Statistics on Investment in Fixed Assets in China, 1950–2000) (Beijing: Zhongguo tongji chubanshe, 2002), 369.

established real estate arms; staked claim to "state" land; and tried their luck in developing commercial real estate. Official speeches and documents refer to an "enclosure craze" (*quandi re*, 圈地热), in which various work units and land occupants parceled out land for development and sale, and "speculative winds" (*chaomai feng*, 炒卖风), in which work units invested substantial capital in property speculation.[50] At the time, the majority of land use was determined by administrative allocation (*huafa*, 划发), by which "the state" (typically the local government but sometimes provincial or central agencies) would assign land-use rights to enterprises or institutions free of charge. After land was "assigned" to an institutional user, the user would then allow the land to enter the real estate market and thereby would "make money through land" (*yitu shengcai*, 以土生财).[51] Figure 2.3 shows that of the increasingly

[50] Liu Weixin, "Lun fangdichan jinrong yu jingji fazhan de guanxi," 8–9; "Guowuyuan Zou Jiahua fuzongli zai quanguo fangdichan kaifa jingyan jiaoliu huishang jiakuai fangdi chanye de gaige fazhan zuole zhongyao zhishi" (Important Instructions by State Council Vice Premier Zou Jiahua at the National Meeting on the Exchange of Experiences in Accelerating Real estate Development), August 10, 1992, in *Zhongguo fangdi chanye qushi* (Trends in Chinese Real Estate), ed. Zhang Yuanduan (Ha'erbin: Ha'erbin chuanbo gongcheng xueyuan chubanshe, 1992), 1–6.

[51] Huang Xiaohu, ed., *Xinshiqi Zhongguo tudi guanli yanjiu*, 18.

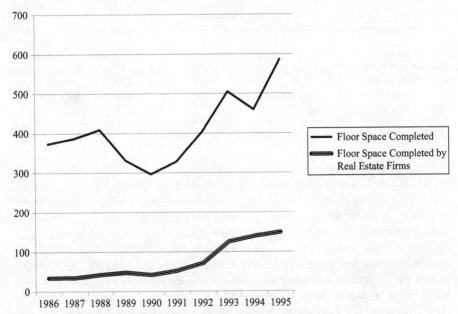

FIGURE 2.3. Annual Floor Space Completed, 1985–1995 (Million Square Meters)
Source: Zhongguo guding zichan touzi shudian, 1950–2000, 351.

large volume of floor space completed in the early 1990s, well less than one-third was completed by officially designated real estate firms.

Massive real estate investment at all levels also was made possible by the decentralized structure of China's financial sector at the time. Before the recentralization of the financial sector under Zhu Rongji in the mid- to late 1990s, discussed in the conclusion to this chapter, China's banking system, although oligopolistic with only several national and state-run banks, was nonetheless dispersed and decentralized, meaning that local bank branches enjoyed independence and discretion over lending practices. Close relationships between local governments and local banks are famously said to have granted strategic advantages to township and village enterprises (TVEs), that is, to "collective" enterprises owned and managed by local governments, but this also meant that the center had very little control over the volume of credit extensions and that local relationships determined the extent of capital available for real estate investment.[52]

[52] See Loren Brandt and Xiaodong Zhu, "Redistribution in a Decentralized Economy: Growth and Inflation in China under Reform," *Journal of Political Economy* 108, no. 2 (2000): 422–39; Christine P. W. Wong, Christopher Heady, and Wing T. Woo, *Fiscal Management and Economic Reform in the People's Republic of China* (Hong Kong: Oxford University Press, 1995); Huang, *Inflation and Investment Controls in China*; Shih, *Factions and Finance in China*.

TABLE 2.1. *Investment Price Indices, 1992–1995*

	1992	1993	1994	1995
Fixed-asset investments	115.3	126.6	110.4	105.9
Construction and installations	116.8	131.3	110.4	104.7
Purchase of equipment, tools, and other instruments	109.4	119.7	109.5	106.3
Other	120.9	123.4	112.1	112.4

Source: *Zhongguo guding zichan touzi shudian, 1950–2000, 7–8.*

Under these conditions, local governments, enterprises, institutions, and banks, as well as foreign investors who poured comparatively astronomical amounts of foreign capital into China after the renewed political commitment to reforms in 1992, all sought to gain from the rising real estate prices. Nationwide, twenty-two thousand hectares – three times the area leased in 1991 and eleven times that leased in 1990 – were leased in 1992. Foreign investment in the real estate sector increased 228 percent between 1991 and 1992.[53] The majority of real estate activity occurred along the east coast, exactly as Chen Yun had feared, and landmark projects attracted both national and international attention. On November 8, 1992, Hangzhou, in Zhejiang province, broke ground on the largest real-estate project west of Shanghai, a project that occupied forty-seven thousand square meters of land and had a combined investment of US$120 million from Taiwan, Hong Kong, Japan, and Singapore.[54] Hainan Island, the provincewide SEZ off the southeastern coast, was the epicenter of foreign investment in real estate development. The island had only one real estate firm in 1987, but by 1991 there were more then 350, or one-tenth of the total number of real estate firms nationwide, and it had the fourth highest level of real estate investment after Beijing, Guangdong, and Fujian provinces.[55]

General inflation between 1992 and 1993 was very high, exceeding20 percent by the end of 1993.[56] In contrast to earlier inflationary cycles during the reform era (the mid-1980s and 1988–1989), land and real estate were the major factors behind the growth in prices. Table 2.1 shows the price indices for elements of fixed-asset investment during the early 1990s: It is clear that the price increases in construction and installation were the drivers behind the general inflation in investment. Comprehensive and comparative data on property or land prices at the time do not exist, and for good reason: From city to city prices varied widely and were determined differently, and nearly no government had full knowledge of the transactions in the sector. Yet, we do know

[53] Liu Weixin, "Lun fandichan jinrong yu guanxi fazhan de guanxi," 5–17.
[54] Ibid., 16. This investment was about 40 percent of Zhejiang province's total FDI in 1992. Comparative data from China Data Center, via China Data Online, accessed July 22, 2013.
[55] Cheng Hu and Zhang Lu, eds., *Zhongguo fangdichan redian datexie,* 206–15.
[56] Shih, *Factions and Finance in China,* 150.

that prices rose nearly everywhere. In Shanghai, as the local government sought international investment for the new district in Pudong, real estate in the city's older districts heated up and prices rose rapidly. Even older structures saw incredible price increases. Peace Garden, an older complex in Jing'an, sold at 900 RMB per square meter in February 1990; by March 1992 the price had risen to 2,600 RMB per square meter and by November of the same year it had reached 3,100 RMB. Developers planned high-rise apartment complexes that sold out within days after being offered and well before construction began. One West Nanjing Road area complex sold out within one hour after the opening of the sales office in late fall 1992, with prices averaging 4,000 RMB per square meter.[57] In Hong Kong, investors were recruited with data that showed average returns on real estate investments at 30 to 40 percent but frequently as high as 50 percent.[58]

Central authorities were surprised at the degree of differences in land and property prices and at the pace of the price changes. A 1992 investigative report by Xinhua News Agency revealed land-pricing differentials and practices that surprised both local and central authorities. The report found that land-pricing practices were full of contradictions and distortions. For example, Xiamen city – one of the original SEZs – had relatively low prices for land, averaging about 175 RMB per square meter. The report alleged that the majority of the 100,000 square meters that had been auctioned had been bought by foreign investors, who were "hoarding and profiteering" rather than developing the land. In Shanghai, however, prices reached as high as US$2,800 per square meter, and averaged US$2,170 per square meter. In other cities, average prices seemed sensible, but averages obfuscate the extremes: In Fuzhou city, average prices in the city center were 1.2 to 1.5 million RMB per *mu* (about one-sixth of an acre, or 667 square meters), but researchers found a similar plot in the same area with a registered price of 10,000 RMB per *mu* and another at a price of 6.6 million RMB per *mu*. The increasing prices were just as alarming as the distortions: The report revealed that the average land price in Shenzhen had increased from 611 RMB per square meter in 1987 to 10,000 RMB per square meter in 1992. Between 1980 and 1992 commercial housing prices had increased on average 5.5 times in the larger cities, a rate of increase far more rapid than that of wages.[59] Officials worried that land and property prices outpacing wages and income changes could constitute a social stability problem; they received the report as a warning call that the real estate sector needed to be disciplined.[60]

[57] Cheng Hu and Zhang Lu, eds., *Zhongguo fangdichan redian datexie*, 37–8.
[58] Loretta Zhang, "Evolution of the Real Estate Market in Southern China" (A.B. thesis, Harvard University, 1993).
[59] "Laizi 'tudi geming' zhanchang de diaocha baogao" (A Report from the 'Land Revolution Battlefield'), in *Zhongguo fangdichan redian datexie*, 212.
[60] "Jianshebu Hou Jie buzhang zai quanguo fangdichan gongzuo huiyishang tan jianshe shiye he fangdi chanye de gaige fazhan guanxi wenti" (Minister of Construction Hou Jie at the National

By the end of 1993, it was painfully clear that the property boom was unsustainable. As the central government began to contract the discretionary flow of lending in the second half of 1993 – part of a "macroadjustment" in response to fears about oversupply and overinvestment in property – empty residential and office buildings peppered the urban landscape in major cities as all kinds of firms and institutions struggled to repay the debt they had taken on to invest in real estate. The Shanghai Municipal Government, in an investigation of the capital requirements of real estate firms with more than 5 million RMB in registered capital, found that 425 of the 505 firms "met basic capital requirements"; the remainder faced liquidity problems and 21 firms faced serious insolvency problems.[61] Reports that cadres, nurses, university professors, and so forth, did not receive their salaries as a result of their employers' forays into real estate alarmed central officials, and vast tracks of land remained undeveloped, even in major urban centers, such as Dalian, Guangzhou, Shenzhen, and Xiamen.[62] Unsold building space remained unsold through the contraction of 1993 and 1994; in fact, remains of the bubble – empty and seemingly abandoned buildings of early 1990s architecture – were still evident in parts of Guangzhou and Shenzhen well into the 2000s.

LESSONS FROM THE BUBBLE

Within a period of twelve years, sentiment in the CCP changed from rejecting the commodity value of land to discovering the power of real estate as a contributor to national growth. Prior to 1986, "real estate" as an economic activity was categorized under social services; providing buildings for workers and enterprises was a "nonproductive" activity associated with welfare provision rather than a central form of economic expansion and capital generation. Song Qilin, a preeminent urban planner and academic at the National Urban Planning Research Institute and one of China's first proponents of land commodification, recalls when, at a conference in 1979, he first presented the idea of land-use fees (nominal annual fees charged to occupants, not the long-term lease fees that emerged in the late 1980s) as a solution to the lack of urban construction funds. He writes: "I hoped to stir just a little debate, but when I finished reading the essay aloud, no one spoke for a long time. When someone did, he laughed and said: 'Land has no value. Marx resolved that a

Meeting on Real-Estate Work Speaks on Construction and Problems Related to the Development of Real Estate Reform), June 25, 1992, in *Zhongguo fangdi chanye qushi*, ed. Zhang Yuanduan, 14–29.

[61] Zhang Zhao, "Shanghai fangdichan shichang xiangzhuang he jinhou ersannian fazhan qushi" (Shanghai Real Estate Market's Current State and Trends for Development in the Next Several Years), in *Zhongguo fangdi chanye yu jinrong fazhan wenti yanjiu*, ed. Yu Yongshun, 75.

[62] Liu Weixin, "Lun fangdichan jinrong yu jingji fazhan de guanxi," 10–12.

long time ago!'"[63] Yet, by 1988, Vice Premier Zou Jiahua stated "We must use the ideas of commodity economics to understand the value of developing the real estate industry ... allowing the state to benefit from the circulation of land as a resource."[64] From the idea of using land to generate revenue for the state to reinvest in urban construction, policy-makers moved on to the idea of using real estate and property development to contribute directly to economic growth and national prosperity.

But the CCP did not stop with the discovery of the power of real estate for the national economy; it also understood the revenue-generating power of land as a state asset. The lessons gleaned from China's first national push toward land commodification and the real estate bubble that ensued built a framework upon which the CCP reorganized economic policy-making and the structure of the political economy. These lessons were first about the real estate industry and second about the nature of economic control and stability.

With respect to the real estate sector, the CCP learned that it was correct about its potential to contribute to GDP growth. Reports in the early 1990s compared the contribution of housing and real estate to GDP in China and other countries, finding that the Chinese economy stood to gain a great deal from real estate development. In 1991, China's rent to GDP ratio (how much citizens spent on housing or rent) was 0.71 percent, compared to 10 percent in Malawi and Kenya, countries with a similar per capita GDP. In Western countries, housing contributed between 15.8 percent (as in England in 1981) and 24 percent (as in France in 1979) of GDP.[65] From these data, central officials, for instance, Minister of Construction Hou Jie, publicly concluded that real estate's contribution to GDP in China, at 2 percent, should be doubled to at least 4 percent.[66] But the contribution of real estate to national growth would not stop there. Real estate, policy-makers proposed (and with good reason), would also generate development in related industries, such as construction, construction materials, metallurgy, and fifty other materials-based industries, as well as electronics, furniture, commerce, transportation, and finance. Researchers at the State Council even calculated a multiplier: Every 1

---

[63] Song Qilin, "Chengshi tudi changyong de qianhouhou," 159. His essay was later published in the leading urban planning journal (*Chengshi guihua*, 城市规划) in 1981, and by 1992 his work on urban land value was receiving awards from the Ministry of Construction.

[64] Quoted in "Guowuyuan Zou Jiahua fuzongli zai quanguo fangdichan kaifa jingyan jiaoliu huishang jiakuai fangdi chanye de gaige fazhan zuole zhongyao zhishi," 2.

[65] Liu Shiyu, "Chengzhen zhufang zhidu gaige yu zhufang jinrong de fazhan" (Institutional Reform of Urban Housing and the Development of Housing Finance), in *Zhongguo fangdi chanye yu jinrong fazhan wenti yanjiu*, ed. Yu Yongshun, 111–16.

[66] Minister of Construction Hou Jie, "Dayou kewei de Zhongguo fangdi chanye" (The Promising Chinese Real Estate Sector), in *Zhongguo fangdichan redian datexie*, ed. Cheng Hu and Zhang Lu, 6.

RMB spent on real estate (property investment and development) was expected to increase GDP by 1.34 RMB.[67]

In coming to understand the growth potential of real estate, policy-makers also revealed its potential to threaten economic stability. Unlike other "productive" sectors (meaning those that produce for product markets), real estate investment must be delicately balanced because of its propensity to "give rise to bubbles and false prosperity."[68] As a leading academic and finance policy-maker said in a conference introductory speech reflecting on the bubble, "The lesson is very clear: abnormalities and over-development of the real estate industry can create an economic bubble and false prosperity, with extremely serious consequences."[69]

How CCP policy-makers understood the causes of the "abnormalities and over-development" had everything to do with the steps they would take to prevent them from occurring in the future. Official speeches and reports reveal that primary blame was attributed to the role of decentralized finance and low barriers to entry in the sector that created the conditions for overinvestment. Officials acknowledged that both the financial and real estate sectors were new in China and that neither sector was yet subject to appropriate regulation and supervision. In addition to the "enclosure crazes" and the "speculative winds" that constituted the real estate bubble, officials cited poor regulation over the establishment of real estate firms that contributed to a "craze of establishing real- estate firms."[70] Officials ascertained that many of these real estate companies lacked discipline and that the proliferation of real estate firms, which were often arms of other firms or institutions, contributed to a lack of control over fixed-asset investments. Decentralized control over the financial sector, and therefore a lack of regulation of the amount of credit available to real estate firms, was also to blame. Reports and speeches decried the "illegal loans" given for real estate development, especially for speculative purposes. Land was leased to firms that borrowed both to lease the land and to develop property on it for residential and commercial sale, leaving the firms vulnerable if they

---

[67] "Jianshebu Hou Jie buzhang zai quanguo fangdichan kaifa jingyan jiaoliu huishang tan shenhua he wanshan fangdi chanye gaige fazhan bixu renqing de jige zhongyao wenti" (Minister of Construction Hou Jie at the National Meeting on the Exchange of Experiences in Developing the Real Estate Market Speaks on the Necessity of Understanding Several Important Issues in Order to Strengthen and Perfect the Reform of the Real Estate Market), August 10, 1992, in *Zhongguo fangdi chanye qushi*, ed. Zhang Yuanduan, 9.

[68] Liu Weixin, "Lun fangdichan jinrong yu jingji fazhan de guanxi," 11.

[69] Zhou Daojiong, "Nuli tansuo Zhongguo fangdi chanye jinrong xietiao fazhan zhilu" (Make Efforts to Explore the Ways to Coordinate the Development of Chinese Real Estate and the Financial Industry), speech to the Real Estate and Finance Working Group of the China Construction Bank and the Urban Management Scholarly Committee, September 1994, in *Zhongguo fangdi chanye yu jinrong fazhan wenti yanjiu*, ed. Yu Yongshun, 1–4.

[70] "Guowuyuan Zou Jiahua fuzongli zai quanguo fangdichan kaifa jingyan jiaoliu huishang jiakuai fangdi chanye de gaige fazhan zuole zhongyao zhishi," 3.

were unable to sell the property quickly enough.[71] The conclusion was that the state had to regulate and limit who could become involved in the business of real estate and at which stages of property development.

Policy-makers also drew conclusions about regulating the supply of land for development. Overheating in the real estate sector has inevitable effects on the real economy and on the structure of the urban built environment. Leaving land development entirely to markets and decisions on land supply to market actors, policy-makers argued would create distortions and endanger the functionality of urban plans for infrastructure, land use, transportation, and so forth.

The policy solution would be dramatic: to unite the power to lease land with the power to create urban plans, and therefore to designate urban governments as the only legal owners of land. Minister of Construction Hou Jie, in a speech reflecting on the lessons from the bubble, is worth quoting at length: "State-owned land use can be transferred for compensation, the goal being to attract domestic and international capital for construction. We must solve the problem of illegal land sales and purchases, especially speculators and the 'uncompleted buildings' [*lou hua*, 楼花]. ... Beginning now, the government will strengthen the building of regulations in the real estate market, establishing rule of law." And, crucially, "From now on, the Chinese government will have a monopoly [*longduan*, 垄断] over the land supply to strengthen economic and land planning. When urban land is transferred, the government will control the macro supply of land."[72]

Conceptually, policy-makers laid out different "levels" of the real estate market: The first would be the leasing of the land itself, and the second would be the sale of the buildings and building space after the land was transferred and construction was completed. The first level of the market would be monopolized and controlled by local governments that would "represent the state" (*daibiao guojia*, 代表国家) as the exclusive owners of the land and therefore had exclusive power to lease land and collect revenue. Municipal governments would only lease land to developers who had clear construction plans, and land lying idle for two years would revert to the state.[73] In essence, the structure of land politics in contemporary China – in which local governments claim exclusive rights of ownership over land and generate revenue directly from land leasing – emerged in these policy clarifications in response to the real estate bubble of the early 1990s.

---

[71] Zhou Daojiong, "Nuli tansuo Zhongguo fangdi chanye yu jinrong xietiao fazhan zhilu," 1–4; and Liu Weixin, "Lun fangdichan jinrong yu jingji fazhan de guanxi," 5–17.

[72] Hou Jie, "Dayou kewei de Zhongguo fangdi chanye," 4–5.

[73] These ideas were circulated at the onset of the 1992 period of overheating, but they did not become official policy until 1994. "Guowuyuan Zou Jiahua fuzongli zai quanguo fangdichan kaifa jingyan jiaoliu huishang jiakuai fangdi chanye de gaige fazhan zuole zhongyao zhishi," 1–6.

The decision to designate municipal governments as landowners was born of the perceived need to designate a central market actor but also of the realization of how much local governments stood to gain. Policy-makers discovered the power of the potential contribution of real estate to national economic growth, but they also discovered its potential to generate revenue for the government. Of course, the power of real estate to generate government revenue through taxes (one-time taxes on real estate exchanges or value-added taxes on real estate) was evident even before the bubble, when cities in the southeast, such as Shenzhen and Guangzhou, saw real estate contributing about 10 percent of annual government revenue through taxes. But if municipal governments were the designated owners of state land, they would access the revenue generated from the sale of land-use rights as well as the taxes, providing local governments with a significant new source of income. In the words of one high-level official in the Ministry of Construction, "Land development and the real estate industry will serve as a secondary source of finance for the cities."[74]

Before the commodification of land and the option to sell land-use rights through competitive auctions, the perception was that land was used inefficiently and given away essentially for free. Now that land had demonstrated an exchange value and land-use rights could constitute a significant portion of local government revenue, policy-makers assumed that local governments would be guided by market pressures to "rationalize the assignment and use of land resources."[75] In 1994, the national Urban Real Estate Law (to be implemented in January 1995) stated that only land for national agencies, military use, special natural resource management, transportation, and infrastructure could be administratively assigned, that is, transferred for free. Land-use rights for any other users or for any other purposes had to be leased. At the same time, the State Council required all cities and counties to publish a land-use plan, clearly designating what land would be available for administrative allocation and what land would be leased. The goal was to eliminate the ability of local governments to obfuscate land use.[76] The push to expand the paid transfer of land-use rights for development was expected to quadruple the tax revenue generated from real estate and land development, and land transfer revenue (the capital generated from local governments' selling land-use rights, preferably through open land auctions) would generate much more.[77] Whereas

---

[74] "Jianshe bu fangdi chanyesi Zhang Yuanrui sizhang zai Zhongguo yanhai kaifa chengshi fangxie huishang tan dangqian fangdi chanye de ruogan wenti" (Speech by Zhang Yuanrui, director of the Real Estate Office of the Ministry of Construction, at the Meeting of the Coastal Cities Housing Association on Several Current Real Estate Issues), in *Zhongguo fangdi chanye qushi*, ed. Zhang Yuanduan, 74.

[75] Zhang Zhao, "Shanghai fangdichan shichang xingzhuang he hou ersannian fazhan qushi," 76.

[76] Huang Xiaohu, ed., *Xinshiqi Zhongguo tudi guanli yanjiu*, 18–19. Nonetheless, the vast majority of land in many places continued to be transferred through administrative allocations. Variations are dealt with in Chapters 4–6.

[77] Hou Jie, "Dayou kewei de Zhongguo fangdi chanye."

real estate taxes constituted from 5 to 10 percent of local government revenue in Guangzhou and Shenzhen, the inclusion of land-use fees would increase the figure to 15–18 percent A National Bureau of Statistics (NBS) report lauded the economic and revenue-generating promise of the sector under government control: "After several years, when virgin land becomes mature land, through real estate markets we can preserve value, add value, and in this way add to the wealth of the country. ... China has 25,000 square kilometers of state-owned urban land. ... This is an indispensable condition for economic and social development and the first great source of national wealth."[78] For local governments, land went "overnight from a 'cold' asset to 'hot' capital."[79]

LAND, THE PARTY-STATE, AND CHINESE CAPITALISM

The real estate bubble of 1992–1993 was followed by nothing short of seismic changes in the larger political economy. These reforms in the 1990s reconfigured the balance of power in both the fiscal and monetary policy arenas in China.

The Fiscal System

Changes to China's fiscal system are considered by many to be the centerpiece of the economic reforms that began under Deng Xiaoping in 1978. In an effort to make local governments fiscally self-sufficient and to provide them with incentives to encourage economic development, the central government steadily decentralized control over tax revenues and expenditures to provincial, municipal, and county governments. By the mid-1980s, "revenue-sharing" fiscal contracts among levels of government throughout the administrative hierarchy determined the share of tax revenue to which each level of government would be entitled and the share it would "send up" to higher levels. In general, lower levels of government were required to contribute a certain quota to higher levels, but they were allowed to retain – and have control rights over – revenue in excess of that quota.[80]

Scholars credit these revenue-sharing arrangements with establishing incentives for "entrepreneurial" local government behavior. Jean Oi has argued that local governments supported rather than preyed upon the collectively owned TVEs because they retained control rights over profits and taxes.[81] Susan Whiting has examined how fiscal contracts permitted local governments to

---

[78] Quoted in in *Zhongguo fangdichan redian datexie*, ed. Cheng Hu and Zhang Lu, 208–9.
[79] Hou Jie, "Dayou kewei de Zhongguo fangdi chanye," 19.
[80] Jean C. Oi, *Rural China Takes Off: Institutional Foundations of Economic Reform* (Berkeley: University of California Press, 1999); Wong et al., *Fiscal Management and Economic Reform.*
[81] Oi, *Rural China Takes Off.*

support various forms of ownership in rural industry, including private as well as collective firms, as local governments established their own extractive institutions as a result of the fiscal decentralization.[82]

Although the decentralized fiscal system probably established the conditions under which local governments could pursue economic growth, it also weakened the fiscal power of the central state. Central power was attenuated in terms of both its extractive ability and its capacity to direct investment and growth policy. The central government's share of fiscal revenue declined steadily from the early 1980s, relative to both the local government's share and GDP. By 1991, central revenue was only 19.4 percent of GDP, down from 26.8 percent in 1985.[83] Moreover, because local governments retained much of the wealth created in their jurisdictions, patterns of regional inequality in China – chiefly the growing prosperity along the east coast relative to the central and western regions – grew progressively starker. The central government found its own revenue insufficient to direct investments in a way to correct these regional imbalances; it was also unable to out-maneuver local governments that were essentially poor agents of the state in terms of extracting revenue.[84]

A recentralization of fiscal revenue proposed in November 1993 and implemented in 1994 upended this system. According to Ministry of Finance estimates, between 1993 and 1994, the share of total fiscal revenue controlled by local governments declined from 78 percent to 44 percent. Incredibly, this recentralization of revenue control was not accompanied by a recentralization of expenditure burdens; the central share of expenditures declined steadily, from 50 percent in the mid-1980s to 30 percent in 2000 and 15 percent in 2010.[85] The lion's share of spending – on public services and welfare provision, public goods, infrastructure construction, and so forth – remained the responsibility of local governments.

It is difficult to overstate the importance of the fiscal reversal of the mid-1990s in terms of reshaping China's political economic landscape. Susan Whiting details how TVEs were privatized en masse in the 1990s: "Like the asteroid and resulting dust cloud that changed the climate in which the dinosaurs lived, a combination of fundamental changes in China's national institutions is transforming the environment for local officials and the rural enterprises they govern."[86] In short, local governments no longer had incentives

[82] Whiting, *Power and Wealth in Rural China.*
[83] Wong et al., *Fiscal Management and Economic Reform,* 48.
[84] Shaoguang Wang and Angang Hu, *The Political Economy of Uneven Development: The Case of China* (Armonk, NY: M. E. Sharpe, 1999). The latter point is from Whiting, *Power and Wealth in Rural China.*
[85] Detailed local fiscal data are available in Tables 2.2 and 2.3; Ministry of Finance, via CEIC, accessed September 2012.
[86] Whiting, *Power and Wealth in Rural China,* 266.

to act as "corporations," managing their localities to pursue economic growth, because the fruits of that growth would now accrue to higher levels of the state. Their efforts were instead directed at the collection of "extrabudgetary revenues," fees and revenues generated outside the planned budgetary tax system.

As policy-makers understood, land-lease fees would now be included in the extrabudgetary category. In 1994, the State Council issued the Urban Real Estate Management Law, clearly designating the municipal government as landowner, but also requiring that land be leased out competitively (*churang*, 出让) rather than freely through administrative allocations.[87] By requiring local governments to manage the exchange of land for capital and removing other sources of revenue, the central government in Beijing hoped to generate efficient, market-based land use and at the same time to recentralize extractive power over taxation.

The discovery of the value of land and the assignment of land control to local governments no more "caused" the fiscal recentralization than did the declining central revenues and the growing calls to correct regional wealth and development disparities. Clearly, the recentralization was a response to a number of economic and political trends that alarmed the center. But the fact is that the recentralization occurred on the heels of the first major experience with land commodification, and simultaneously with the designation of municipal governments as representatives of the state in land management. The reliance of local governments on land revenues as extrabudgetary funds, a dependence that would become greater throughout the 1990s and 2000s, was not an "unintended consequence" of institutional change. On the contrary, the "fiscalization of land" – "the management of land resources by political authorities for the purpose of generating fiscal revenue" – during the mid-1990s *was* the institutional change.[88]

Financial Reforms

The real estate bubble was also followed by a seismic effort at recentralization in the financial sector. Those efforts were spearheaded by Zhu Rongji, a brash reformer from Shanghai who served as vice premier (1993–8) and then premier (1998–2003) under Jiang Zemin.

Prior to these reforms, China's banking system was highly decentralized, in terms of the autonomy afforded to both large, national banks and to the local

---

[87] Exceptions included allocation of land for national agencies, the military, some natural resources, transportation, and infrastructure, all of which still could be administratively assigned. Huang Xiaohu, ed., *Xinshiqi Zhongguo tudi guanli yanjiu*, 18.

[88] Definition from Whiting, "Values in Land," 570.

branches of these banks. In the 1970s and 1980s, what would become the "Big Four" national banks – China Agricultural Bank, Bank of China, China Construction Bank, and the Industrial and Commercial Bank of China – broke off from the ministries that had controlled them to become independent financial institutions that could extend credit for investment projects. Local governments that wanted to spur economic development through investment in fixed assets had close relationships with these banks, whose decisions were subject to a mostly unenforced "credit plan." As a result, the reform era was marked by distinct inflationary cycles, characterized by runaway local government spending followed by periods of austerity brought about by changes in central policy. Critically, these cycles were managed not through "traditional" instruments of monetary control, such as interest-rate changes, but rather through political directives to lend more or less as signaled in the speeches and statements by major leaders.[89]

The 1993 inflation cycle, driven primarily by investments in real estate through a decentralized financial system, provided an unprecedented opportunity for Zhu Rongji and others who desired more central control over monetary policy. At the zenith of the asset bubble and crisis in the spring of 1993, Zhu proposed "sixteen measures" that would limit fixed-asset investment, real estate investment, and the flow of foreign capital and would crack down on illegal financial institutions and steadily recentralize lending authority under the People's Bank of China (PBoC), the central bank.[90] Although there had been momentum for transitioning to "macroadjustments" – the use of indirect, central tools of economic adjustment rather than "microcontrols" over prices, investments, and so forth – since the late 1980s, the 1992–1994 asset bubble and the inflationary cycles solidified this approach in the minds of many central policy-makers. Over the course of the mid- to late 1990s, Zhu capitalized on this momentum and the crisis essentially to eliminate local financial discretion and to subordinate major financial institutions, including the Big Four, under the administrative control of the central party-state.[91] As local governments lost their influence over credit extensions and levels of investment, they increasingly turned to their control over land as an instrument with which to spur local investment and growth.

---

[89] Scholars on China's financial sector may disagree about the political forces behind the changes in policy (factional conflicts, the relative power of central and local governments, and so forth), but they agree on the paramount importance of political directives from the center. Huang, *Inflation and Investment Controls in China*; Shih, *Factions and Finance in China*; Brandt and Zhu, "Redistribution in a Decentralized Economy."

[90] Shih, *Factions and Finance in China*, 76–80, 147–53.

[91] Huang, *Inflation and Investment Controls in China*, preface; Shih, *Factions and Finance in China*; and Sebastian Heilmann, "Regulatory Innovation by Leninist Means: Communist Party Supervision in China's Financial Industry," *China Quarterly* no. 181 (2005): 1–21.

TABLE 2.2. *Local Budgetary, Extrabudgetary, Tax, and Land Revenues,*
1990–2010

	Local budgetary revenues	Local extrabudgetary revenues	Local tax revenues	Land lease revenues	Land revenues: Local budgetary revenues	Land revenues: Local tax revenues
	RMB million	RMB million	RMB million	RMB million	%	%
1990	194,468	163,536				
1991	221,123	186,220				
1992	250,386	214,719				
1993	339,144	118,664		4.05		
1994	231,160	157,921		3.59		
1995	298,558	208,893		3.32		
1996	374,692	294,568				
1997	442,422	268,092				
1998	498,395	291,814		4.996		
1999	559,487	315,472	493,493			
2000	640,606	357,879	568,886	62,490	9.75	10.98
2001	780,330	395,300	696,276	131,810	16.89	18.93
2002	851,500	403,900	740,616	245,430	28.82	33.14
2003	984,998	418,743	841,327	570,580	57.93	67.82
2004	1,189,337	434,849	999,959	645,880	54.31	64.59
2005	1,510,076	514,158	1,272,673	594,170	39.35	46.69
2006	1,830,358	594,077	1,522,821	810,910	44.3	53.25
2007	2,357,262	628,995	1,925,212	1,224,720	51.96	63.61
2008	2,864,979	612,516	2,325,511	1,041,440	36.35	44.78
2009	3,260,259	606,264	2,615,744	1,728,510	53.02	66.08
2010	4,061,304	539,511	3,270,149	2,939,700	72.38	89.89

Source: *Zhongguo guotu ziyuan nianjian* (China Land and Resources Yearbook) (Beijing:
Zhongguo guotu ziyuan nianjian bianjibu), various years. Data on budgetary and extrabudgetary
revenues are from the Ministry of Finance, via CEIC.

FROM COMMODIFICATION TO FISCALIZATION: LAND
AND THE MACROECONOMY

Over the course of the 1990s and 2000s, local governments became ever more
reliant on "extrabudgetary revenues," collected outside the tax system and
consisting mainly of fines and land-lease revenues, to finance expenditures on
social and public services and growth-generating policies. The fiscalization of
the banking sector and "local state corporatism" were steadily replaced by the
fiscalization of land. Tables 2.2 and 2.3 reveal the progress of fiscalization
during the 2000s; by 2010, the revenue that county and municipal governments

TABLE 2.3. *Land- and Property-Related Revenue, 1999–2010 (Million RMB)*

	Local budgetary revenue	Urban construction tax	Urban land-use tax	Land value-added tax	Occupancy tax on arable land	Real-estate tax	Land-lease fees	Total land-related revenue	Land-related revenue: Budgetary revenue
1999	559487	31257	5906		3303		52170	92636	16.6
2000	640606	34896	6476		3532		62490	107394	16.8
2001	780330	38062	6615		3833		131810	180320	23.1
2002	851500	46711	7683		5734		245430	305558	35.9
2003	984998	54671	9157		3990		570580	638398	64.8
2004	1189337	66974	10623		12008		645880	735485	61.8
2005	1510076	79102	13734		14185		594170	701191	46.4
2006	1830358	93343	17666		17112		810910	1014708	55.4
2007	2357262	114870	38549		18504		1224720	1396643	59.2
2008	2864979	133630	81690	53743	31441	68034	1041440	1409978	49.2
2009	3260259	141992	92098	71956	63307	80366	1728510	2178229	66.8
2010	4061304	173627	100401	127829	88864	89407	2939700	3519828	86.7

Source: Zhongguo guotu ziyuan nianjian, various years. Data on budgetary and extrabudgetary revenues are from the Ministry of Finance, via CEIC. Aggregate tax composition data are from the Ministry of Finance, via CEIC and *Zhongguo caizheng nianjian* (China Finance Yearbook) (Beijing: Zhongguo caizheng zazhishe), various years.

generated though land development nearly equaled the revenue raised through transparent taxation-based sources.

Over the course of the 1990s, land was a tool with which local governments managed their budgets and economies as well as means that central authorities used to regulate the macroeconomy. Realizing the potential of land development as a tool for economic expansion, the Ministry of Land Resources (MLR) imposed a land control hierarchy that would leave local governments as owners but would organize administration of land supply such that the center could determine how much land would be available for development in the various regions and in the country as a whole. Beginning during the late 1990s Asian financial crisis, the MLR, in cooperation with other central state agencies, began to manipulate the supply of land available for local governments to lease and to develop as a form of indirect macroeconomic management.

Despite the State Council's 1994 decision that most land should be distributed through paid transfers, the vast majority of urban land during the remainder of the 1990s changed hands without formal compensation because it was used by state or collectively owned firms, which typically paid land-use fees but did not pay for long-term rights to lease state-owned land (see Table 2.3). In the late 1990s, central authorities adopted land-based policies to implement massive ownership reforms in the state sector and to avoid the effects of the Asian financial crisis. Housing commodification removed the heavy burdens of facilities maintenance from ailing enterprises, provided subsidized housing for many soon-to-be-laid-off workers, and lifted aggregate demand during a period of economic slowdown.[92]

TABLE 2.4. *Selected Data on Land Transfers by Lease and Administrative Allocations, 1993–2002*

	Leased land (hectares)	Assigned land (hectares)
1993	57,338	89,750
1994	49,432	91,413
1995	43,092	87,608
1998	62,058	235,194
1999	45,390	54,163
2001	90,394	73,979
2002	124,229	88,052

Source: *Zhongguo guotu ziyuan nianjian*, various years.

[92] Huang Xiaohu, ed., *Xinshiqi Zhongguo tudi guanli yanjiu*, 19–20. For more on the 1998 housing reform, see Ya Ping Wang, "Recent Housing Reform Practice in Chinese Cities: Social and Spatial Implications," in *China's Housing Reform and Outcomes*, ed. Joyce Yanyun Man (Cambridge, MA: Lincoln Institute for Land Policy, 2011), 19–44; Youqin Huang, "Low-Income Housing in Chinese Cities: Policies and Practices," *China Quarterly* no. 212 (2012): 941–64; Lan Deng, Qingyun Shen, and Lin Wang, "Housing Policy and Finance in China:

At the same time, authorities at the center were becoming painfully aware of the extent of urban development and encroachment on rural land for cultivation, a process that began primarily during the 1992–1994 real estate inflation cycle. Landsat photos alerted the authorities to the rapid pace of urbanization and farmland loss, leading to a reorganization of land management under a hierarchically organized MLR.[93] The 1998 revision to the Land Management Law – the same law that initiated markets in land-use rights in 1988 – established quotas of land available for development for every level of government from top down, requiring that all local governments preserve more than 80 percent of the total arable land under their respective administrations and receive approvals for conversion of farmland into land for urban construction. Importantly, local governments could maintain the base levels of arable land by replacing or reclaiming land as arable land. Since the late 1990s, local governments all over China have succeeded at innovating ways to maximize land for lease and urban development while also maintaining their assigned quotas. Some of these innovations are institutional, such as transferring development rights among jurisdictions to preserve quotas at higher (e.g., provincial) levels, establishing elaborate systems in which rural residents may trade their land certificates and land rights for urban citizenship, and selling those land certificates in government-sponsored markets.[94] Other innovations are less transparent and involve potential abuses of farmers, such as the "village redevelopment" projects that consolidated villagers into high-rise housing developments, frequently displacing them from their farms in the process, to maximize the amount of transferrable land.[95]

In addition to spurring local-level innovations, quotas became a way in which central authorities could direct regional and national economic expansion and contraction. The national land-use plan details land-use plans for various social and economic purposes as well as which regions and subregions are entitled to more or less land for development and other purposes. Land-use plans are also used as a form of industrial policy. For example, in 2006 the MLR and the National Development and Reform Commission (NDRC) jointly

A Literature Review" (Washington, DC: U.S. Department of Housing and Urban Development, 2009).

[93] Hui Wang et al., "Farmland Preservation and Land Development Rights Trading in Zhejiang, China," *Habitat International* 34, no. 4 (2010): 456. George C. S. Lin and Peter Ho, "China's Land Resources and Land-Use Change: Insights from the 1996 Land Survey," *Land Use Policy* 20, no. 2 (2003): 87–107.

[94] Ibid. "Land certificate exchanges" are a policy component of the bundle of social, economic, and political reforms propagandized as the "Chongqing model" before Bo Xilai's fall from prominence in 2012. Su Wei, Yang Fan, and Liu Shiwen, *Chongqing moshi* (The Chongqing Model) (Beijing: Zhongguo jingji chubanshe, 2010), ch. 6.

[95] See Kristen Looney, "China's Campaign to Build a New Socialist Countryside: Village Modernization, Peasant Councils, and the Ganzhou Model of Rural Development," *China Quarterly*, no. 224, (December 2015).

used land-use regulations to limit the proliferation of industrial development zones and to promote land-use projects that would be more environmentally friendly, ostensibly as part of Hu Jintao's drive for "scientific development."[96] Throughout the 2000s, as part of the "opening to the west" regional development policy, the national land-use plan allocated greater quantities of land for development in the western and central provinces – and away from the east coast – in an effort to enhance investment there.[97]

The predominant view of central–local relations in China's land politics envisions the center as a disciplining agent of unruly and hard-to-monitor local governments. Observers point to episodes in which Beijing and the MLR have restrained local governments from land development. For example, in 2004, in response to what was called the "blind" declaration of development zones, which by August of 2004 had resulted in 6,886 development zones that collectively occupied more space than China's entire urban built-up area, the MLR declared a moratorium on the declaration of new zones.[98] But the center also deploys land as a tool of expansion and policy adjustment, encouraging real estate development and investment in specific places at specific times to achieve central political and economic objectives.

At levels of government throughout the administrative hierarchy, land-use plans (*guihua*, 规;划) play a role similar to that played by the economic plan (*jihua*, 计划) during the era of the command economy. Land-use plans signal where investments are likely to be politically supported and to be accompanied by infrastructure investment; they allocate resources to sectors and regions on the basis of changing political and development objectives; and they establish the strategic intentions and goals for various time frames. The distribution of land resources and the content of land-use plans determine local government fiscal revenues and, more indirectly, how much banks will loan for investment and the amount of funds available for local government investment. In short,

---

[96] Wang Shiyuan, "Bawo xin xingshi, mingque xin renwu, dali tisheng tudi guanli tiaokong de zhicheng baozhang nengli: Dui dangnian quanguo tudi kance guihua yuan yewu de sikao" (Understand the New Circumstances, Determine the New Tasks, and Greatly Improve the Ability to Support and Secure Control of Land Management: Some Thoughts on the Professional Activities of Land Exploration and Planning Institutes in Our Country), in *Zhongguo guotu ziyuan nianjian, 2007* (China Land and Resources Yearbook, 2007) (Beijing: Zhongguo guotu ziyuan nianjian bianjibu, 2008), 19–23. See also the speech by Vice Minister of Land Resources Li Yuan, January 10, 2006, "Yi kexue fazhanguan wei tongling quanmian tuijin guotu ziyuan guanli yifa xingzheng tixi jianshe" (Use the Scientific Development Concept to Comprehensively Promote a Land Source Management System for Administrative Building), ibid., 62–7.

[97] Sun Wensheng, "Wei shishi xibu kaifa zhanlüe fuwu" (Serving the Great Western Development Strategy), in *Zhongguo guotu ziyuan nianjian, 2000* (China Land and Resources Yearbook, 2000) (Beijing: Zhongguo guotu ziyuan nianjian bianjibu, 2001), 3–5.

[98] Wen Jiabao, "Shenhua tudi guanli zhidu gaige yifa qieshi jiaqiang tudi guanli" (Deepening the Reform of the Land Management System by Legally Enhancing Land Management), October 28, 2005, in *Zhongguo guotu ziyuan nianjian, 2005* (China Land and Resources Yearbook, 2005) (Beijing: Zhonghua renmin gongheguo guotu ziyuan bu, 2005), 26–30.

since the 1990s, land has become a form of fiscal, industrial, and financial policy for the CCP in its attempts to recentralize economic and political power without entirely snuffing out local initiative.

Land and Institutional Change

Land politics in China has been incorrectly described as either a simple evolution toward increasingly liberal land markets or an accidental slide toward land predation as the CCP supposedly has been unwilling or unable to clarify property rights.[99] An examination of this early period reveals that both narratives are incorrect. We see that land policies were much more liberal at the outset. First, the period of land politics between 1988 and 1994 appeared a great deal more like privatization of property rights over land than anything since. The next four chapters, which analyze the birth of land markets in three cities, show what this looked like in practice. Second, the national land regime, we find, was not at all an accident, but the intentional reaction to a real estate crisis by a CCP that wanted to benefit from the growth generated from the real estate sector but not be subject to its vicissitudes.

By examining the early period of land commodification in this chapter, we begin to see the logic of recentralizing fiscal and financial control in light of the discovery of land as an asset. The institutions of land control, fiscal relations between local and central levels of the state, and financial-sector management seem to fit uncomfortably to generate perverse incentives, but in fact they fit together logically to create a political economy in which the center controls capital and local governments control land. While central officials no longer trusted local governments with power over investment or revenue extraction, they thought that ceding them control over land would rationalize land use and land markets and provide a stable revenue stream for local governments.

Advocates of decentralization propose that fiscally or financially empowered local governments serve as a check on a central government whose power could be, devastatingly, without limit.[100] They would expect, then, that this

---

[99] Peter Ho, "Who Owns China's Land? Policies, Property Rights and Deliberate Institutional Ambiguity," *The China Quarterly* no. 166 (2001): 394–421; Ho, *Institutions in Transition*; Samuel P. S. Ho and George C. S. Lin, "Emerging Land Markets in Rural and Urban China: Policies and Practices," *China Quarterly*, no. 175 (2003): 681–707; Xiaolin Guo, "Land Expropriation and Rural Conflicts in China," *The China Quarterly* no. 166 (2001): 422–39; Wooyeal Paik and Kihyun Lee, "I Want to Be Expropriated! The Politics of Xiaochanquanfang Land Development in Suburban China," *Journal of Contemporary China* 21, no. 74 (2012): 261–79; Chiew Ping Yew, "Pseudo-Urbanization? Competitive Government Behavior and Urban Sprawl in China," *Journal of Contemporary China* 21, no. 74 (2012): 281–98.

[100] Yasheng Huang writes: "Fiscal decentralization is like purchasing an insurance policy. It is costly in financial terms but it may help prevent catastrophic failures by checking and balancing the enormous political power of the central government." Huang, *Inflation and Investment Controls in China*, xx–xxi. This is also the assumption of the "market-preserving federalism"

incredible recentralization of economic power would fuel the growth of a central government incapable of restraint and of respect for property rights of many kinds. The greatest irony is that these reforms did exactly the opposite, turning local governments that previously "entrepreneurially" nurtured local enterprises of all forms of ownership and, as we will see in Chapters 5 and 6, negotiated with their constituencies into fiscally desperate and land-hungry organizations that expanded, physically and administratively, without limit.

The dependence on land, construction, and real estate was born after China's first experience in land commodification in the 1980s and 1990s. By examining the rise of land politics and the institutional changes in fiscal and monetary management together, it becomes clear that some of the proposed reforms for land conflict in China – from judicial enforcement of property rights claims to transferrable rural rights to increasingly strict limits on urban growth – seem unlikely to alter the basic system of local state dependence on land. Because land is an institution at the heart of the Chinese economy, effective reform of China's land system would require reform of the fiscal and financial systems. The following chapters show how initially ambiguous national institutions permitted the development of local property-rights regimes during the first decade of land liberalization.

school. Gabriella Montinola, Yingyi Qian, and Barry R. Weingast, "Federalism, Chinese Style: The Political Basis for Economic Success in China," *World Politics* 48, no. 1 (October 1995): 50–81; Barry R. Weingast, "The Economic Role of Political Institutions: Market-Preserving Federalism and Economic Development," *Journal of Law, Economics, & Organization* 11, no. 1 (1995): 1–31.

3

The Political Economies of China

The three provinces that constitute the northeastern region of China (东北, Dongbei) are not the most obvious places in which to study land politics and property rights, particularly for a political scientist. The land conflicts that have escalated and attracted international attention, such as the case of Wukan discussed in Chapter 1, most frequently have occurred in the southeast in the Pearl River Delta region or in the Yangzi River Delta region. These areas are the most urbanized in China, comprising agglomeration regions where large urban centers are separated, if at all, by increasingly sparse rural areas.[1] By contrast, the constellation of cities in the Northeast today is much the same as it was thirty years ago. The region has attracted the attention of scholars interested in unemployment and labor politics in China, but land, for the most part, has not figured into the narrative of the rise and fall of China's rust belt.[2]

Yet, I propose we can learn more about land politics and conflict over property rights in reform-era China from a controlled comparison of Northeastern cities than from either single case studies or treating "China" as a single unit of analysis. To be sure, other studies have identified and explained variation in patterns of land conflict, examining how differently situated urban,

---

[1] Zheng Zhu and Bohong Zheng, "Study on Spatial Structure of Yangtze River Delta Urban Agglomeration and Its Effects on Urban and Rural Regions," *Journal of Urban Planning and Development* 138, no. 1 (2012): 78–89.

[2] Some research on labor conflict does indeed identify property rights over housing as a key source of contention, but it envisions this more as a grievance related to the decay of the "socialist social contract" rather than to land politics as such. Ching Kwan Lee, *Against the Law: Labor Protests in China's Rustbelt and Sunbelt* (Berkeley: University of California Press, 2007); Feng Chen, "Industrial Restructuring and Workers' Resistance in China," *Modern China* 29, no. 2 (2003): 237–62; William Hurst, *The Chinese Worker after Socialism* (Cambridge: Cambridge University Press, 2009); William Hurst and Kevin J. O'Brien, "China's Contentious Pensioners," *The China Quarterly* no. 170 (2002): 345–60.

periurban, and rural residents interact with state land policies and whether citizens pursue distributive or procedural justice claims in response to threats to their land rights.[3] Yet, few studies – if any – have attempted to explain variation in the approaches that different local governments adopt toward land property rights.[4] Indeed, a longitudinal analysis of the use of land as a political resource in the three cities in this study uncovers two critical processes that have heretofore been absent from discussions of land politics. First, the controlled comparison reveals that very different subnational property-rights regimes emerged in the 1980s and 1990s as land markets were liberalized and land-use rights were commodified. This finding is the subject of the following three chapters. Second, the longitudinal comparison also reveals a national shift in land politics, after which most urban governments throughout the country adopted a predatory and expansionist approach to land. I return to this second insight in the conclusion.

Clearly, a long list of factors can be said to influence the emergence of property-rights regimes and the nature of land politics in any given place. The extensive literature on the relationship between property rights and political and economic development trajectories examines technological change over the very long term. Geography, in the sense of land quality and output, clearly matters tremendously in terms of how different groups value land and therefore their different ways of governing land.[5] These large, structural explanations typically operate at the level of the nation-state or at least the macroeconomy and therefore do not explain variation within a single country or region. In contrast, here I employ a research design that identifies variation in a single region with a shared political-economic legacy. This strategy permits maximum attention to the political choices and contingencies that shape property-rights regimes as they emerge at the local level.

[3] You-tien Hsing, *The Great Urban Transformation: Politics of Land and Property in China* (Oxford: Oxford University Press, 2010); Susan Whiting, "Values in Land: Fiscal Pressures, Land Disputes and Justice Claims in Rural and Peri-Urban China," *Urban Studies* 48, no. 3 (March 2011): 569–87.

[4] One major exception is George Lin's book on regional diversity in patterns of urbanization and expansion. Lin uses cadastral surveys and satellite images to show different patterns of land use and agricultural land conversion in the cities of Guangzhou and Hefei and the provinces of Guangdong and Jiangsu, which he explains in terms of political and economic pressures of accumulation. A geographer, Lin is more interested in land-use change, whereas the present book looks at property-rights institutions. George C. S. Lin, *Developing China: Land, Politics and Social Conditions* (London: Routledge, 2009).

[5] Douglass C. North and Robert Paul Thomas, *The Rise of the Western World: A New Economic History* (Cambridge: Cambridge University Press, 1973); Douglass C. North, John Joseph Wallis, and Barry R. Weingast, *Violence and Social Orders: A Conceptual Framework for Interpreting Recorded Human History* (Cambridge: Cambridge University Press, 2009); Elinor Ostrom, *Governing the Commons: The Evolution of Institutions for Collective Action* (Cambridge: Cambridge University Press, 1990); Daniel H. Cole and Elinor Ostrom, eds., *Property in Land and Other Resources* (Cambridge, MA: Lincoln Institute of Land Policy, 2012).

Different subnational property-rights regimes emerged, I argue, as a function of the underlying local distribution of political power as configured by the sequencing of the reforms to state socialism and the opening to global capital. Land control and property-rights rules were resources over which local governments and social groups bargained during the process of economic reforms. Different local experiences with economic reforms and global opening empowered some groups and disempowered others, giving rise to local approaches to land and property and to different local narratives that legitimated these approaches. Once patterns of land control and property-rights rules emerged, they were hardened and reproduced as property-rights claims acquired a moral content, envisioning land as either a moral entitlement for specific social groups or a state resource to be put toward the pursuit of collective prosperity.

THE NORTHEAST REGION BEFORE THE REFORMS

The provinces of Heilongjiang, Jilin, and Liaoning compose the Northeast macroregion, referred to in China as the "old industrial base" (*lao gongye jidi*, 老工业基地), or what Westerners may call "a rust belt." The three provinces were at the heart of Japanese Manchuria between 1931 and 1945: Changchun was the capital of Japanese Manchukuo, and Dalian was the foothold for the Japanese-held Kwantung Lease Territory beginning in 1905. Despite the atrocities of the Japanese imperial project, the three northeastern provinces had already inherited a substantial infrastructural and industrial capacity by the beginning of the PRC period. Barry Naughton notes that "the *majority* of China's industrial output was in Manchuria" by the end of World War II.[6]

That inherited capacity, as well as the region's historic connections to Russia and its proximity to the PRC's close ally in the 1950s, made the Northeast the heartland of Maoist, state-led industrialization. In the First Five-Year Plan (FYP), the three provinces were designated for more than 40 of the 156 "key" nationwide industrialization projects.[7] The growth rates of Heilongjiang, Jilin, and Liaoning provinces were among the highest in the country between 1952 and 1978.[8] Beyond growth and state investment, it was in the Northeast where the socialist model of urban organization was most thoroughly developed because of the region's heavy share of state-owned enterprises

---

[6] Barry Naughton. *The Chinese Economy: Transitions and Growth* (Cambridge, MA: MIT Press, 2007), 48 (emphasis in the original).

[7] *Dongbei jingjiqu tongji nianjian, 1987* (Northeast Economic Region Statistical Yearbook, 1987) (Beijing: Zhongguo tongji chubanshe, 1987), 12.

[8] Zeng Juxin and Liang Bin, "Zhongguo quyu jingji zengzhang bijiao yanjiu" (Comparative Research on Regional Economic Growth in China), *Jingji dili* (Economic Geography) no.1 (1994): 16–20.

(SOEs) and formal state workers. According to available data, Harbin's GDP grew sevenfold between 1949 and 1957 (from 266 million RMB to 1.488 billion RMB), and that of the city of Shenyang, the capital of Liaoning province, was ten times greater in 1957 than it was in 1949. These trends are on par with national trends, again according to the relevant data for this period. But these two cities, having inherited a mature industrial structure, began the PRC period with economies orders of magnitude much larger than those of cities of comparable size.[9]

Since the onset of the economic reforms, however, the northeastern provinces have certainly lost their place of privilege as the cradle of Chinese industry and investment. The region's share of industrial output has declined steadily from its height at about one-quarter of industrial output in the 1950s to less than 10 percent in the 2000s (see Figure 3.1). The region's share of GDP has similarly declined. This shared fate is not a product of the region's inability to compete in a market economy, but rather a direct consequence of the nature of the economic reforms and the global opening policies that were introduced at the beginning in 1978.

REFORM AND OPENING: PREFERENTIAL POLICIES
AND SEQUENTIAL STAGING

The Third Plenary Session of the Eleventh Chinese Communist Party (CCP) Central Committee in 1978 marked the beginning of the "reform and opening" (*gaige kaifang,* 改革开放) – the general policy of introducing gradual market reforms and permitting private enterprise while also opening to investment and trade with the global economy. China's global integration began with limited experiments in "opening up" concentrated in specific cities. In 1979, the CCP established four "special economic zones" (*jingji tequ,* 经济特区) (SEZs) along the southeastern coast in Shenzhen, Zhuhai, and Shantou of Guangdong province and in Xiamen of Fujian province. The entire island of Hainan was designated an SEZ in 1988.[10] On the basis of evidence from the early 1980s that the open-door policy in the SEZs was successful and politically

---

[9] *Xin Zhongguo chengshi wushinian, 1949–1999* (Fifty Years of Chinese Cities, 1949–1999) (Beijing: Xinhua chubanshe, 1999), 153.

[10] Policies toward investors in the SEZs and investors in the Economic and Technology Development Zones differ somewhat from place to place. In general, the zones offer preferential income-tax rates (at about 15 percent, as opposed to 33 percent), flexible wage systems, and preferential land-use and acquisition fees and policies, flexible import and export taxes, and administrative flexibility. "Softer" institutional benefits include streamlined administration to ease registration, labor recruiting, contracting, and so forth, as well as the establishment of training institutes. Some of the specific policies are formulated at the local levels, whereas some are determined at higher levels, often in order to experiment with new policies. This was especially the case in Shenzhen. See Naughton, *Chinese Economy*, 407–8.

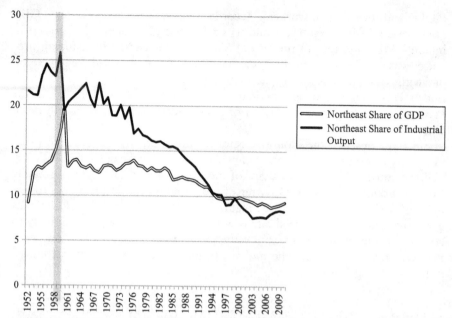

FIGURE 3.1. Northeast GDP and Industrial Output (GVIO) as a Share of National Output, 1952–2010

Source: China Data Online, accessed September 9, 2013. The shaded area indicates the period of the Great Leap Forward. Whether the spikes indicate real jumps in output or simply overreporting, these years are not representative of general trends.

manageable, the CCP expanded the "opening up" by designating fourteen coastal open cities (*yanhai kaifang chengshi*, 沿海开放城市) in Dalian, Qinhuangdao, Tianjin, Yantai, Qingdao, Lianyungang, Nantong, Wenzhou, Shanghai, Ningbo, Fuzhou, Guangzhou, Zhanjiang, and Beihai. In addition to opening these cities to international investment, the fourteen coastal open cities were allowed a group of preferential policies that afforded them more autonomy in attracting and approving foreign investment projects through lower tax rates, preferential land-use policies, and so forth. In designating these specific cities as open cities, the central government in Beijing sent a clear signal that it was committed to reform and that it would support international investment. This signal of commitment was just as important as the specific policy packages to attract foreign capital. By the mid-1980s, the constellation of preferential policies allotted to cities along China's eastern seaboard became a more definite "coastal development strategy." The strategy was codified in the Seventh Five-Year Plan as the country was divided into "three economic belts" (*sanda jingji didai*, 三大经济地带). The plan designated the East for export-oriented industrialization, the center for agriculture and energy, and the West for animal husbandry and natural resource extraction. Planners began to refer to the strategy as the "eastern mission" (*dongbu juezhan,* 东部决战) and to the eastern seaboard as the "golden coastline" (*huangjin haiyan,* 黄金海岸).[11]

Though policy-makers and officials articulated a number of reasons why development first of the coastal areas constituted an economically "natural" growth strategy for China, designating preferential policies for specific coastal cities was also a way to experiment with opening up while limiting the geographic scope of the reach of global capital. Initially confining foreign investment to a series of discrete locations obviated the need for what would have been protracted and painful negotiations over national policy, permitting gradual steps toward global integration and more generally following the Chinese policy-making approach of "experimentation under hierarchy."[12] Barry Naughton characterizes this process simply: "Zones permitted incremental progress within a rigid system."[13]

The sequential staging of reform policies continued apace into the second decade of the twenty-first century (see Table 3.1). By the time of China's entry into the World Trade Organization in 2001, almost every location in the country was open to global capital and nearly every city (and most counties) had established development zones that offered preferential tax and land policies to attract global and domestic investment. Contemporary preferential policies, such as the creation of "national-level development zones" in Tianjin and Chongqing and urban-rural integrated planning sites in Chengdu and Chongqing, are as closely associated with guaranteeing Beijing's support for a particular area as they are with the actual effects of policy preferences. During the thirty years after the initiation of reforms, preferential policies from Beijing have remained both the key manifestation of the regime's credible commitment to support investment and the clearest signal of the direction of central government development efforts.

DIVERGENCE IN THE NORTHEAST

Although Dalian, Harbin, and Changchun began the reform era as part of the same regional political economy, their fates diverged irrevocably after Dalian was declared a coastal open city in 1984. With earlier access to global capital and a commitment on the part of Beijing to support the city's growth, Dalian's economy expanded as a result of foreign investment and a growing export-

---

[11] C. Cindy Fan, "Uneven Development and Beyond: Regional Development Theory in Post-Mao China," *International Journal of Urban and Regional Research* 21, no. 4 (1997): 623.

[12] Sebastian Heilmann, "Policy Experimentation in China's Economic Rise," *Studies in Comparative International Development* 41, no. 1 (2008): 3. For the origins of experimentation in China, see idem, "From Local Experiments to National Policy: The Origins of China's Distinctive Policy Process," *China Journal* no. 59 (January 2008): 1–30; see also Sebastian Heilmann and Elizabeth Perry, eds., *Mao's Invisible Hand: The Political Foundations of Adaptive Governance in China* (Cambridge, MA: Harvard University Asia Center, 2011).

[13] Naughton, *Chinese Economy,* 406.

TABLE 3.1. *Selected Preferential Policies Related to Opening Up, 1979–2010*

Preferential policy	Geographic area	Year
Special economic zones 经济特区	Shenzhen, Zhuhai, Shantou, Xiamen (Hainan)	1979 (1988)
Coastal open cities 沿海开放城市	Dalian, Qinhuangdao, Tianjin, Yantai, Qingdao, Lianyungang, Nantong, Wenzhou, Shanghai, Ningbo, Fuzhou, Guangzhou, Zhanjiang, Beihai	1984
Coastal open areas	Pearl River Delta, Yangzi River Delta, Minnan River Region	1985
Eligibility for Economic and Technology Development Zones (ETDZs) expands widely	Nationwide – ETDZs must be approved by the State Council All provincial and autonomous region capitals All coastal cities	1992
National-Level Development Zones	Binhai in Tianjin, Liangjiang Zone in Chongqing (Shenzhen and Pudong in Shanghai)	2010 (1979, 1992)
Shanghai Free Trade Area	Shanghai	2013

processing sector. Figure 3.2 shows the growth progress in terms of per capita GDP in each city compared to China's national per capita GDP and urban averages. The three cities – as did urban China more generally – began at relatively similar levels (per capita GDP: Changchun, 1,055 RMB; Dalian 2,022 RMB; Harbin 1,317 RMB; China's national per capita GDP 1,112 RMB), but they began to diverge, especially in the early 1990s. By 2010, Dalian's per capita GDP was nearly twice the national urban average, whereas Changchun was close to the national average and Harbin was slightly below. Figure 3.3 reveals a similar story with respect to regional GDP (labeled GRP), though clearly all three cities grew substantially, especially after 2000.

A look at the flows of foreign direct investment lays bare the sources of these divergences (see Table 3.2). As we would expect, Dalian's inclusion along the "golden coastline" afforded the city access to foreign capital in orders of magnitude in excess of the two other cities. We see that the levels of FDI in Changchun and Harbin were basically on par until the late 1990s, when FDI in Changchun's auto sector, as discussed in Chapter 6, took off. Even by 2010, Harbin enjoyed well less than 10 percent of the FDI that flowed into Dalian in that year.

FDI and the early opening certainly made Dalian richer than the other cities in the region, but I do not argue that the greater wealth on its own led to a certain type of property-rights regime. On the contrary, it was the reliance on a different form of capital, rather than a different degree of capital, that made Dalian a vastly different political economy. In a material sense, Dalian's local

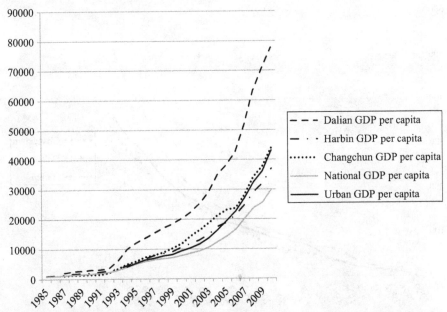

FIGURE 3.2. GDP per Capita, Nationwide, Urban, Dalian, Harbin, and Changchun, 1985–2010 (RMB)

Sources: Dalian, Harbin, and Changchun data are from the respective city statistical yearbooks (*tongji nianjian*, 统计年鉴), various years, except for 2005–10, which are from China Data Center (CDC), University of Michigan, via China Data Online (CDC). The national average includes the urban and rural areas, also via CDC. The urban average indicates average per capita GDP for all prefectural-level cities and above, from NBS via the CEIC.

government acted as arbiter between desperate local firms (and their workers) and potential foreign investors. Competition for local state support for technical upgrading and capital investment – factors that would determine firm survival – allowed the local government to pressure firms and residents to relinquish land claims and thereby consolidate the state monopoly over urban property rights. In a less material sense, early urban physical expansion in the form of a development zone, in which export-oriented manufacturing enterprises were staffed primarily by migrant workers, reoriented the struggle over reforms from one of local government versus firms and workers to one of market competition versus the "old" thinking. Authorities in Dalian embraced competitive pressures and the language of state-directed market development as an alternative to the moral economy of state socialism. As the next section makes clear, Dalian suffered no fewer job losses than did Harbin or Changchun, but the nature of the local political economy created vastly different stakes, with the distribution of political power tilted toward the local state.

Municipal governments in Changchun and Harbin, in contrast, had no such external capital base. Figure 3.4 shows the budgetary revenue and expenditure

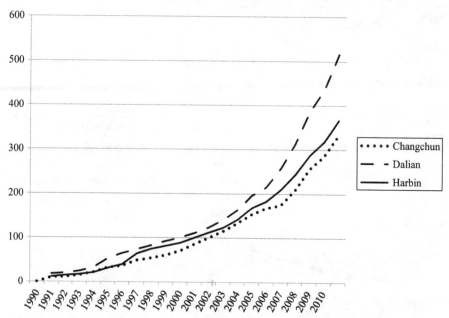

FIGURE 3.3. GRP, Changchun, Dalian, Harbin, 1990–2010 (Billion RMB)
Sources: Changchun, Harbin, and Dalian City Yearbooks, various years; NBS, via CEIC, accessed September 2013.

data as a share of the regional GDP in each city. All three cities suffered the same massive drop in revenues in 1994 (as a result of the fiscal reforms discussed in the previous chapter). Changchun's revenue to GDP ratio was consistently much lower than that in the other two cities because most of the revenue generated by its largest firm—a joint venture of Volkswagen and a massive centrally owned and centrally controlled auto SOE – accrued to Beijing. Dalian spent slightly more relative to GDP than the other two cities, but in general, its trajectories of revenues and expenditures did not differ dramatically. The differences among these local political economies were not in the amount of economic activity or the levels of government spending, but rather in the nature of their economic activity and how the local governments made use of nonbudgetary resources to meet both their own needs and the expectations of local political groups. These differences were generated by the extent of global exposure but also by the sequencing of the opening and reform.

Reforms to the State Sector

Opening to global capital was delayed in Changchun and Harbin, as it was in much of the country, but the reforms to the state sector and the socialist system

TABLE 3.2. *Foreign Direct Investment, 1990–2010 (US$ million)*

	Changchun	Dalian	Harbin
1990	0.66	201.29	2.24
1991	3.03	261.11	17.43
1992	25.81	311.48	32.00
1993	70.97	667.38	68.00
1994	82.03	814.81	110.00
1995	181.61	709.62	131.50
1996	67.18	1005.92	150.00
1997	75.70	1319.44	162.00
1998	284.91	1237.52	150.00
1999	331.45	1174.15	150.95
2000	143.83	1305.97	203.14
2001	506.66	1454.00	223.84
2002	626.66	1603.09	205.00
2003	751.01	2211.26	226.03
2004	901.96	2203.28	405.00
2005	1170.60	3004.15	366.04
2006	1407.34	2244.77	317.20
2007	1687.87	3162.76	372.00
2008	2035.56	5006.78	573.41
2009	2432.88	6011.97	622.02
2010	698.79	10030.25	700.10

Sources: China Data Center of the University of Michigan, via CDC; 2009 data are from *Changchun tongji nianjian, 2010* (Changchun Statistical Yearbook, 2010) (Beijing: Zhongguo tongji chubanshe, 2010), 549; *Dalian tongji nianjian, 2010* (Dalian Statistical Yearbook, 2010) (Beijing: Zhongguo tongji chubanshe, 2010), 515; *Ha'erbin tongji nianjian, 2010* (Harbin Statistical Yearbook, 2010) (Beijing: Zhongguo tongji chubanshe, 2010), 271.

of collective consumption and welfare provision were not. All cities – and especially those saddled with large loss-generating state enterprises – experienced internal enterprise reforms, including layoffs, structural ownership reforms, and, eventually, privatization. These reforms were implemented – and likely conceptualized – gradually, in contrast to the rapid, "big bang" style of privatization and departure from economic planning undertaken by the transitional economies in Eastern Europe and the former Soviet Union.

The initial SOE reforms, implemented as early as 1979, involved greater enterprise autonomy, allowing enterprise managers to sell output above the plan and to retain a share of the profits (rather than remitting all the profits to the level of government that owned the enterprise). Barry Naughton writes that these reforms were popular ones, since they involved assigning autonomy over profits, and they were "overimplemented" beyond the six thousand largest firms in the state budget that had initially adopted them. Although firms had little autonomy in relation to labor, in terms of both the quantity of the

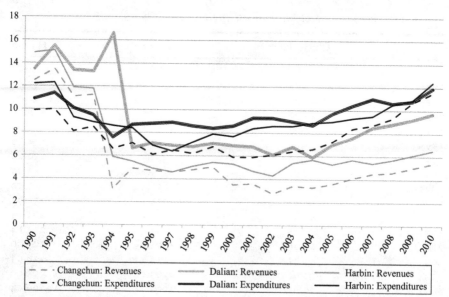

FIGURE 3.4. Budgetary Revenues and Expenditures as a Percentage of GDP, 1990–2010
Source: Xin Zhongguo chengshi wushinian, 1949–1999 (Fifty Years of Chinese Cities, 1949–99)
(Beijing: Xinhua chubanshe, 1999), 425–30; 1999 data are from the China Data Center, University
of Michigan. The data have been verified in the city statistical yearbooks, various years.

workforce and the wages, they enjoyed "significant freedoms to engage in
outside plan activity and to deflect implementation of government commands
in ways that suited their interests."[14] These reforms, as I will detail in the case
chapters, entailed enhanced autonomy over the use of land and the built
environment as enterprise assets, strengthening claims to enterprise property
rights vis-à-vis local governments.

Additional reforms in the early 1980s included expanded autonomy over
enterprise investments, fueled by the retention of profits. Naughton tracks how
the retained earnings went to new worker bonus programs and investments in
fixed assets, including worker housing. Although the bonuses and investments
were intended to incentivize workers to work harder, in reality they served to
enhance worker claims over housing and the built environment, especially since
many of the same enterprises encountered partial privatization or bankruptcy
during the decade.[15] Although these early reforms were arrested when, perhaps

[14] Barry Naughton, *Growing Out of the Plan: Chinese Economic Reform, 1978–1993*
(Cambridge: Cambridge University Press, 1995), 99–100. These six thousand firms accounted
for 60 percent of output and 70 percent of profits under the state budget.
[15] Ibid., 103–6. Naughton shows that retained funds increased from less than 15 percent of GNP in
1981 to more than 20 percent in the mid-1980s.

predictably, they generated inflationary pressures and were presumed to challenge the existence of the plan, such moves toward greater enterprise autonomy
generated support for the growth of markets "outside the plan." That the
reforms were not accompanied by serious reforms of prices or of budget
constraints left the state sector at a stage of only partial exposure to markets
during most of the 1980s.[16]

City-level public finance data show how the ailing enterprises drastically
drained urban budgets in the late 1980s and 1990s. Local governments were,
on the one hand, required to implement the reforms, while, on the other hand,
they were eager to protect local enterprises and therefore their own coffers.
A new round of reforms initiated in the late 1980s entailed moving from profit
remittances to taxation, longer-term profit contracting, and decreased rigidity
in workforce requirements. These reforms were intended to support enterprise
commercialization further and to allow enterprise management to respond to
longer-term incentives and competitive pressures. For the purpose of understanding land politics and property rights, the introduction of contract labor
(replacing lifetime job security) and worker redundancy programs are critical.
Although few workers were officially laid off, many became "unemployed
in-house," receiving partial wages or shifting to municipal government programs to await reassignment.[17] Even though these workers remained tied to the
state socialist welfare and job security systems for the time being, the future of
the place of labor was becoming clear. Moreover, these reforms coincided with
urban China's first major experience with land commodification and real estate,
presenting some local governments with a way to assuage workers' concerns
and to generate funds for enterprises and for local public revenues.

Reform momentum in the early to mid-1990s was generated by increased
labor flexibility and ownership structural reforms. Beginning in 1992 and
1993, as extensive reforms eroded enterprise-provided social welfare (especially
unemployment insurance and pensions), contract labor grew rapidly, and many
firms began to lay off workers in earnest and some even entered bankruptcy.[18]
Ownership reforms entailed the issuance of stocks as well as the creation of
joint ventures with international investors. Enterprise assets – including land
and buildings – were under some new controls and were seen in a new light,
especially during the early 1990s real estate boom.

SOE reforms reached a height in the mid- to late 1990s, when the central
authorities in Beijing at last adopted extensive privatization efforts and

---

[16] For this reason, Naughton assesses the early 1980s' reforms as a failure. See also Edward S.
Steinfeld, *Forging Reform in China: The Fate of State-Owned Industry* (Cambridge: Cambridge
University Press, 1998).
[17] Naughton, *Growing Out of the Plan*, 209–12. See also Mary Elizabeth Gallagher, *Contagious
Capitalism: Globalization and the Politics of Labor in China* (Princeton, NJ: Princeton University Press, 2005), ch. 4.
[18] Naughton, *Growing Out of the Plan*, 295–8; Gallagher, *Contagious Capitalism*, 76–82.

enterprises collectively laid off millions of workers. Under Zhu Rongji's program of "grasping the large and releasing the small" (*zhuada fangxiao*, 抓大放小), small and medium SOEs were instructed to lay off workers and to consider firm exit or bankruptcy.[19] These layoffs and firm closures coincided with the first national drive to privatize housing; the goals were to reduce the state's burden to maintain residential facilities linked with enterprises and to stimulate macroeconomic demand in the midst of the 1998 Asian financial crisis. The politics of these painful layoffs and firm closures would affect the distribution of housing and land during these years.

Abandoning the Socialist Social Contract

These reforms, however incremental, chipped away at the socialist social contract, the understanding since 1949 that the state would provide employment security and birth-to-death social welfare. In return for this provision, Chinese citizens submitted to the political authority of the CCP and accepted limits on consumption and individual aspirations. This understanding was replaced by a market social contract, which promised more individual autonomy, better jobs, and a growing piece of the economic pie, but also required the dismantling of the social welfare regime, the "iron rice bowl," on which much of society had come to rely.[20]

Nowhere were the bonds of the socialist social contract stronger than in the Northeast, the region where socialism had taken shape in the early decades of the PRC and whose citizens were considered the core force behind the building of the "New China." Moreover, the promises of the new market order were slow to materialize in much of the region, which had few links with overseas Chinese communities who were potential investors and had little access to the preferential policies that catalyzed growth along the coast. In Deng's famous adage that "some will get rich before others," much of the population in the Northeast may have been viewed optimistically as the "others" and more pessimistically as those who would bear the costs of the market transition.

The provinces that make up the Northeast lost 4.7 million industrial jobs between 1996 and 1998 (see Tables 3.3 and 3.4). These data include only the officially registered numbers of unemployed; millions of others were unemployed "in house," on reduced wages, suffering wage arrears and underemployment, or had exited the workforce rather than registering as unemployed. Ching Kwan Lee, in her book on labor protest in the Northeast and Southeast regions, cites a

---

[19] See Hurst, *Chinese Worker after Socialism*, 49–56.
[20] This idea originally appeared in Wenfang Tang and William L. Parish, *Chinese Urban Life under Reform: The Changing Social Contract* (Cambridge: Cambridge University Press, 2000). See also Lee, *Against the Law*, 71.

TABLE 3.3. *Workforce Data, Case Cities, 1993–2001*

	Dalian			Harbin			Changchun		
	Employed persons	Unemployed persons	Unemployment rate	Employed persons	Unemployed persons	Unemployment rate	Employed persons	Unemployed persons	Unemployment rate
1993	1,619,920	39,890	2.4	1,996,638	49,604	2.4	1,121,400	10,567	0.9
1994	1,635,000	44,047	2.6	1,941,200	75,084	3.8	1,050,881	9,727	0.9
1995	1,640,000	46,800	2.8	1,660,000	46,000	3.1	1,079,859	9,867	0.9
1996	1,683,000	49,500	2.9	1,640,000	47,008	2.8	1,053,219	11,963	2.3
1997	1,594,000	65,874	4.0	1,630,000	52,208	3.5	1,234,866	5,822	0.5
1998	1,584,000	43,265	2.7	1,580,000	66,392	4.0	1,071,394	22,588	2.1
1999	1,672,000	70,000	4.0	2,157,000	80,000	3.0	1,420,000	39,000	2.7
2000	1,558,000	63,000	3.9	2,127,000	81,000	3.1	1,470,000	45,000	2.9
2001	1,558,000	81,700	5.0	2,106,000	81,000	4.04	1,394,000	22,100	1.6

Sources: All data are from *Zhongguo laodong tongji nianjian* (China Labor Statistical Yearbook) (Beijing: Zhongguo tongji chubanshe), various years; employed persons (*chengzhen congye renyuan nianmo renshu*, 城镇从业人员年末人数) indicates people on the job at year end, including those laid off and reassigned within the year. Unemployed persons (*nianmo shangyou shiye renyuan renshu*, 年末尚有失业人员人数) refers to people who were registered as unemployed at year end. These numbers are very conservative since they do not include the informally unemployed and do not reveal the turnover within the year. Harbin 1999, 2000, and 2001 data are from *Ha'erbin tongji nianjian* (Harbin Statistical Yearbook) (Beijing: Zhongguo tongji nianjian), various years.

TABLE 3.4. *Industrial Workers and Public-Sector Employees in the Northeast,*
1990–2000 (Million)

	Liaoning (Dalian)		Jilin (Changchun)		Heilongjiang (Harbin)	
	Industrial workers	SOEs and urban collectives	Industrial workers	SOEs and urban collectives	Industrial workers	SOEs and urban collectives
1990	7.8	9.9	3.3	5.2	5.0	8.5
1991	7.9	10.1	3.4	5.3	5.3	8.7
1992	7.9	10.2	3.5	5.4	5.4	8.7
1993	8.3	9.9	3.4	5.3	5.3	8.5
1994	7.7	9.7	3.3	5.1	5.4	8.3
1995	7.7	9.7	3.3	5.0	5.3	8.1
1996	7.5	9.4	3.1	4.9	5.3	7.8
1997	7.2	9.1	2.3	4.8	5.1	7.7
1998	5.2	6.1	2.2	3.4	3.8	5.6
1999	4.9	5.5	2.1	3.1	3.7	5.2
2000	4.8	4.9	1.9	2.9	3.4	4.6

Sources: Data are from the China Data Center of the University of Michigan, via China Data
Online, accessed October 2013. SOEs and urban collectives, my own calculations, include
nonindustrial firms and institutions.

popular jingle in the region: "We gave our youth to the Party; now in our old age
no one cares for us. Can we turn to our children? They are also laid off."[21]

The formerly privileged workers of the urban Northeast did not passively
accept the dismantling of the socialist social contract. As several scholars on
popular protest and labor politics have documented, the cities in the Northeast
were plagued by sit-ins, street marches, work stoppages, petitions, and occa-
sions of collective violence as urban enterprises were unable to pay wages and
pensions or to manage worker housing and ancillary facilities and eventually
entered into bankruptcy and underwent privatization.[22]

Local governments in these cities were situated uneasily between the expectations of Beijing – that they carry out economic reforms, generate growth, and
maintain social stability – and those of the urban citizens, whose hardships,
grievances, and sense of moral economic justice intensified as the reforms

[21] Lee, *Against the Law*, 72–3.

[22] Ibid.; Hurst and O'Brien, "China's Contentious Pensioners"; Hurst, *Chinese Worker after*
Socialism; Chen, "Industrial Restructuring and Workers' Resistance in China." See also Mun
Young Cho, *The Specter of "the People": Urban Poverty in Northeast China* (Ithaca, NY:
Cornell University Press, 2013). With the exception of Lee's volume, which looks at workers'
grievances related to housing and collective property rights at factories facing bankruptcy, land
and property rights have not figured prominently in the literature on labor protests in the
Northeast or elsewhere.

proceeded. Land, a resource nominally under the control of local governments and without much oversight from the higher levels of the administrative hierarchy, was adopted as a political resource by local governments. They made varying use of land control as a vehicle by which to coerce compliance with the economic reforms, as a resource for distribution to the losers from the reforms, or as an arena in which to project local government administrative power over the local economy.

LIMITS OF THE STUDY

The selection of cities within a single region has allowed me to isolate the effects of the different political economies that were forged during the process of China's post-Mao reforms. The following three chapters will explain why different cities adopted different roles for local governments in the arena of land control and why the emergence of property rights in terms of the resources and constraints available to them was the result of the sequencing of the economic reforms and opening. The goal is to provide a systematic way of describing different local political economic orders and explaining their origins so that the argument may hold outside the specific cases.

With an eye to preventing unnecessary disappointment, it is worth stating what this approach neglects or ignores before delving into the cases. First, I treat as exogenous the distribution of preferential policies, that is, which cities secured which privileges from Beijing and when. That is to say, I do not attempt to explain why Dalian was chosen as a coastal open city in 1984, whereas Harbin and Changchun had to wait until the early 1990s to open in earnest to global capital. What is obvious is that Dalian is on the coast and Harbin and Changchun are not. Less obvious, in general, is why some cities seemed to enjoy greater privileges and perhaps the backing of Beijing, whereas others did not.

Chinese local officials – to state the obvious – serve at the pleasure of those above them in the hierarchical party-state. Part of what makes a local leader effective or popular is how successful he or she is in attracting resources, attention, and support from the higher levels of government. At the same time, individual careers within the CCP are made and broken on the basis of their local achievements. Particularly promising lower-level leaders are often placed in specific jurisdictions such that those leaders and jurisdictions are both picked as winners. The story of Dalian and its most famous politician, Bo Xilai, can certainly be described in this way. Chapter 4 tells the story of the city's rise as well as Bo's ascent to power within the PRC. Bo's connections perhaps afforded Dalian more central support than that enjoyed by Changchun or Harbin, meaning that Dalian authorities had more maneuverability in terms of implementing reforms and growth projects. However, central support and elite political connections did not guarantee any outcome with regard to local property-rights rules and enforcement. The connections and central support certainly ensured Dalian's access to global capital, which, I argue, is the main mechanism by which the power of the municipal state was enhanced.

The second outcome I do not aim to explain is economic growth, or why some cities grew wealthier than others. Even within a single region, the answer is surely overdetermined for the cases at hand. Dalian was a beneficiary of the preferential policies, which were correlated with a geographic location that would predict a better growth outcome than that of the other two cities. As should by now be clear, economic growth figures into the resources or constraints that urban officials face and therefore has clear effects on what kinds of property-rights regimes they embrace. Unfortunately for readers who are more interested in the differences in these cities' long-term trajectories, the causal process I outline here is limited to how the growth processes interacted with the emergence of land markets and changes in the configuration of property rights. My goal is to explain the emergence of different land regimes rather than to describe in full the process through which specific Chinese cities moved from state socialism to where they are now. This focus is an analytical choice, and one I make in hopes that more general lessons about Chinese capitalism and state–society relations do not become lost in the particularities of individual experiences.[23] Nonetheless, the case chapters, to which I now turn, delve into the relationships between political economic reforms and land politics in these three cities.

---

[23] Atul Kohli writes, "the chain of causation stemming from the phenomena to be explained can stretch back continually. One has to cut into the chain of causation somewhere to undertake manageable research. Given this inevitability, where one cuts into the causal chain is then a matter of analytical judgment." Atul Kohli, *The State and Poverty in India: The Politics of Reform* (Cambridge: Cambridge University Press, 1987), 13.

4

"Land as a State Asset"

Global Capital and Local State Power in Dalian

Dalian, a city of a little more than six million people on the tip of the Liaodong peninsula in Liaoning province, is most frequently mentioned outside China for one of two reasons. First, as the host of the "Summer Davos," Dalian has a reputation as one of China's cleanest and most beautiful cities. Dalian is also noted for its connection to one of China's most recognizable and notorious contemporary politicians: Bo Xilai. Before Bo attracted global attention for "smashing" corruption and singing Red songs as part of his populist reform campaign in Chongqing, and notoriety for the murder scandal that felled him in 2012, he served in the city of Dalian from 1984 through 2000 in various positions, and ultimately as mayor. However, Bo's populist turn in Chongqing was not at all predictable in terms of his tenure in Dalian, during which he presided over the city's opening to foreign direct investment (FDI) and its transformation from a socialist industrial base to an area for global corporate outsourcing.

Dalian's two reputations are, to be sure, deeply intertwined. Under Bo's leadership, the city initiated a massive transformation of the urban built environment and undertook a substantial public relations campaign to highlight its success in urban planning and economic reforms. Dalian's rise, both economically and publicly, coincided with Bo's political rise such that we cannot disentangle the effect of one from the other. The same is true of the mutual dependence of the city's economic trajectory and its pursuit of land and real estate development. As Dalian grew out of the rust belt into a global capital hub, the local government monopolized property rights and deployed land development as a tool for government financing, a model that almost all Chinese cities would replicate in the 2000s. This chapter narrates Dalian's economic growth and physical transformation, illustrating how its statist property-rights regime emerged as a result of the sequencing of global opening and economic reforms.

THE ARGUMENT IN BRIEF

The integral relationship between economic strategies and property-rights practices experienced throughout China is on particular display in Dalian. Dalian's reform era economic performance was made possible by a dramatic reorganization of its political economy from a state socialist heavy industry base to a global capital hub. This reorganization, itself possible because of Dalian's preferential status and therefore early access to global capital, generated a shift in local political alliances. The municipal government became more reliant on foreign capital and less dependent on the city's traditional power base: state-owned industrial firms and their workers. The division between the "new" economy – comprising foreign-owned firms chiefly employing migrant workers – and the "old" economy became even more pronounced as a result of the city's land policies, which physically segregated these two economies into a downtown core and a suburban development zone.

Dalian, a beneficiary of the preferential policies bestowed on several coastal cities as outlined in the previous chapter, pursued global opening and economic reform in that order, first establishing a thriving, foreign capital–supported economic base and then later executing politically painful economic reforms to the public sector. Beginning in 1984, the same year that it established a large development zone on converted farmland thirty-five kilometers from the downtown city center, Dalian was granted power to negotiate independently for FDI. As global firms sought domestic partners, the local government positioned itself as middleman, directing much-needed capital to specific firms and industries and rendering faltering public-sector enterprises dependent on the local government for survival. When, in the 1990s, the city enforced reforms to public-sector enterprises, such as layoffs, bankruptcies, and privatization, competition among firms for local government assistance to locate capital and foreign partners reduced potential opposition to local government plans. Workers in these enterprises competed to secure jobs in the newly restructured firms and were similarly discouraged from political organizing.

Dalian's property-rights regime is statist; regulatory authority is concentrated exclusively in the hands of the municipal government, and the state is the sole legitimate claimant to landownership rights. Dalian Municipal Government consolidated monopoly control over urban land by encouraging other potential claimants – such as residents and firms – to bargain away their claims through both positive inducements and threats of force. The local government used its status as an intermediary between global capital and local firms to induce firms to relinquish their property. Enterprise reform and restructuring frequently involved moving enterprises to the development zone or reconstituting them there, allowing the municipal government to reclaim downtown land while foreclosing opportunities for firms to assert their property rights over land or the built environment. Workers faced similar incentives with respect to property rights over housing; relinquishing claims and accepting relocation better positioned workers for reemployment, thereby deterring political organization and opposition. Moreover, a lack of enterprise support for workers' claims and competition among workers for reemployment discouraged efforts to assert property-rights claims.

These economic growth and land strategies were carried out alongside political campaigns that involved massive propaganda and ideological efforts to focus public attention on collective prosperity. Declaring the city to be the "Hong Kong of the North," Dalian authorities, with Bo Xilai at the helm, repositioned the city's plight as one of competing with other global capital hubs for investment and recognition. The built environment – and the use of land as a "state asset" – would become a primary symbol of the achievement and transformation of Dalian, both to city residents and to potential investors, tourists, and outside audiences more generally. These ideological campaigns established legitimacy for the local government's claims to urban property: State control over land was considered necessary to attract global investment and to project an image of a modern, global city. Ironically, the state monopoly over urban property rights was regarded as a requisite for capitalist growth.

Perhaps counterintuitively, Dalian's early and wide opening to global markets shored up local state power to intervene in markets and to direct local economic and political behavior. Dalian's statist property-rights regime emerged simultaneously with its new political economic order that privileged the local state as the economic and physical planner and that favored global capital over the domestic private and erstwhile public sectors. Groups in Dalian – firms, workers, investors, and agents of the state – formed their preferences about property rights in the midst of massive and uncertain social and economic change. The property-rights regime emerged from political bargains in which potential challengers to the local state's claims on land relinquished their own claims in pursuit of economic security under the reforms and from moral campaigns that promoted state claims to land as necessary for collective prosperity.

THE UNMAKING OF A RUST BELT CITY: POWER AND GLOBAL CAPITAL IN DALIAN'S RISE

Over the course of the 1980s and 1990s, Dalian was transformed from a rust belt city "well known for its concentration of state-run heavy-industry units in power generation, oil refining, shipbuilding, and chemical and machinery production"[1] to the so-called Bangalore of north Asia and "China's best business city."[2] As described in the previous chapter, Dalian is by far the

---

[1] Lisa M. Hoffman, *Patriotic Professionalism in Urban China: Fostering Talent* (Philadelphia: Temple University Press, 2010), 32.

[2] Rachel Morajee, "No Dilly Dalian: Dalian," *Monocle* 4, no. 31 (March 2010): 95–9.

wealthiest city in Northeast China, and it also boasts a reputation as a business-friendly center and a great place to live and work. In the early 1990s, the city began to attract the attention and envy of many cities as it amassed prestigious awards and titles related to its achievements in livability and its construction of the urban environment: "Sanitation Model City" in 1991, "Environmental Protection Model City" in 1992, one of China's "Ten Most Beautiful" cities in 1992, and the first city in China and the second city in Asia to be included among the UN "Global 500" livable environments in 1995.[3]

Positive views of Dalian's urban management and built environment abound in the Western media. Thomas Friedman of the *New York Times* praised Dalian as "one of China's Silicon Valleys because of its proliferation of software parks and its dynamic, techie mayor, Xia Deren."[4] In addition to the city's rapid growth, Dalian is praised for its evident control over the urban environment. Coverage of the first ever "Summer Davos," a World Economic Forum meeting that took place in Dalian in 2007, is worth quoting at length:

Growth has been achieved without many of the problems seen in some rapidly growing Chinese urban areas and the city remains less chaotic than elsewhere. Traffic stops at red lights here allow pedestrians to cross the road without dodging cars and cyclists. Street merchants sell toys and souvenirs like everywhere else in China, but they are fewer in number than in other places and wait for you to ask rather than press-ganging you into buying their goods.[5]

Details like bans on taunting opposing teams in soccer competitions and fines for spitting in the train station are relayed with frequency and a tone of admiration in English-language media.[6]

Mary Gallagher has argued that the sequencing of reform and opening at the national level introduced competitive liberalization pressures while also precluding the organization of reform "losers" to challenge the CCP's hold

[3] *Dalian shi aiguo weisheng yundong zhi, 1988–1998* (Dalian City Patriotic Sanitation Movement Gazetteer 1988–1998) (Dalian: Dalian shi aiguo weisheng yundong zhi bianweihui, 2001), 2–3; *Dalian shi zhi: Huanjing baohu zhi* (Dalian City Environmental Protection Gazetteer) (Dalian: Dalian ligong daxue chubanshe, 2003), 1–2.
[4] Thomas Friedman, "Doha and Dalian," *New York Times*, September 19, 2007, at www.nytimes.com/2007/09/19/opinion/19friedman.html?pagewanted=print&_r=0, accessed February 6, 2015. Friedman describes how Dalian "already had a mini-Manhattan" on his last visit, in 2004, and by 2007 "seems to have grown two more since – including a gleaming new convention complex built on a man-made peninsula." The latter refers to Xinghai Square, which I discuss later.
[5] Duncan Mavin, "From Davos to Dalian," *Financial Post*, September 1, 2007, at www.financialpost.com/story.html?id=de8a188d-8f00-43ba-a3f4-e49083758336, accessed February 6, 2015.
[6] Conor O'Clery, "Comrade Mayor Sporting Old-School Tie," *Irish Times*, November 10, 1997, 12; You Jin, "Pearl of the Liaodong Peninsula," *Straits Times* (Singapore), October 12, 1994, 14; Edward Cody, "Striving to Be 'Spiritual': Chinese Campaign Seeks to Combat Western Values," *Washington Post*, January 30, 1997, A13.

on power. She focuses in particular on labor, examining how the recruitment of a new pool of laborers (migrant workers from the countryside), in addition to the prospect of Chinese enterprises losing out to their more competitive foreign counterparts, created conditions for politically difficult reforms to public enterprises and for shedding the state's welfare burden. In her view, opening to the global economy (i.e., FDI) before large-scale public-sector reform unleashes "competitive pressure across regions and different types of ownership for deeper reform, provides a laboratory for sensitive and difficult reforms, and leads to the ideological reformulation of the public-versus-private industry debate."[7]

Dalian's experience demonstrates how the sequencing of reform and opening emboldened the state at the local level. In Dalian, the specter of highly competitive foreign-invested enterprises outside the city center introduced pressures on the state sector, and the presence of a sizable and growing group of rural-to-urban labor migrants at the city's periphery dampened the potential for labor activism in the urban core. Dalian's strategy for economic growth was to expand the city into its surrounding countryside and to locate new forms of economic activity – mostly foreign-invested enterprises – well outside the downtown core. Only after the city enjoyed a new and vibrant foreign-dominated economic base did Dalian officials begin the politically difficult process of dismantling socialism. As we see in the sections that follow, this economic strategy enabled the emergence of a statist property-rights regime, in which the local government was both owner and regulator of urban land.

Dalian's economic dynamism and urban reputation propelled the career of its famous leader, Bo Xilai, who, before 2007, had been invoked as an example of China's new, forward-thinking, and technocratic corps of leaders. After 2007, when he was appointed party secretary of the provincial municipality of Chongqing, Bo gained fame for his populist campaigns against organized crime and his revival of Maoist-era mobilization tactics. In March 2012, in the most spectacular and visible conflict among China's elite since Tiananmen, Bo was arrested in association with a murder scandal involving his wife and the death of a British businessman.

Bo Xilai was born into the apex of Chinese politics. His father was Bo Yibo, one of the "eight immortal" party elders who took part in both the founding of the PRC and the reforms of the 1980s and 1990s, making Bo Xilai a member of the "princeling group" (*taizidang*, 太子党), descendants of the party elite who have achieved great degrees of wealth and power in contemporary China. But Bo Xilai's ties with Beijing were not limited to those with his family. He served for two years (1982–4) as a staff member in the Research Office of

---

[7] Mary Elizabeth Gallagher, *Contagious Capitalism: Globalization and the Politics of Labor in China* (Princeton, NJ: Princeton University Press, 2005), 10.

the Secretariat and the General Office of the Chinese Communist Party (CCP), working directly with those at the commanding heights of power in China.[8] This well-educated member of a prominent political family moved from the research office of the highest group in the country to a relatively obscure county outside a strategically uncertain city just before that area was to become the most important location within one of the country's fourteen designated coastal open cities. Ultimately, this clearly was not a coincidence; nor was it a story of a visionary local politician or a Beijing crony, but rather a case that highlights the assignment power by Beijing in determining what space exists for officials maneuvering at the local levels to create conditions for growth and success.[9]

A good deal of the global narrative on Dalian's economic rise, before Bo's fall, referenced its dapper, English-speaking, cosmopolitan mayor. *Time* magazine, declaring Bo one of the "100 most influential people in 2010," wrote that "in an era of drab Chinese politicians, Bo Xilai stands out."[10] Educated at Peking University and the Chinese Academy of Social Sciences in international journalism and world history, Bo made his name as a cosmopolitan, visionary local leader who looked far beyond the Chinese domestic experience for inspiration to transform the city of Dalian. Bo's first post as an official was that of a deputy party secretary in Jin county in Liaoning province.[11] More specifically, he worked as the party chief of Maqiaozi village. He was placed in charge of the village in 1984, but in 1985 the area was designated as part of China's first Economic and Technology Development ment Zone, the key locus for economic growth in the city of Dalian. Bo first appears on the rolls of the Dalian City Party Committee in July 1985, already having been designated deputy mayor of Dalian, a status automatically given to the director of the management committee of the Dalian Economic and Technology Development Zone.[12]

Having stewarded the growth of the Dalian Development Area between 1985 and 1992, Bo was promoted to first party secretary and mayor of Dalian

[8] "Chinese Agency Profiles Politburo Standing Committee Member Bo Xilai," Xinhua (New China News Agency), October 22, 2007, in BBC Monitoring Asia Pacific: Political, October 22, 2007. See also "Bo Xilai," at www.chinavitae.com/biography/72, accessed September 29, 2010.

[9] See Sebastian Heilmann, "Policy Experimentation in China's Rise," *Studies in Comparative and International Development* 43, no. 1 (March 2008): 5.

[10] Austin Ramzy, "Leaders: Bo Xilai," *Time*, April 29, 2010, at http://content.time.com/time/specials/packages/article/0,28804,1984685_1984864_1985416,00.html, accessed February 12, 2015.

[11] A county outside yet controlled administratively by Dalian city. See "Liaoning's Experience of Putting Counties under Jurisdiction of Cities," Xinhua, January 20, 1983, in BBC Summary of World Broadcasts: The Far East, FE/7242/C/2, January 27, 1983.

[12] See Jae Ho Chung, "Preferential Policies, Municipal Leadership, and Development Strategies: A Comparative Analysis of Qingdao and Dalian," in *Cities in China: Recipes for Economic Development in the Reform Era*, ed. Jae Ho Chung (New York: Routledge, 1999), 121.

city in 1992, coinciding with Deng Xiaoping's "Southern Tour," after which Bo initiated sweeping changes to the city's political, economic, and physical landscape, including a campaign to privatize and relocate public enterprises out of the downtown area, the creation of seventeen smaller "economic development zones," city beautification and "spiritual" behavior modification campaigns, as well as a propaganda effort to establish Dalian's national and global reputation as a cosmopolitan and modern city. Under the slogan "Make Dalian into the Hong Kong of the North" (*beifang Xianggang*, 北方香港), Bo earned credit for the city's physical and public relations facelift. Nearly every publication that focuses on the city's transformation refers to his pioneering leadership, and his city planning efforts were profiled frequently in national urban planning journals and magazines. One such interview is worth quoting at length:

Reporter: "You are a planner, and Dalian is your art. What is planning?"

Bo: "It is an idea. The environment can be converted into an economic advantage; it has a fundamental value. A beautiful city with complete infrastructure and function is an important national resource. Public assets are not just public enterprises, but also include the city itself. Planning is the lynchpin of the city's construction. It is not just about having enough money, technology, or the skilled hand of a planner. I believe that planning and culture should be brought together and fused, and planning should demonstrate cultural flair and show the status of culture. A pioneer has to have style and status. This is why planning is an ideological venture."[13]

To be sure, Bo was never a planner (his academic training was in journalism), but rather he was a politician with an interest in urban planning as a political strategy and with a grasp of how to market and brand a city. Bo's remarks here show how he staked his own political career on Dalian's built environment; urban planning and spatial transformation were both tools and evidence of the political power of the local state.

Bo's career trajectory after Dalian is evidence that his superiors approved both of the achievements of Dalian and of Bo's hand in them. Bo left Dalian in 2001 for the provincial capital of Shenyang to become the governor of Liaoning province and the deputy secretary of the party committee in the province. As provincial governor through 2004, Bo presided over extensive corruption investigations and the "cleaning up" of the province and its capital.[14] In

---

[13] Hu Xin, "Dalian shi shizhang Bo Xilai jiu chengshi guihua da benkan jizhe wen" (An Interview with Bo Xilai, the Mayor of Dalian, about City Planning), *Renmin luntan* (People's Forum), December 1999, 30–1.

[14] Wen Shizhen, "Zhenxing Liaoning laogongye jidi de silu yu shixian" (Thought and Practice on Revitalizing the Liaoning Industrial Base), speech by the Liaoning Provincial Party Secretary at the Fourth Session of the Eighth Party Congress of Liaoning Province, 2004, in Liaoning Provincial Archives. See also John Pomfret, "One Corrupt City Reflects Scourge Plaguing China: Political System Infected, Some Say," *Washington Post*, March 6, 2002, A10.

2004, Bo Xilai rode his success in opening Dalian to the national level, earning a promotion to the position of minister of commerce under Hu Jintao and Wen Jiabao. He served in this post until 2007, when he was elevated to membership on the Politburo of the CCP Central Committee and sent to the Southwest provincial-level city of Chongqing as party secretary.

Bo would gain notoriety and adoration in equal parts during his tenure in Chongqing, where he presided over phenomenal economic growth fueled by real estate growth, state investment generated from land financing, and global capital in a new development zone, as well as political campaigns to "sing Red songs" and to wipe out corruption and crime.[15] In the eyes of many, Bo's popularity and populism, although perhaps initially acceptable to the central leadership, would account for his eventual political ouster. Perhaps, at first glance, the substance of Bo's policies in Dalian and Chongqing can be contrasted as technocratic versus populist and can be viewed as mostly incompatible. But a deeper look at both ideology and economic policy in Dalian under Bo reveals greater commonalities: securing acquiescence with local economic objectives through campaigns and ideological framing, situating the local government as the spatial and economic planner, and ultimately consolidating local government control over urban and suburban land as the main source of financial and political power for the local government. By conscientiously deploying "land as a state asset," Bo's experience with land politics and property rights in Dalian laid the foundation not only for his later experiments in Chongqing but also for a national model of local government dependence on land-based financial revenue and land-based political power.

"Pass over the Old City; Build a New City": Dalian under Reform

Dalian's initiation into the "winners' circle" of the reform period began with its designation as a coastal open city and a central economic city (*jihua danlie chengshi*, 计划单列城市) in May of 1984. These designations gave the city's leadership autonomy to form economic policy. They also supplied a direct link to Beijing that enabled Dalian policy-makers to circumvent the Liaoning Provincial Government in Shenyang. Municipal officials had lobbied hard for this status over the objections of the Liaoning provincial authorities, who did not wish to see the province's second-largest city wrested

---

[15] See Su Wei, Yang Fan, and Liu Shiwen, *Chongqing moshi* (The Chongqing Model) (Beijing: Zhongguo jingji chubanshe, 2011). See also the contributions to a special issue of the journal *Modern China* devoted to Chongqing, especially Philip C. C. Huang, "Chongqing: Equitable Development Driven by a 'Third Hand'?" *Modern China* 37, no. 6 (2011): 569–622; Ivan Szelenyi, "Third Ways," *Modern China* 37, no. 6 (2011): 672–83; and Zhiyuan Cui, "Partial Intimations of the Coming Whole: The Chongqing Experiment in Light of the Theories of Henry George, James Meade, and Antonio Gramsci," *Modern China* 37, no. 6 (2011): 646–60.

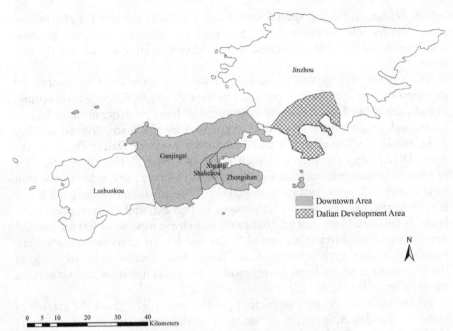

FIGURE 4.1. Dalian Downtown and Development Area

from their control.[16] The designation handed over decision-making power regarding large influxes of foreign capital in the form of foreign-invested enterprises (FIEs) or FDI to the municipal authorities.

The city authorities looked outside the four core urban districts – Zhongshan, Xigang, Shahekou, and Ganjingzi – for physical space to accommodate new forms of economic activity. Officials within the municipal party committee and the government, chiefly in the Urban Planning Bureau, conceived of the "construction ideology" of "pass over the old city, build a new city" to guide the city's development and planning orientation[17] (see Figure 4.1). Even

---

[16] *Dalian nianjian, 1987–1989* (Dalian Yearbook, 1987–1989) (Dalian: Dalian chubanshe, 1990), 13. The yearbook suggests that Dalian was actually to achieve open city status in the fall of 1983, but the policy was delayed. Another source indicates that Dalian's "1980 plan," a ten-year master urban plan, which was completed as early as the end of 1980, included a provision for a development zone in Maqiaozi village of Jin county, but the city waited nearly two years for provincial approval. See Liu Changde, ed., *Dalian chengshi guihua 100 nian: 1899–1999* (One Hundred Years of Dalian City Planning: 1899–1999) (Dalian: Dalian haishi daxue chubanshe, 1999), 103–4. Jae Ho Chung suggests that Dalian was still obligated to remit to Liaoning province 25 percent of its shared revenues, in addition to 500 to 600 million RMB in "road maintenance fees." See Chung, "Preferential Policies, Municipal Leadership, and Development Strategies," 112.

[17] Wang Zhenggang, chief of the Dalian Urban Planning and Land Resource Management Bureau, quoted in "Jianfu kaituo de shiming yu zeren: Fang Dalian shi guihua he guotu ziyuanju Wang Zhenggang juzhang" (Taking on the Opening Mission and Responsibility: An

before Beijing conferred special status upon Dalian, the city's 1980 master plan included the preliminary designation of a development zone in what had been Maqiaozi village located a full thirty-five kilometers from the city center.[18]

Though the strategy of designating a specific space for foreign-oriented development may strike any present observer of urban China as unexciting, in 1984 the idea of directing new investment an hour's driving distance from a traditional urban center was novel. Approved by the State Council in May 1984, the Dalian Development and Technology Zone (or Dalian Development Area [DDA]) was the very first such space in China.[19] The DDA offered a number of formal benefits to foreign firms so as to entice them either to invest in local enterprises or to relocate to the DDA. These advantages included a lower corporate tax rate (15 percent rather than 33 percent) and an exemption from land-use fees and taxes (not an exemption from lease fees, however) for the first three years of the investment period.[20] Beyond formal guarantees, the Dalian municipal leadership, headed by Mayor Wei Fuhai, crusaded tirelessly to signal the commitment of the local government to potential investors and to harness the support of Beijing.[21]

Beginning in the 1980s, municipal publications highlighted the establishment of the DDA, proudly showing that the zone was the first of its kind in China. Explanations for establishing the zone outside the city, however, made no mention of the economic benefits of clustering and instead invoked reasons such as avoiding the problems of the downtown area and establishing a new place to absorb migrant labor. In an explanation of the benefits of Dalian's novel development zoning strategy in a flagship national urban planning journal, members of the Urban Planning Bureau write:

The new area has an extraordinary number of benefits. Principally, it avoids the downtown area's "urban heart disease." Population density is declining (it is already

Interview with Dalian Urban Planning and Land Resource Management Bureau Chief Wang Zhenggang), in *Chengshi jiaoxiang: Dalian chengshi linian yu shixian* (Urban Symphony: Dalian City Theory and Practice), ed. Liu Changde (Beijing: Qinghua daxue chubanshe, 2003), 19.

[18] On the 1980 city plan, see Liu Changde, ed., *Dalian chengshi guihua 100 nian: 1899–1999*, 112. This was made in anticipation of its special-status designation.

[19] The larger SEZs, established in 1979, were the entire cities of Shantou, Shenzhen, Zhuhai (all in Guangdong province), and Xiamen (in Fujian province). I refer here to a smaller development zone (*kaifaqu*, 开发区) within a city.

[20] See Chung, "Preferential Policies, Municipal Leadership, and Development Strategies," 105–40. See also *Dalian shi zhi: Waijing waimao zhi* (Dalian City Foreign Trade and Opening Gazetteer) (Beijing: Fangzhi chubanshe, 2004), 518–39.

[21] Shenyang Liaoning Provincial Service, November 9, 1986 (available in Foreign Broadcast Information Service [FBIS], CHI-86-218, November 12, 1986).

lower than the national standard). The migrant populations will threaten the low population density, so it is best to attract them to the new urban area.[22]

They go on to specify the symptoms of the "urban heart disease": dated transportation arrangements, insufficient water facilities, proximity of polluting factories to residential areas, and so forth.[23] Even as the practice of development zoning gathered steam nationally, there were lengthy discussions of how Dalian's experience suggests that expansion was best for absorbing labor and "avoiding" (*bimian*, 避免) the problems of the inner city and took precedence over the economic benefits of agglomeration.

The strategy of development zoning well outside the battleground of traditional urban politics gained greater momentum in the early 1990s, after Deng Xiaoping's Southern Tour reassured reform-minded officials of Beijing's commitment to introduce market principles, especially through development zones, the number of which exploded in the period between 1992 and 1994. In October 1992, the Dalian Tax Free Zone (*baoshuiqu*, 保税区) was established adjacent to the Maqiaozi Development Zone in suburban Jinzhou, China's first economic area to be treated as duty-free (*jingnei guanwai*, 境内管外).[24] Land was also requisitioned and designated for high-technology parks around the DDA and to the southwest of the city center; only one of the special zones was located within the three core urban districts (Zhongshan, Xigang, and Shahekou). During the period between 1986 and 1992, the total land area controlled by the Dalian Municipal Government more than doubled, and the land designated for urban construction increased 240 percent (see Table 4.1).

In expanding its land control and concentrating new economic activities outside the downtown areas, Dalian succeeded in creating parallel societies as well as parallel economies. The forms of economic activity in the new zones were novel, and the residents and workers were new to Dalian. The city has been a leading destination for rural-to-urban and interurban migration in the Northeast throughout the reform era. According to official data, Dalian had by far the largest "floating population" (*liudong renkou*, 流动人口) in the Northeast. The official growth rate of the migrant population between 1980 and 1989 grew an average of 12 percent per year, increasing

---

[22] Cai Xuefu, Wang Fang, and Zheng Jiazhan, "Chu yi jiang Dalian shi jianshe chengwei xiandaihua guoji xing chengshi de fazhan moshi" (Consider Building Dalian City's Form to Become a Modern International City), *Chengshi guihua* (Urban Planning) no. 4 (1992): 52–5.

[23] Ibid.

[24] *Dalian shi zhi: Waijing waimao zhi*, 549. The benefits of the tax-free zone include exemption from domestic taxes as long as partial assembly is carried out in the bonded zone, and access to warehousing and transport provided by the city. Though the translation is literal, the area was not, of course, under the sovereign authority of any entity other than that of the PRC. The phrase is meant to convey the idea that the area was the first space intended solely for the use of foreign firms within Chinese territory.

TABLE 4.1. *Dalian Land Area and Designation, 1985–2000 (Square Kilometers)*

	Total land area	Urban area	Urban built-up area
1985	12,574	1,063	84
1986	12,574	1,062	90
1987	12,574	2,415	103
1988	12,574	2,415	113
1990	12,574	2,415	131
1992	12,574	2,415	200
1994	12,574	2,415	200
1995	12,574	2,415	218
1996	12,574	2,415	227
1997	12,574	2,415	227
1998	12,574	2,415	234
1999	12,574	2,415	234
2000	12,574	2,415	234

Source: *Zhongguo guotu ziyuan nianjian* (China Land and Resources Yearbook) (Beijing: Zhongguo guotu ziyuan nianjian bianjibu), various years.[25]

the total population by a quarter of a million people.[26] A 1988 Public Security Bureau (PSB) survey reveals even more dramatic numbers. The PSB estimated a "floating population" of 388,000 people, of whom 205,000 were employed, 118,000 were dependents of workers, and the remainder were in Dalian for other reasons. The PSB estimated that 61 percent were below the age of thirty, 75 percent were male, and most worked in the construction or handicrafts industries. It estimated that more than 80 percent resided outside the city core (i.e., not in Zhongshan, Xigang, Shahekou, or Ganjingzi districts).[27]

In the 2000s, popular conceptions of the differences between the "new" and "old" city underscored the importance of the population distribution. Officials in the DDA insisted that the DDA was similar to an "immigrant city," its population "young, open-minded, and part of China's transform-ation."[28] People in downtown Dalian, especially in Shahekou and Ganjingzi districts, which are now home to most of the former working-class and many middle-aged longtime residents of the city, harbored some resentment toward the DDA and the people who lived and worked there. Many people, especially the victims of layoffs, often remarked that the city is biased toward the new areas and that Dalian's new wealth only benefits people not originally from Dalian. Rather than blaming the state or the city authorities for a lack of opportunities during the reform period, the "losers" of the reform directed

[25] Data for 1989, 1991, and 1993 are unavailable.
[26] Liu Changde, ed., *Dalian chengshi guihua 100 nian: 1899–1999*, 154.   [27] Ibid.
[28] Group interview with DDA management committee members, March 2008, Dalian.

their frustrations against another population in the city. Yet, the spatial distribution of Dalian's economic transformation prevented these populations, laid-off workers and migrant workers, from actually living and working alongside one another.

Opening before the Reforms: Dalian's Growth through Foreign Partnerships

Foreign partnerships and access to global capital figured prominently in Dalian's efforts to implement state-sector reforms. Dalian's enterprise reform strategy from the outset was one of "grafting" (*jiajie shi*, 嫁接式) to attract foreign investments in facilities, technology, and management before downsizing and shedding public ownership.[29] Coordinating foreign investment in the city's public enterprises allowed the municipal party committee and government to appear to "save" these enterprises and some of the jobs of those they employed by infusing investment rather than allowing them to fail. One former Municipal Bureau of Industry and Commerce (MBIC) official explained that in the mid- and late 1980s, he and his colleagues would tour large- and medium-sized SOEs with potential foreign investors (typically from Japan or Hong Kong) to find ways in which the enterprises could "upgrade or renovate facilities or production processes to increase efficiency within the next few years." Enterprise managers were eager to exchange management stakes for scarce investment resources, and investors knew that impending management and ownership reforms would enhance both enterprise viability and their own ownership stake.[30] By 1992, the city had 456 such technology renovation projects, and 1.2 billion RMB was invested in FIEs[31] (see Figure 4.2).

Although investment was channeled into upgrading the older public enterprises, attracting new FIEs was the primary focus of the city's growth strategy. In 1985 the municipal party committee decided that the industrial layout should be divided between the old industrial base and the new enterprises, with the "new enterprises as the leaders in implementing new technology, which would eventually be introduced to invigorate the old enterprises."[32] In 1986 alone, the city boasted fifty-eight approved FDI projects, with a total value of US$319 million. Of that, twenty-six projects and US$55 million were in FIEs, and the remainder were solely foreign ventures.[33] By channeling foreign investment to starved enterprises and limiting the growth of the public sector both physically and

---

[29] The metaphor is medical, i.e., "grafting foreign investment over ailing enterprises," like a skin graft over a burn. *Gaige kaifang shiqi de Dalian* (Dalian in the Era of Reform and Opening) (Beijing: Zhonggong dangshi chubanshe, 2004), 7–8.

[30] Interview with MBIC official, February 2008.   [31] *Gaige kaifang shiqi de Dalian*, 7–8.

[32] Ibid., 7–8.

[33] *Dalian nianjian, 1987–1989* (Dalian Yearbook, 1987–1989) (Dalian: Dalian chubanshe, 1990), 52.

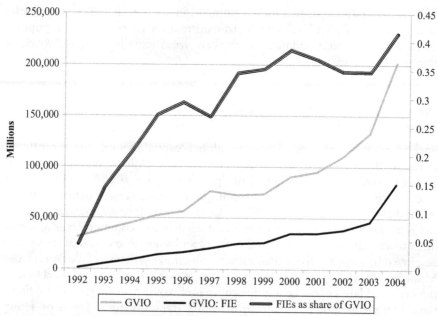

FIGURE 4.2. Dalian GVIO (GDP and Industrial Output) and FIE GVIO (Yuan)
Sources: Dalian nianjian (Dalian Yearbook), various years.

economically, city authorities essentially opted to increase foreign influences while staving off reforms to the public sector until new forms of economic production, that is, export-oriented manufacturing, had time to mature.

Major reforms did not begin in the city until at least 1992, even as neighboring cities (especially Harbin and Shenyang) were undergoing politically difficult urban public-sector reforms. Though the city established goals in its "1980 plan" – the city's decennial master plan – to begin the large-scale relocation of industrial enterprises from downtown, it was decided to hold off until funds were sufficient to offer higher compensation to the relocated employees and managers. The 1980 plan designated twenty-four industrial relocation projects, involving 62.3 hectares of space and at least 5,775 workers, for reasons ranging from "pollution" to proximity to parks. In some cases, the land was designated for alternate projects (a sports arena or a residential area). However, by 1989, only eleven of those projects had been completed, and the remainder were delayed until the mid-1990s.[34] Other reforms to the state sector proceeded slowly or not at all. By 1986, only eighteen public enterprises had been encouraged to implement a (nationally devised) wage reform that tied wages to the taxes and profits

[34] Liu Changde, ed., *Dalian chengshi guihua 100 nian: 1899–1999*, 114–15, 124.

of the enterprises, but the city had increased its investment in SOE technological upgrading to 833 million RMB (up nearly 40 percent from 1985).[35] The city's focus during the early period of reform was on opening and attracting foreign capital rather than enacting potentially unpopular reforms.

INITIATING LAND MARKETS TO GENERATE REVENUE

Dalian's approach to property rights and land management was born during the building of the development zone, the timing of which coincided with the opening of real estate nationally and the amendment of the Land Law. Logistically, converting rural farmland into a modern, well-planned, and strategic industrial and commercial base demanded a great deal of investment. The new area required transportation facilities, basic public infrastructure, highways, storage facilities, and telecommunications, not to mention residential facilities for the potential workers in the FIEs. Dalian official statistics estimate that 38 billion RMB (about US$5 billion) in fixed-asset investments (FAI) flowed into the DDA during its first ten years (1984–94).[36] The official policy at the time was to "make money through land" (*yitu shengcai*, 以土生财).[37]

The execution of such a policy required the municipal authorities to acquire rural land, convert that land into urban land for construction, and attract investors. As many cities did, Dalian established a Land Management Office in 1986 after implementation of the 1986 Land Law. Unlike in most cities, however, Dalian's office was organized to unify the planning and allocation of urban and rural land, which prior to 1986 were governed by the real estate and agriculture authorities, respectively. The new Dalian City Land Management Office (hereafter, the Land Office) established authority over construction approvals and legal investigations into property rights, and it set up a deed processing station. In 1988, the same year that land-use rights could be exchanged on markets, the Land Office established the Dalian Land Acquisition Service Station, with responsibilities for rural land conversions and contracting. More than one-half of the total staff in the Land Office was assigned to the Acquisition Station in 1988.[38] The Land Office began to establish local

---

[35] *Dalian nianjian, 1987–1989*, 115. This investment in technological upgrading was obtained directly from municipal investments, financed through municipal revenue (from corporate taxes, SOE profits, or central transfers) and/or borrowing from local financial organs, i.e., banks. See ftn. 41.

[36] *Dalian shi zhi: Chengshi jianshe zhi* (Dalian City Construction Gazetteer) (Beijing: Fangzhi chubanshe, 2004), 478. Another source states that 400 million RMB went to basic investment during the first two years. "Dalian jingji jishu kaifaqu fazhan gaikuang" (The Situation in the Development of the Dalian High Technology Development Zone), in *Gaige kaifang shiqi de Dalian*, 197.

[37] Dalian shi shizhi bangongwu, (Dalian City Gazetteer Office), ed. *Dalian shi zhi: Tudi zhi* (Dalian City Land Gazetteer) (Dalian: Dalian chubanshe, 1998), 6–7.

[38] Ibid., 302.

branches in districts and counties, beginning in December 1986 in what was
then Jin county – the location of the DDA.

To "make money through land," the Land Office requisitioned rural land
and then converted it to urban land for leasing after clearing it and readying it
for urban construction, including connecting the land to urban public infrastructure systems, such as water, gas, heat, roads, and so forth. The necessary
infrastructure financing was provided through municipal debt taken on by
various DDA construction and infrastructure companies, semipublic financing
platforms that bear great similarities to the local investment financing vehicles
(*touzi pingtai*, 投资平台) that emerged throughout China in the 1990s.[39] These
companies would borrow from banks, invest in land readiness, repay loans
with the money generated from land leasing, and reinvest further revenues in
additional land development projects.[40] Typically, the DDA authorities leased
land to industrial partners at very low costs and generated revenue from
residential and commercial projects surrounding the industrial developments.
Frequently, the DDA authorities would solicit investment in land development
projects from foreign and domestic partners, some of whom would also take
part in development efforts, whereas others would simply provide investment
capital.[41] In this way, the Dalian authorities used lease revenue from the
deployment of "land as a state asset" to generate the capital required to create
a development zone from farmland. This model of revenue generation and
state-initiated capital accumulation that began outside the city in the 1980s
would be applied inside the traditional city in the 1990s, bound tightly to the
city's efforts to restructure the public sector.

Turning Land into Capital

The removal of the industrial enterprises and the accompanying housing
compounds that dominated the downtown left prime real estate available for

---

[39] See Victor C. Shih, "Local Government Debt: Big Rock-Candy Mountain." *China Economic Quarterly*. Vol. 12, no. 2. (June 2010): 26–32. Christine Wong, "Paying for Urbanization in China: Challenges of Municipal Finance in the Twenty-First Century," in *Financing Metropolitan Governments in Developing Countries*, ed. Roy W. Bahl, Johannes F. Linn, and Deborah Wetzel (Cambridge, MA: Lincoln Institute of Land Policy, 2013), 273–308; Weiping Wu, "Fiscal Decentralization, Infrastructure Financing, and Regional Disparity," in *China's Public Finance in Transition*, ed. Joyce Yanyuan Man and Yu-Hung Hong (Cambridge, MA: Lincoln Institute of Land Policy, 2011), 41–56.

[40] "Dalian jingji jishu kaifaqu fazhan gaikuang," 197.

[41] For example, the case of the West Pacific Petro-Chemical Factory (Xi Taipingyang shiyou huagong youxian gongsi, 西太平洋石油化工有限公司), established in October 1990 jointly by Sinopec, the Dalian Urban Construction Company (the development wing of the Dalian City Construction Bureau), Daqing City Foreign Trade Conglomerate, China Chemical Engineering Corporation, Zhonghua Oil International (Hong Kong), and Daodaer (France). These parties invested a total of 1.03 billion RMB, 20 percent of which was foreign-contributed. *Dalian shi zhi: Chengshi jianshe zhi*, 478.

land leasing and commercial development. Dalian city officials managed to consolidate control over urban downtown territory by leasing land for retail, commercial, and high-end housing development. In this way, they sought to segregate the downtown as a commercial center from the DDA as the city's manufacturing base. These activities generated a tremendous amount of wealth for the city government and, presumably, some of its officials. Dalian officials, in interviews and in public materials, were explicit that revenue generation through land leasing was a principal urban planning and public management strategy from the early 1990s. While the opening of the real estate sector in some cities took the form of various economic actors stumbling haphazardly into land markets as they attempted to placate urban constituencies, Dalian officials initiated large-scale markets in real estate for the explicit purpose of growing the value of state assets. In an interview, Mayor Bo Xilai bragged that real estate prices in downtown Dalian increased 500 percent between 1994 and 1999, a process engineered by local government authorities for the financial benefit of the state.[42] Revenue from real estate activities totaled between 40 and 60 million RMB annually between 1988 and 1992, but quickly grew to 1.3 billion RMB by 1997 and to more than 2 billion RMB by 2000.[43]

The fact that Dalian by 1992 had managed to become a successful hub for foreign investment did not mean that funds for urban construction were unrestricted. According to Chief Wang Zhenggang of the Urban Planning and Land Resources Management Bureau (the reincarnation of the Land Office), only 80 million RMB was available for urban construction in 1992, despite the fact that the city's GDP exceeded 2 billion RMB. At this time, Bo Xilai advanced the idea of "managing the city as an important state asset" (*ba chengshi zuowei zhongyao de guoyou zichan*, 把城市作为重要的国有资产). This idea, which appears again and again in discussions of Dalian's 1990s transformation, generally means using a good urban environment to attract more investors. But officials and planners, as well as Bo himself, were also explicit about generating revenue by using land as "a key state-owned resource."[44] In August 1992, the Dalian City Real Estate Development Company (Dalian shi dichan kaifa zong gongsi,大连市地产开发总公司) was established under the auspices of the local Land Office with a staff of fifty – more than the staff in all the other Land Office departments combined.[45] This semipublic real estate development company would develop and sell land requisitioned by the city government, generating revenue directly for the state coffers and further generating investment capital.

---

[42] Bo Xilai, "Ruhe jingying chengshi zhefen guoyou zichan" (How to Operate a City as a State Asset), in *Chengshi jiaoxiang*, ed. Liu Changde, 9.

[43] Data compiled from *Dalian tongji nianjian* (Dalian Statistical Yearbook) (Dalian: Dalian shi tongjiju), various years

[44] "Jianfu kaituo de shiming yu zeren: Fang Dalian shi guihua he guotu ziyuanju Wang Zhenggang juzhang," 15–16. See also Bo Xilai, "Ruhe jingying chengshi zhefen guoyou zichan."

[45] Dalian shi shizhi bangongwu, ed., *Dalian shi zhi: Tudi zhi*, 65.

For example, Xinghai Square, which was completed in 1999 for the centen-
nial celebration of the city's founding, is described by the city as "the work of a
great calligrapher," representing the modernity of contemporary Dalian.[46] The
project, about five kilometers from the city's downtown center, began in
1994 as a result of a direct request from the mayor's office as part of a greater
push to create green spaces and to beautify the urban areas. More than 150,000
square meters of space, Xinghai Square is the second largest public square in
Asia, second only to Tiananmen Square in Beijing. The space includes several
statues and monuments commemorating the city's history, a seaside dock area,
vast lawns of synthetic grass that are off-limits to visitors and pedestrians, and
few benches or seats on which visitors can rest or linger. The area is frequented
by tour buses and is home to Dalian's exhibition center and attendant hotel
facilities, and it hosts the Dalian International Beer Festival each summer.

The construction of the large plaza illustrates the logic of statist land
development in Dalian. In 1993, the area was simply "empty shoals" (*huang
tan*, 黃滩), with a land value of no more than 700 RMB per 10,000 square
meters. Irrigated and landscaped by the city, less than ten years later the land
was valued at 10,000 RMB per square meter, or 15,000 times its original value.
Moreover, the value of the surrounding land was enhanced by the creation of
the park and the placement of the exhibition center. The director of the Dalian
Urban Planning and Land Resource Management Bureau estimated that the
city earned more than 6 billion RMB by leasing out land surrounding Xinghai
Square.[47] In Dalian, powers to regulate property rights, claim ownership rights,
and plan for the urban built environment were all concentrated in the municipal
government. As they were elsewhere in China, land-use rights were leased to
actors inside and outside the state, but the municipal government consolidated
exclusive landownership rights in the process of remaking the city, opening it to
global capital, and carrying out market reforms.

The strategy of generating capital from land repurposing was the same with
occupied land, requiring city authorities to articulate exclusive property rights
over downtown land. Shengli Bridge North is an area to the north and across
the tracks of the Dalian Train Station. To permit the forced relocation of
residents, the area was designated a "shantytown" (*penghuqu*, 棚户区) because
of housing conditions, and in 1993 it was earmarked for historical preservation
by the Urban Planning Bureau (UPB). The problems listed by the UPB that
precipitated its designation as a slum were its high population density (living
space per capita was 3.7 square meters prior to renovation, well below the
national standard of 5 square meters per capita), a lack of "green areas," and
a good deal of "temporary" (*linshi*, 临时), i.e., illegal, construction. The UPB,
however, faced the problem of meeting contemporary construction standards

---

[46] *Dalian shi zhi: Chengshi jianshe zhi*, 382–3.
[47] "Jianfu kaituo de shiming yu zeren: Fang Dalian shi guihua he guotu ziyuanju Wang Zhenggang
     juzhang," 15.

while also preserving the historical architecture, which it proudly solved by renovating and commodifying the surrounding housing and by converting historical buildings into tourist centers. The plan drafted by the UPB called for a restoration of the "original" layout of the areas, with additional open spaces (green areas) and the establishment of a "cultural center." The bureau arranged for the establishment of the Dalian History Museum and the Dalian Local Resources Museum on the sites of the former Natural History Museum and a steam engine waiting room from the Japanese era, respectively. Bordering buildings were converted into foreign-language schools, souvenir shops, Western restaurants, coffee shops, and other commercial ventures appropriate for tourist areas. Importantly, the surrounding factories were also relocated, reducing factory space in the neighborhood from 68,000 square meters to 33,000 square meters.[48]

The process of marketing Dalian as a brand, enhancing the urban built environment to suit Dalian's particular strategy of capital accumulation (foreign investment and commercial redevelopment), and multiplying city resources by enhancing the exchange value of urban land were part of the explicit strategy of "managing the city as an important state-owned asset." It is worthwhile to quote Bo Xilai at length:

Where do we get the capital to renovate a city?... For example, "July 7" Street, in order to renovate a street to that extent, we used a great deal of brains and muscle. Don't think about actual resources – brick and mortar, a highway, lights, and so forth – we used our own resources, compressed the expense of the project, and then turned it into a resource itself. The road made it passable, the bridge made it usable, the building required heat, and at a more advanced economic stage we turned a part of it into a stock option and received back our investment many times over. This is our fundamental thinking.[49]

BUILDING THE "HONG KONG OF THE NORTH": IDEOLOGY, LAND, AND GROWTH

After 1992, Dalian authorities continued their strategy of development zoning and remained committed to anchoring new industrial activities outside the city in the DDA. Linking access to foreign capital to firm survival was the primary strategy for restructuring public enterprises throughout the 1990s, and especially during the massive restructuring campaign to "grasp the large and release

---

[48] This principally involved relocating a plastics plant that employed most of the residents in the area, true to the logic of tying employment to relocation, as I detail earlier. Xiao Zongyi and Fu Handong, "Dalian Shengli qiao bei xiaoqu lishi jianzhu de baohu yu zai kaifa" (Protecting and Reopening Dalian City's Shengli Bridge North Community's Historical Architecture), *Chengshi guihua* (Urban Planning), no. 4 (1990): 32–5.

[49] Hu Xin, "Dalian shi shizhang Bo Xilai jiu chengshi guihua da benkan jizhe wen," 30–1. "July 7" Street is an area of creatively renovated "Japanese houses." They look quite like Western-style, stand-alone homes, and the street is a pedestrian area intended for tourists.

TABLE 4.2. *Real Estate in Dalian, 1985–2000*

	Fixed-asset investment (million RMB)	Real estate investment (million RMB)	Real estate income (million RMB)	Building area under construction (million m²)	Building area with completed construction completed(million m²)
1985	2,181			5.80	2.09
1987					
1988	2,560		4,037	7.76	3.31
1989			4,614		
1990	2,960	470	5,493	5.51	2.83
1991	5,406		5,493	6.02	3.96
1992	8,912		5,866		
1993	21,060			14.27	5.45
1994	24,620			18.00	7.41
1995	23,710	7,320		16.18	7.74
1996	23,720	6,421	133,313	14.71	6.48
1997	26,220	6,423	103,506	13.65	5.71
1998	26,350	6,286	154,584	14.31	6.79
1999	22,280	6,758	173,134	14.29	6.83
2000	26,850	10,687	216,700	16.68	8.19

Sources: Fixed-asset investment data are from *Dalian tongji nianjian* (Dalian Statistical Yearbook), various years, and China Data Online. All other data are from *Dalian nianjian* (Dalian Yearbooks), various years.

the small" of 1997 and 1998. Although these key political economic strategies persisted, the nature of urban politics in Dalian changed substantially when Bo Xilai was appointed mayor in 1992. Bo's ascent coincided with the widespread growth of real estate markets throughout the country, as described in Chapter 2. During this period, Dalian's model of state dominance of property rights would become renowned nationally.

Opening Real Estate in Downtown Dalian

Dalian's experience during the real estate boom in the early 1990s (see Table 4.2), especially compared to that of the other cities under study in this book, rivaled the experiences of the cities along the east and southeast coasts. Dalian had only 4 real estate companies in 1985; by 1993 there were 301. The city saw the construction of at least sixty residential neighborhoods (*xiaoqu*, 小区) between 1986 and 1993.[50] Because the municipal authorities had already

---

[50] "Dalian fangdichan guanli gongzuo" (The Work of the Dalian City Real Estate Bureau), in *Gaige kaifang shiqi de Dalian*.

experienced the commodification of land in the development area and had established bureaucratic authority over land, they were eager to capitalize on the large-scale initiation of real estate markets in the downtown area.

After organizing initial land offices to coordinate land sales in the DDA, municipal authorities expanded their work to survey urban landholdings and to establish municipal control over land rights. The Land Office conducted aerial cadastral surveys between 1987 and 1989, and in 1989 it established a "land investigative team" to deal with illegal uses, to resolve disputes, and to deal with petitions and letters from citizens about land. The Land Office worked under the office that authorized state requisitions of land rather than under the Ministry of Civil Affairs, giving Dalian land authorities greater control with fewer administrative barriers.[51] Massive land and property registration drives began in the early 1990s to "clarify" ownership of commercial, industrial, and residential buildings, and the "land administrative office" of the Land Office was established in 1993 with authority to deal with land allocations, conveyances, and pricing for both urban and rural land.[52] The opening of real estate was coordinated by the "the leading group for managing the opening of real estate" (*Dalian fangdichan kaifa guanli lingdao xiaozu*, 大连房地产开发管理领导小组), which set the administrative division of labor: The Urban Planning Bureau would draw up the detailed plans; the Land Office would acquire and price the land; and the Real Estate Bureau would deal with relocation and compensation issues.[53] Although, as I detail in Chapter 2, it was not until the mid-1990s that there was a national push for land exchanges to go through the municipal government, Dalian's initial experiences with land and real estate were dominated by the local state.

Whereas other cities entered the real estate boom and bubble with little fanfare or knowledge of how the new industry would work, Dalian considered the "opening of real estate" to be a primary task of the local state. Bo Xilai declared real estate opening, along with TVEs and attracting FIEs, to be the "city's future."[54] Various building sales and notices to encourage the real estate sector appeared daily in the city's flagship newspaper throughout 1992 and 1993, especially since the growth in real estate coincided with the campaign to make Dalian the "Hong Kong of the North." Notices warned residents and enterprises against "arbitrary" or "self-initiated" transfers of land and buildings, confirming that any transactions that did not go through the real estate management office would not be recognized and the occupants would not be compensated.[55] Advertisements for newly constructed "commodity

[51] Dalian shi shizhi bangongwu, ed. *Dalian shi zhi: Tudi zhi*, 61–5.
[52] Ibid., 65. Information on deed registration is from *Gaige kaifang shiqi de Dalian*, 596–8.
[53] Zhang Tianshou, "Fangdichan da remen" (The Big Start of Real Estate), *Dalian ribao* (Dalian Daily), January 1, 1993.
[54] "Yuandan xianju" (New Year's Word), *Dalian ribao*, January 1, 1993.
[55] *Dalian ribao*, January 9, 1992; June 26, 1992.

homes," encouraging families to turn their savings into investments in new homes sold by the Dalian Real Estate Development Company, appeared under exposés about Deng Xiaoping's Southern Tour.[56]

Reform through Relocation: The Banqian Campaign, 1993–2001

The most important mechanism by which city officials, chiefly from the MBIC, induced public firms to relinquish their physical property and assets and to undertake large-scale layoffs was part of a campaign to "relocate the enterprises" (*qiye banqian*, 企业搬迁, henceforth the "relocation" campaign). Having established thriving development zones with expanding foreign-owned or foreign-invested enterprises, city officials offered incentives in the form of coordinating joint-venture partners (i.e., investment capital) and corporate tax incentives to relocate from the downtown and to the city's periphery.

Efforts to limit growth downtown began in the 1980s, but the policy did not become binding until the 1990s. Citing reasons of "density" and pollution, the "1990 plan" essentially prohibited new industrial construction in the urban core. Instead, all new projects were to be based in Jinzhou; extant industrial clusters (ten had been established in the 1950s) could be upgraded, but no new land acquisitions or large-scale construction projects were to be approved.[57] The "guiding philosophy" of the 1990 plan was to "unite construction and renovation of the new and old city, taking construction of the new city as the key." The 1990 plan, or at least its public version, did not designate specific spaces and neighborhoods as "slums," but rather it made broad references to "old housing" surrounding the "polluting enterprises."[58] The plan to move public-sector enterprises out of the city also called for moving their workers and their housing compounds.

The year 1992, the same year that Dalian authorities declared the "opening" of real estate markets in the city, became a turning point, after which the "old" city area became a key target for redevelopment rather than an area to be avoided in favor of the outlying areas. The relocation campaign began in earnest when Bo Xilai assumed the city's leadership in 1993, as more general campaigns to "beautify the city" and enhance green space and public parks and squares (these goals were all aimed at the "old" city area) as well as to transform Dalian's industrial character into a "commercial and trade, finance, tourism, and informational city" were implemented.[59] The campaign was carried out jointly by the MBIC, the Urban Planning and Land Resource Management Bureaus, and the Dalian Municipal Housing Authority, which

[56] Ibid., March 31, 1992.
[57] Liu Changde, ed., *Dalian chengshi guihua 100 nian: 1899–1999*, 142.   [58] Ibid.,146.
[59] "Jianfu kaituo de shiming yu zeren: Fang Dalian shi guihua he guotu ziyuanju Wang Zhenggang juzhang," 16.

held authority over approximately 83 percent of the residential housing in the downtown core area.[60] United under Bo's leadership, between 1994 and 2001 these institutions relocated 115 enterprises from Zhongshan and Xigang districts alone, freeing more than 3 million square meters of land space.[61]

Relocation especially targeted enterprises desperate for capital infusions. The typical process involved leasing development zone or industrial cluster land at very low prices to enterprises (in an interview an MBIC official insisted that land was essentially "given away" to the enterprises), and leasing former space with the promise that a good deal of the acquired capital would be released to the relocated enterprise for facility upgrading and technological investments.[62] Critically, the city would also assist with locating foreign joint-venture partners for enterprises that agreed to move, enabling the city both to reclaim downtown land from enterprises and to execute management and ownership restructuring. For example, the Bohai Beer Factory, which occupied thirty thousand square meters in Zhongshan district, was designated for relocation in 1995. The factory was in need of technological upgrading, so the MBIC negotiated its acquisition by a Hong Kong investment firm, turning more than half of the land-lease fee to the factory when the Land Management Bureau secured the former area for a Korean commercial venture (a large mall).[63] More spectacularly, when Sanyo located production facilities in the DDA in 1996, the DDA assisted with the creation of a large conglomerate (the Bingsheng Jituan), in which Sanyo was partnered with sixteen SOEs relocated from the downtown core. The joint-venture partnership encouraged the SOEs to compete in raising the technological capabilities of the workers so that they would not suffer layoffs.[64]

Securing the acquiescence of factory managers who faced underperforming enterprises and painful downsizing was not especially challenging. The thorny parts of the relocation campaign, and the ones rarely discussed in public celebrations of the remaking of the city, were related to the movement of the housing compounds that had dominated downtown neighborhoods for at least twenty years and relocating the workers who occupied them.[65] In interviews,

---

[60] Interview with former MBIC official (serving from 1991 to1997), January 2008, Dalian. Housing data are from the 1985–6 National Housing Survey. Total housing space was 38,820,626 square meters, and housing managed by work units (under the Dalian Housing Authority) and the Land Management Bureau totaled 32,264,487 square meters. Cited in *Dalian nianjian, 1986* (Dalian Yearbook, 1986) (Dalian: Dalian chubanshe, 1986), 62.

[61] Exhibit at the Dalian Modern Museum (Dalian xiandai bowuguan, 大连现代博物馆), visited in February 2008. Note that, citywide, there were only 282 large and medium SOEs in 1993. *Dalian nianjian, 1993* (Dalian Yearbook, 1993) (Dalian: Dalian chubanshe, 1993).

[62] Interview with former MBIC official (serving from 1991 to 1997), January 2008, Dalian.

[63] Example cited in "Jianfu kaituo de shiming yu zeren: Fang Dalian shi guihua he guotu ziyuanju Wang Zhenggang juzhang," 16.

[64] Group interview with DDA management committee members, March 2008, Dalian.

[65] It is difficult to find credible estimates of the number of residents relocated in the 1990s. The December 1995 "Dalian City Residential Neighborhood Work Law" set an agenda of creating 95 small residential districts in 1995 and 175 more in 1996, relocating more than 280,000

officials and urban planners referenced opposition and objections to the demolition and relocation (*chaiqian banqian,* 拆迁搬迁) work of the 1990s. One urban planner recalled many petitions and attempts at disruption (*naoshi,* 闹事) in 1994 and 1995,but said that because the local party organizations, residential committees, and work units did not back the residents, their efforts at collective organization failed.[66] Another official clearly stated the dilemma faced by residents: They stood to lose both their homes and their jobs should they choose to resist relocation. Enterprises often laid off a substantial portion of their workforces when they relocated and underwent management and ownership restructuring. Since the work units and factory managers supported the relocation plans, residents and workers wanted to demonstrate loyalty by accepting the relocation compensation packages. As a result, in some situations, residents were actually competing with one another to accept the compensation and relocation arrangements.[67]

Political Campaigns, Ideology, and Moral Legitimacy

Dalian's strategy of establishing local government property rights operated partly via providing positive inducements (linking employment and capital to relinquishing land rights) and partly by indirectly deploying the coercive power of a strong local state. In Dalian, both positive inducements and coercive powers were evident in the use of political campaigns to transform the built environment and in the way that residents and investors thought about urban land and property. Political campaigns, which make use of mass mobilization, intensive propaganda, and heightened uncertainty, were used throughout the Maoist era as the primary way to achieve production goals and political objectives. But, as scholars such as Elizabeth Perry, Tyrene White, and Kristen Looney have pointed out, the use of campaigns has extended to the reform era, albeit with fewer revolutionary objectives.[68] In Dalian, city authorities carried out campaigns to relocate firms from downtown, beautify the city, involve citizens in urban reform efforts, and relocate residential housing. Heightened political mobilization and intense propaganda efforts facilitated the city

---

people in less than one year, which indicates some idea of the scale. "Dalian shi aiguo weisheng yundongzhi, 1988–1998."

[66] Interview with an urban designer at the Dalian Urban Planning Bureau, October 2007, Dalian. The support of local organizations, as evidenced in similar situations in Harbin and Changchun, was necessary for successful efforts at collective action to preserve occupancy.

[67] Interview with former MBIC official (serving from 1991 to 1997), January 2008, Dalian.

[68] Sebastian Heilmann and Elizabeth J. Perry, eds., *Mao's Invisible Hand: The Political Foundations of Adaptive Governance in China* (Cambridge, MA: Harvard University Asia Center, 2011); Kristen E. Looney, "The Rural Developmental State: Modernization Campaigns and Peasant Politics in China, Taiwan and South Korea" (PhD diss., Harvard University, 2012); Tyrene White, *China's Longest Campaign: Birth Planning in the People's Republic, 1949–2005* (Ithaca, NY: Cornell University Press, 2006).

government's conquest of urban land and limited opportunities for nonstate actors to stake urban property claims.

Dalian's efforts at urban beautification began in earnest with the 1988 decision to launch a "Patriotic Cleanliness Campaign" and the 1991 introduction of the campaign to build Dalian into a "modern, international, green city."[69] These campaigns involved not only efforts at afforestation (*lühua*, 绿化) and environmental protection, but also broader attempts to enhance the city's infrastructure with regard to residential area planning, the creation of parks and public squares, regulation of market areas, and so forth. Early on during the movement (in the late 1980s), the city government set the goals for Dalian's overall achievement: to be recognized as one of China's ten most beautiful cities, as a garden city, a nature tourism city, an environmental model city, and so forth.[70] Substantial propaganda campaigns accompanied these efforts. The Urban Planning and Land Resource Management Bureau chief at the time recalls Bo Xilai's own efforts to soften the term "demolition" (*chai*, 拆): "Bo Xilai himself said that the greening of Dalian will emerge from '*chai*' and '*ba*' [stripping away]. Don't look down on the word '*chai*,' because this is really tearing down people's closed hearts and old ideas."[71] The combination of entwining employment prospects with relocation acquiescence, the offer of substantial compensation packages for residents by leasing out land, and ideological campaigns to pressure compliance foreclosed any viable attempts at collectively resisting eviction and relocation.

Municipal authorities promoted state claims to land as necessary for collective development and prosperity; ironically, state control over land was deemed to be required for both retaining elements of socialism and pursuing a future of "market socialism." In announcing the opening of the real estate sector, Party Committee Secretary Zheng Hongliang described the "major breakthrough" in land management: No land had been leased in the past ninety years; thus cities and governments were to forfeit the potential revenues and assets that never entered the market. Leasing land, he argued, would allow a new stage of development, not the end of state ownership, but rather the "strengthening of state supervision."[72] Commodifying land under state control, officials emphasized, was necessary to "build the nest to attract the bird"; just as in the DDA, downtown Dalian needed to attract investment to prosper, and that process required making use of land assets.[73] The local

---

[69] "Dalian shi aiguo weisheng yundongzhi, 1988–1998," 2–3.   [70] Ibid., 72.

[71] "Jianfu kaituo de shiming yu zeren: Fang Dalian shi guihua he guotu ziyuanju Wang Zhenggang juzhang," 15–16.

[72] Zheng Hongliang, "Tudi guanli zhidu de zhongda tupo" (Major Breakthroughs in the Institutions of Land Management), *Dalian ribao*, June 10, 1992, 3.

[73] For example, an article by City Construction Committee Secretary Chen Xuezhu. See Ming Da and Tian Mu, "Liyong waizi kaifa fangdichan" (Use Foreign Capital to Develop Real Estate), *Dalian ribao*, May 21, 1992, 1.

state's exclusive access to land capitalization was the only legitimate way to manage land as a special resource: "The best way to protect land as a source of capital and a national resource is to be sure the owner is always the state; in this way the Land Management Bureau (LMB) can entrust its own real estate companies and local investment companies to develop the land in the social interest."[74]

By contrast, claims that emphasized individual or even collective entitlements to the state were regarded as backward and conservative elements of Dalian's past. Officials, and especially Bo Xilai, sought to compare Dalian not to other cities in the Northeast, but rather to Shenzhen and Shanghai, where "old mind-sets" did not hinder creativity and development.[75] At the same time, newspapers ran editorials by managers located in the DDA, all from outside Dalian, who argued that Dalian workers could improve their efficiency and attitudes: "Shenzhen people would certainly not expect the kind of social welfare handouts and breaks that Northeasterners are accustomed to."[76] The threat, frequently explicit, was that if the city did not do more to make the investment environment attractive, investments would flow to the Southeast and the gap between those cities and Dalian would grow.[77] The dislocation and relocation experienced by firms and individuals, particularly those associated with efforts to "remove industry" and "build services" in the downtown center, were categorized as "growing pains" – necessary sacrifices for the city's growth:

Some grass-roots work units may complain when their land plans are changed or canceled, and that will influence other residents. Many who move will not want to leave the city center, but these growing pains cannot be avoided. ... Building a normal [nonluxury] housing building in the middle of the narrow and crowded city center is a great waste and will limit the area's growth potential in finance, commerce, and trade, which will eventually influence the level of social welfare enjoyed by every resident of Dalian.[78]

Announcements about successful reclamations of factory land and the resettlement of firms and residents abounded, frequently declaring that various

---

[74] Dalian Foreign Investment Land Use Office, "Qiye shixing gufenzhi tudi zichan ruhe jiejue?" (How Should the Land Assets Be Resolved When Enteprises Are Undergoing Ownership Restructuring?), *Dalian ribao*, April, 21, 1993.

[75] "Zai kaifang zhong zhao zhun Dalian de weizhi" (Searching for Dalian's Place Under Reform), *Dalian ribao*, April 5, 1993.

[76] "Kaizhan 'Dalian ren yu da kaifang' de taolun huodong" (Kickstarting the "Dalian People and the Grand Opening" Discussion Event), *Dalian ribao*, June 26, 1993.

[77] Lu Jun, "Ba liyong waizi gongzuo tigao dao yige xin shuiping" (Improve FDI Work to a New Certain Level), *Dalian ribao*, March 8, 1992, 1.

[78] The phrase "growing pains" (*zhentong*, 阵痛) appears frequently in newspapers and official speeches. This quote is from Zhang Tianshou, "Fangdichan Dalian remen," *Dalian ribao*, January 1, 1993. See also "Dichan jiang gei Dalian lai shenme? (What Will Real Estate Bring Dalian?), *Dalian ribao*, July 3, 1993.

projects were executed without a single "nail house," a term referring to holdouts in property negotiations. Whether this claim is true is beside the point; successful holdouts inspired imitators, and Dalian authorities never portrayed local land politics as state goals versus social actors, but always as the benevolent local state acting on behalf of society.

LAND AND THE STATE IN DALIAN AND BEYOND

In Dalian, land was commodified and fiscalized at the same time: Land markets were initiated by the local state for the purpose of generating state revenue, and from the outset capital from real estate and land exchanges accrued primarily to the local state, which secured its monopoly over urban property rights by linking the fates of firms and workers, or residents, to compliance with relocation and casting state dominance over land allocations as the only legitimate way to ensure social interests and collective prosperity.

After the fiscal, financial, and land reforms of the mid-1990s detailed in the last chapter, most cities in China aspired to establish the sort of statist land regime that Dalian had created early on. In the Northeast, and indeed nationally, many cities looked to Dalian as a model when they sought to expand into their rural peripheries and to use land "as a state asset." Dalian had become a successful growth hub and had won national acclaim as an urban environment. Throughout the 1990s and into the 2000s, a popular phrase advised that "the South should look to Shenzhen, and the North should look to Dalian" (*nan kan Shenzhen, bei kan Dalian*, 南看深圳,北看大连). As this chapter has demonstrated, the use of land as a state asset constituted a main part of Dalian's pursuit of wealth as well as the city officials' pursuit of national and international recognition. Dalian's land management work did indeed gain national recognition and approval as the LMB received a number of "model" designations throughout the late 1980s and early 1990s.[79]

As an early mover in globalization and urban expansion through the creation of a development zone, the Dalian Municipal Government began its territorial conquest of urban and periurban land earlier than most cities, and certainly earlier than its regional counterparts. Much of the land that Dalian acquired in the late 1980s and early 1990s was not immediately developed; rather it was reserved in "land banks" for the city to tap into for fiscal revenue and economic development in later periods. Indeed, in the 2000s, the ratio of land financing to local government budgetary revenue averaged about 75 percent (see Table 4.3); in 2004 and 2006, revenue generated from land development (including land-lease fees and taxes

---

[79] Xiu Chengguo, "Chuangye jiannan baizhan duo: Dalian tudi guanli jishi" (Entrepreneurship Is the More Difficult Battle: Notes on Dalian Land Management), *Zhongguo tudi* (Chinese Land), no. 23 (2008): 60–1.

TABLE 4.3. *Dalian Land Finance, 2000–2009*

	Land-lease fees (RMB billion)	Land finance (RMB billion)	Local revenue (RMB billion)	Land-lease revenue: local revenue	Land finance: local revenue
2000	.86	1.68	7.76	11.18	21.63
2001	2.40	3.22	9.52	25.26	33.87
2002	5.27	6.29	9.86	53.37	63.66
2003	7.91	9.14	11.05	71.52	82.67
2004	12.56	14.15	11.72	107.17	120.79
2005	7.08	9.43	15.14	46.78	62.27
2006	17.88	20.96	19.61	91.15	106.84
2007	17.73	22.31	26.79	66.19	83.24
2008	21.35	27.19	33.91	62.98	80.18
2009	26.55	35.75	40.02	66.33	89.31

Sources: Dalian tongji nianjian (Dalian Statistical Yearbook), various years; *Zhongguo guotu ziyuan nianjian* (China Land and Resources Yearbook), various years; Wang Yu, "Dalian shi tudi caizheng de jingji shehui yingxiang jiqi lixing lujing fenxi" (Multidimensional Analysis of the Economic and Social Influence and the Rational Path of Dalian Land Finance), *Dongbei caijing daxue* (Northeast Finance University) (November 2012), 58.

generated from land sales and real estate development) was in fact greater than local government budgetary revenue.[80] In 2004, the MLR issued a moratorium on the declaration of new development zones, which dramatically restricted most local governments, preventing them from converting farmland to land for construction. Dalian, however, continued to lease land from 2004 to 2009 by tapping into its vast reserves.[81] In the Conclusion to the volume, I will follow up on Dalian's land strategies into the 2000s and after the global financial crisis of 2008.

Dalian's statist land regime emerged as the city became open to global markets and embarked on a transition from a command economy to "socialism with Chinese characteristics." Throughout the 1990s, Dalian and cities like it along the eastern coast became increasingly reliant on land and real estate development for local economic growth and local fiscal revenue, a model that would apply to almost all Chinese cities in the 2000s. From that vantage point – near-universal urban reliance on land development – it is easy to assume that

---

[80] Taxes typically part of "land finance" include the land value-added tax, the rural land-use tax, the urban land-use tax, the deed tax, the real estate tax, and corporate and enterprise taxes from construction and real-estate firms.

[81] See Wang Yu, "Dalian shi tudi caizheng de jingji shehui yingxiang jiqi lixing lujing fenxi," 27–8. To reach this conclusion, Wang analyzes the total amount of land leased, the land supply, and the amount of newly converted land.

state domination of property rights has been a feature of urban land politics for decades. But Dalian's statist model was but one way of organizing urban property rights over land. The next two chapters will describe alternate arrangements in the cities of Harbin and Changchun, where policies more closely resembling private-property rights over land emerged in the wake of state socialism.

5

Property Rights and Distributive Politics

Urban Conflict and Change in Harbin, 1978 to the Present

> The state-owned enterprises are faced with many burdens of reform. We must allow them to succeed economically and relieve them of their social welfare burdens. But most importantly, Harbin cannot betray her workers.
>
> Zhou Wenhua, vice party secretary of Harbin, 1989[1]

The urban landscape in Harbin, a city of about ten million in China's northernmost Heilongjiang province, confronts the visitor with a visual pastiche of the last century of Chinese political history. Harbiners often refer to the three core urban districts of the city, Daoli, Nangang, and Daowai, as "Heaven" (*tiandi*, 天地), "Purgatory" (*lianyu*, 炼狱), and "Hell" or the "Inferno" (*diyu*, 地狱), respectively. Daoli district is home to much of the city's characteristic Russian architecture, the commercial and retail center of the city, and numerous new development projects that capitalize on prime real estate prices through high overhead commercial centers or high-rise residential buildings. Many of the city's universities and research institutes, as well as its embryonic Central Business District, are located in Nangang district, where main arteries house department stores and modern residential neighborhoods (*xiaoqu*, 小区) next door to informal street markets, decayed prereform and even prerevolutionary housing units, and buildings associated with now-closed factories, with the character for "demolition" (chai, 拆) displayed prominently on every surface. Many of these areas slated for demolition remain untouched by bulldozers and are occupied by former residents, even without heat in China's harshest winters.

[1] "Speech to the Heilongjiang Academy of Social Sciences," April 1989, in Heilongjiangsheng kexue xuehui lianhehui (Joint Science Society of Heilongjiang Province), *Heilongjiangsheng: Sheng kexue xuehui lianhehui diwuci daibiaohui* (Heilongjiang Province: Fifth Provincial Joint Science Society Representative Meeting) (097), June 1989, HMA C262.1.

This variegated urban landscape is a product of the property-rights regime that evolved in Harbin over the course of the economic reforms. Like local authorities everywhere, Harbin urban authorities face constant incentives to transform the urban landscape in ways that suit the pursuit of economic growth, the display of political power to higher government organs, and control over the exchange value of urban land. Yet, unlike in Dalian, city officials in Harbin have encountered significant resistance to enforcing their plans for urban renovation and relocation. A great deal of this resistance has arisen from occupants of neighborhoods who perceive themselves as de facto – if not de jure – claimants to the property rights over urban land that the city has sought to appropriate or reallocate. More often than not, the Harbin bureaucracies charged with carrying out transformation of the urban landscape recognize these claims, even when multiple claims to urban land thwart the city's own efforts at spatial restructuring. Examining these battles today, without understanding their generation, would leave observers wondering how some groups of occupants have acquired such a degree of power whereas others are left without it.

THE ARGUMENT IN BRIEF

Because Harbin had nearly no access to foreign capital early during the reform period, reforms to the public sector were introduced in a climate of resource scarcity. Layoffs and factory closures, particularly in the late 1980s through the mid-1990s, created potentially destabilizing sets of "losers" to the market reforms, and the use of urban land and control of property constituted a key resource for redistribution to these groups. Laid-off workers, whose future access to pensions and reemployment prospects were precarious at best, were granted de facto and sometimes de jure control over their homes in factory compounds, where they continue to reside although the factories have been defunct for decades. Similarly, the informal appropriation of urban property for entrepreneurial activities was tacitly permitted and later legitimated by both the Urban Planning Bureau and the Municipal Bureau of Industry and Commerce (MBIC), allowing the organic growth of a tertiary sector and a petite bourgeoisie.

In contrast to the empowered local state as landlord in Dalian and the bureaucratic coherence in Changchun (documented in the following chapter), Harbin's local state was politically fragmented both vertically (among municipal-, district-, neighborhood-, and enterprise-level officials) and horizontally (among various municipal agencies).[2] In Harbin, while some state agencies (chiefly the Bureau of Land Planning Management and the Real Estate Bureau,

---

[2] Yue Zhang, in explaining why authorities in Beijing declare some buildings and streets as sites for historical preservation while razing others, invokes the concept of political fragmentation. In her formulation, Beijing is "functionally fragmented," with authorities charged with historical preservation pitted against those responsible for housing development and economic growth. See Yue Zhang, "The Fragmented City: Politics of Urban Preservation in Beijing, Paris, and Chicago"

and sometimes the Urban Planning Bureau [UPB]) worked toward consolidating municipal authority over urban land, other state agencies (enterprises, the Municipal Bureau of Industry and Commerce, the Ministry of Construction, and the Urban Planning Bureau) used urban land control as a form of redistribution and decentralized control over land use and planning.[3] Harbin's spatial policies emphasized decentralization and local autonomy, thus creating a pattern of fragmented authority over urban territory and giving rise to property claims that were imbued with moral entitlements. These groups of claimants have proven difficult to dislodge long after the conditions that produced their leverage vis-à-vis state agents have disappeared. In other words, the moral credibility of their claims endures despite the evaporation of their power resources.

Authorities in Harbin pursued reforms without a coherent strategy or grand design, instead experimenting with different approaches, permitting self-directed action from below, and adapting policy to respond to local group needs and changes in circumstance. On the one hand, such an approach left room for the emergence of market activities, as in the case of local entrepreneurship, and permitted the local state to pivot when policies met with resistance or failure. On the other hand, such a decentralized approach – if indeed we may characterize the actions of Harbin authorities as an "approach" at all – left the local state open to the particularistic lobbying of various groups that sought political and economic accommodations as the market reforms proceeded. Harbin's fragmented property-rights regime is a product of seemingly infinite bargains among various agents of the state and social groups. These bargains were driven not only by the actors' interests in property and land, but also as part of a larger process of economic reform that upended nearly every formal and informal institution that structured local society. The positions adopted by the state and social actors with regard to control of urban land and property were not simply a function of their own expected distributional gains, but also of the broader pursuit of political stability, compliance, social recognition, and economic prosperity during a period of rapid political economic change and deep uncertainty.

THE MORAL ECONOMY OF THE ERSTWHILE WORKING CLASS

Political accommodations, especially in the form of distributed resources or claims, prove difficult to retract. In Harbin, claims to property rights over land and the urban built environment acquired moral as well as political

---

(PhD diss., Princeton University, 2008); idem, "Steering towards Growth: Symbolic Urban Preservation in Beijing, 1990–2005," *Town Planning Review* 79, no. 2–3 (2008): 187–208.

[3] The UPB experienced conflicts between goals for citywide transformation and plans drawn up and implemented for specific neighborhoods or districts, a product of the intentional decentralization of urban planning and land use.

TABLE 5.1. *Harbin Firms and Workforce, 1982*

	No. of firms	No. of workers	Share of labor force
Harbin total	3,102	1,087,786	100.00%
By ownership			
SOEs		655,547	60.26%
Collectives		432,239	39.70%
By ownership level			
Central SOEs	150	84,786	12.9%
Provincial SOEs	558	175,209	26.7%
City SOEs	2,952	570,761	52.5%
By type			
Industrial units	314	317,981	
Commercial units	385	65,616	

Source: Laodong gongzi tongji nianbao, 1982 (Labor and Wages Statistical Annual Report, 1982) (Ha'erbin: Heilongjiangsheng tongjiju, 1983), 2–3, 38–9, 50–1.

content; laid-off workers, the erstwhile revolutionary and protected class, articulated emotional and morally grounded reasons for their rights to occupy and own urban land. The substantive content of the debate about the built environment was therefore quite different in Harbin than it was in Dalian, where an ideological framing of competition and globalization painted "socialist" claims to urban property as backward or selfish. In battles for land control under vague institutional rules, the persuasive power of claims to land matters tremendously.

The majority of scholarly work on the Northeast region – and Harbin in particular – focuses on the plight of the erstwhile working class.[4] Within the SOE-heavy Northeast, Harbin's economy has been dominated by public enterprises and its city by residents employed in these enterprises. In 1982, the city owned 253 industrial enterprises, in addition to those owned by the provincial and national levels.[5] Some 60 percent of its industrial workforce was employed by SOEs, and another 40 percent by collective enterprises (see Table 5.1).[6]

---

[4] Mun Young Cho, *The Specter of "the People": Urban Poverty in Northeast China* (Ithaca, NY: Cornell University Press, 2013); William Hurst and Kevin J. O'Brien, "China's Contentious Pensioners," *China Quarterly* no. 170 (2002): 345–60; William Hurst, *The Chinese Worker after Socialism* (Cambridge: Cambridge University Press, 2009); Ching Kwan Lee, *Against the Law: Labor Protests in China's Rustbelt and Sunbelt* (Berkeley: University of California Press, 2007); Dorothy J. Solinger, "Labour Market Reform and the Plight of the Laid-Off Proletariat," *China Quarterly* no. 170 (2003): 304–26.

[5] "Heilongjiangsheng: Chengzhen jumin jiating yici xing ziliao 1984" (Heilongjiang Province: Results from the Inaugural Urban Household Survey of 1984), HMA C832.35/03.

[6] *Ha'erbin nianjin, 1987* (Harbin Yearbook, 1987) (Ha'erbin: Heilongjiang renmin chubanshe, 1987), 191.

As I discuss in Chapter 3, this once-privileged group of workers experienced a devastating decline all over the Northeast as public-sector firms underwent ownership restructuring, privatization, and bankruptcy beginning in the 1980s and continuing through the 2000s. In Harbin and in other cities with limited access to global capital, control over property rights and urban space became contested resources in struggles between workers and firms, firms and the state, and workers and the local state. During the early period of reforms, especially as the new rules of land-use commodification were uncertain, control over property – in the form of urban residential housing associated with socialist work units as well as informal appropriation of urban space for alternate uses – was imagined as a relatively inexpensive resource to distribute to workers and firms in the context of uncertain economic change. Housing, in particular, was often distributed (that is, sold at very low prices) to workers because the firms could not afford severance packages. As enterprises underwent ownership restructuring and even bankruptcy, the housing compounds surrounding the enterprises survived, becoming ecosystems of postsocialist organization and survival for the erstwhile working class. Many of these neighborhoods became territories of poverty and destitution, whereas others became relatively thriving areas of commerce and private economic activity.[7]

Whether economically powerful or not, these distributed claims to urban property acquired a moral legitimacy because of their association with the demise of the Maoist working class. In the 1980s, local governments and enterprises distributed land and property as a form of political accommodation, a policy that imbued property claims with a moral economic entitlement that proved difficult to revoke. The spatial organization of these communities also facilitated collective action in response to plans to reorganize property rights – collective action to which local officials more frequently capitulated than sought to overcome.[8] Efforts at reclaiming property rights for the state – frequently manifested as "neighborhood redevelopment" or slum clearing – were seen as illegitimate interventions to benefit a corrupt private sector at the expense of the downtrodden and rightful occupants. Land and property rights were at the center of the moral economy of industrial decline.

Ching Kwan Lee, in her study of labor protest politics in China's sun belt and rust belt, characterizes labor activism in the Northeast as "protests of desperation." She writes: "In the reform era, the transition from social contract to legal contact has been stalled in the rustbelt, and therefore workers still leverage mass action as a means of political bargaining. Betrayed by the state

---

[7] I detail the trajectory of a relatively thriving neighborhood in Daowai district later. On the less fortunate, see Cho, *The Specter of "the People."*

[8] On this mechanism, see Dingxin Zhao, *The Power of Tiananmen: State–Society Relations and the 1989 Beijing Student Movement* (Chicago: University of Chicago Press, 2001); Yongshun Cai, *Collective Resistance in China: Why Popular Protests Succeed or Fail* (Stanford, CA: Stanford University Press, 2010); Cho, *Specter of "the People."*

and excluded from the labor market, their protests are fueled by moral outrage and desperation."[9] Protection of formal and informal property rights, perceived as political accommodations earned by the former working class during the process of its demise, is imagined as a part of the local state's moral responsibility to the "masses."

PROPERTY POLITICS AND ECONOMIC REFORMS IN THE 1980s

Harbin was the center of the regional economy during the Maoist period as well as during the prerevolutionary period. Any Harbiner will boast of the city's eighteen consulates and embassies in the 1920s, when Harbin was sometimes called the "Paris of the East" (not to be confused with China's other Paris of the East – Shanghai) and home to a twenty-thousand-strong community of Jewish Russian émigrés. With a robust public infrastructure and a strong industrial base, in addition to the city's storied international past, Harbin's post-Mao stagnation is better explained by national policies adopted during the reforms than by previously existing structural conditions. Whereas Dalian was allocated preferential policies for opening to foreign investment in 1984, Harbin, despite being the backbone of the regional planned economy, is said to have "dropped off the central government's radar screen" after 1979.[10]

In 1983, the Harbin Municipal Government signaled its intention to become "the cultural, tourist, and advanced scientific production center of the North."[11] In 1984 the Harbin Municipal People's Government formed a special committee to "investigate Harbin municipal economic development," which adopted as its purpose "to investigate Harbin city's competitive advantage and to develop a strategy for economic growth and modernization."[12] Though the committee recommended in 1984 that the leaders of the Harbin Municipal People's Government seek permission for Harbin to become an "experimental city" in science research and development,[13] Harbin did not have much, if any, access to foreign capital or a base of wealth outside the state sector until much later during the reform period. The city did, however, undertake efforts to reform the public economy and state-owned enterprises throughout the 1980s, privatizing small and medium state- and collectively owned enterprises, diversifying economic

---

[9] Lee, *Against the Law*, 12.

[10] Jonathan Woetzel et al., "Harbin: Moving On from Central Planning," in *Preparing for China's Urban Billion* (McKinsey Global Institute, 2009), at www.mckinsey.com/mgi/publications/china_urban_billion/, accessed February 9, 2015.

[11] Ha'erbinshi jingji fazhan diaocha weiyuanhui (Harbin Economic Development Investigation Committee), *Ha'erbin shi zhi: Chengshi guihua, tudi, shizheng gongyong jianshe* (Harbin City Gazetteer: Urban Planning, Land, and Municipal Utilities) (Ha'erbin: Heilongjiang renmin chubanshe, 1998), 30.

[12] Ibid., 31–3.   [13] Ibid., 34–7.

activities, decentralizing power and decision making to suburban levels, and encouraging the growth of a nascent private and entrepreneurial sector. The land and property-rights strategies that accompanied these reforms created powerful constituencies of legitimate claimants to urban land, namely, public enterprises, workers, and entrepreneurs. The next sections take up each group in turn.

Conglomeration and Decentralization: Empowering Firms as Landlords

In April 1989, when 92 percent of Dalian's US$66.3 million in FDI was flowing to its newly established development zone thirty-five kilometers outside the city center, Harbin Party Secretary Zhou Wenhua said that "reinvigorating large and medium enterprises is the guarantee of economic development."[14] By the end of the 1980s, Harbin had taken few steps toward targeting foreign capital to inject much-needed capital into the city's socialist industrial base. Yet, enterprise management reforms began in Harbin much earlier than in other regional cities. As early as September 1979, forty-two enterprises had begun experimenting with self-management (including the manager responsibility system), a program that had expanded to 129 work units by the end of 1980.[15] The devolution of control over enterprise management and enterprise performance would empower public enterprises and their managers as the rightful claimants to firm assets, including land.

A push for firm consolidation began as early as 1980, with rounds of conglomeration supported by high-profile municipal and provincial officials.[16] Industrial plants were encouraged to develop links with plants producing similar products as well as to diversify by enhancing and enlarging the commercial functions of neighborhood enterprises within their compounds. Gong Benyan, who became mayor of Harbin in 1985, stated clearly in a speech at the municipal congress of the party committee in December 1986 that the city's first economic goal would be "to rehabilitate traditional industry," noting that "traditional industry is the foundation of the city's economy" and the "staying power" of the city. He laid out plans to renovate facilities and upgrade technology in seventy-three large and medium SOEs in Harbin – SOEs that

---

[14] Heilongjiangsheng kexue xuehui lianhehui, *Heilongjiangsheng: Sheng kexue xuehui lianhehui diwuci daibiaohui*. Statistics on Dalian are from *Dalian shi zhi: Waijing waimao zhi* (Dalian City Foreign Trade and Opening Gazetteer) (Beijing: Fangzhi chubanshe, 2004).
[15] Zhao Peixing, ed., *Zhonggong Heilongjiang jian shi* (Brief History of the Heilongjiang CCP) (Beijing: Zhongyang wenxian chubanshe, 2003), 308–9.
[16] There were reports that the Harbin Joint-Management Industrial Bearings Company, a conglomeration of industrial bearings producers in several parts of the city and other nearby cities, was established during a ceremony attended by the provincial party secretary, Chen Lei. Heilongjiang Province Service (Harbin), May 31, 1980, in Foreign Broadcast Information Service, FBIS-CHI-80-107, June 2, 1980. The key operations of the new company were to be headquartered in an enlarged complex in Xiangfang district of Harbin.

accounted for 63 percent of the city's GDP and industrial output (GVIO).[17] This policy involved a clear land strategy: "Taking large enterprise colonies or clusters as key points," the city would invest in facilities for transportation, infrastructure, and worker welfare in large industrial colonies.[18]

Harbin's 1985 master plan, its first during the reform period, provides a strong contrast to Dalian's experience during the same period. Harbin's plan aimed to limit industrial "sprawl" by concentrating industrial infrastructure investments in extant compounds, mostly located in industrial clusters created in the 1950s for heavy industry enterprises and well within the city's six core urban districts. Harbin's four major industrial areas – Pingfang, Sankeshu, Haxi, and Dongli – and its three central districts – Daowai, Daoli, and Nangang – were slated to receive investments to "rehabilitate" facilities and housing.[19] Harbin's city plans expressly avoided the acquisition of new urban land and confined new industrial construction to adding on to existing compounds. In the 1980s, the city officially acquired only four plots of new land for urban construction, all of which surrounded major industrial compounds within Daoli and Nangang districts (see Table 5.2).[20]

The practical effect of this strategy was to distribute control over urban land to longtime occupants and managers. As municipal and provincial officials channeled increasing funds to the upgrading and expansion of firm-controlled real estate, public enterprises saw their de facto control over urban land become entrenched, even absent de jure permission to convert or lease land. As early as 1986, the city's highest officials were wrestling with firm managers over infrastructural investments and large-scale planning, to say nothing of attempts to reclaim the land that would occur later. A 1986 project to build a new transport tunnel through Nangang and Xiangfang districts interfered with the land operated by a local factory, whose manager asked for more than 8 million RMB in compensation. Its compliance required the intervention of the mayor, who went to the factory manager with the money and personally counted out each bill to reach a "mutual understanding."[21]

---

[17] *Ha'erbin nianjian, 1987* (Harbin Yearbook, 1987) (Ha'erbin: Heilongjiang renmin chubanshe, 1987), 14.
[18] Ibid., 15.
[19] Harbin City Management Department, "Harbin City 1985 Master Plan," 1984 (Archives of the Urban Planning Society of Harbin Municipality), 6–7. Each of the industrial clusters in Pingfang, Sankeshu, Haxi, and Dongli was one of the national 156 "key point" projects for industrial construction in the First Five-Year Plan. See Ha'erbinshi jingji fazhan diaocha weiyuanhui, *Ha'erbin shi zhi: Chengshi guihua, tudi, shizheng gongyong jianshe.*
[20] "Harbin City 1985 Master Plan," 8; Yu Binyang, ed., *21 shiji Ha'erbin chengshi guihua duice yanjiu* (Research on Harbin City Planning Measures for the Twenty-First Century) (Ha'erbin: Ha'erbin chubanshe, 2002), 11.
[21] Gu Wanming, "Yizhi chengshi bing: Ha'erbin chengshi gaizao lueji" (Treating Urban Illness: Harbin City's Renovation Strategy), *Liaowang xinwen zhoukan* (Outlook News Weekly) no. 44 (1987): 21–2.

TABLE 5.2. *Harbin Land Area, 1985–2000*

	Total land area	Urban area	Urban built-up area
1985	6,929	1,637	156
1986	6,929	1,637	156
1987	6,929	1,637	156
1988	6,929	1,637	156
1990	6,929	1,637	156
1991	18,376	1,637	156
1992	18,466	1,637	156
1994	18,466	1,637	156
1995	53,068	1,658	220
1996	53,068	1,658	220
1997	53,068	1,658	220
1998	53,068	1,658	220
1999	53,068	1,660	165
2000	53,068	1,660	168

Source: Zhongguo guotu ziyuan nianjian (China Land and Resources Yearbook) (Beijing: Zhongguo guotu ziyuan nianjian bianjibu), various years.

Housing, Renovation, and Redistribution: Workers as Claimants

The logic of distributing property rights as part of larger political bargains accompanying the economic reforms is on clearest display in Harbin's housing policies. According to the results of the first national urban housing survey, carried out in December 1985, about 93 percent of Harbin residents lived in housing owned by an SOE (73.63 percent) or a collective or directly managed by the public housing authority.[22] In the 1980s, Harbin gained national attention for rehabilitating dilapidated housing compounds that were part of major industrial clusters but not relocating the residents. As officials and work units in Harbin began to draw up plans for distributing the funds and allocating housing, workers at large enterprises voiced concerns through the Trade Union Council about unfair housing assignments, accusing managers and officials of reserving the best and biggest apartments for themselves and their cliques. The Trade Union Council negotiated with the municipal party committee to issue a circular reserving the right to distribute housing for enterprise-based worker congresses (*gonghui*, 工会), not enterprise managers or officials.[23]

[22] "Heilongjiangsheng: Chengzhen jumin jiating yici xing ziliao 1984" (Heilongjiang Province: Results from the Inaugural Urban Household Survey of 1984), HMA C832.35/03.

[23] "Ha'erbin dangshi ziliao" (Harbin Party History Materials), part 3, HMA, D235.351/01-3. It is difficult to know how independent in practice the workers' congresses were from managers and party officials, but the fact of the directive demonstrates the logic of decentralizing decision making as a political strategy.

In Harbin, new funding for housing was dispersed directly to enterprises that, in conjunction with the Municipal Construction Bureau, used the money to renovate old work-unit housing and to build new worker housing within compounds. The city's mayor pledged in 1986 to "attack the slums" and renovate 21 million square meters of the city's residential space, of which 4 million square meters had been left unconverted from the pre-1949 period and 1.25 million square meters qualified as "slums" (棚户).[24] The slogan for housing renovation was "Unite the Renovation of the Old City and the Building of New Areas; Take the Renovation of the Old City as the Key and the Renovation of the Slums as the Most Important." In 1986 alone, the city renovated 7,346 households, moving only 2,000 of these households into new homes. The rest were offered upgraded facilities where they already lived.[25]

The flagship projects were the renovation of Harbin's two most famous slums, the "36 corner" and "18 corner" slums, both of which were turned into work-unit housing compounds attached in the 1950s to either the Ministry of Railways or machinery plants under the Harbin Municipal Bureau of Industry and Commerce. These plants were some of Harbin's first to undergo privatization and layoffs in the 1990s, culminating in massive protests in 1997.[26] There is a political logic evident in investing in housing renovation in compounds that were soon to face layoffs: to assuage the formal-sector workers who constituted a group of potentially contentious "losers" of the reforms and to placate the politically powerful managers of these enterprises. One Harbin urban planner in charge of such a project in Nangang district in the late 1980s viewed renovating housing as a form of "insurance" for the soon-to-be laid-off workers, since they would assume ownership of an apartment that they could then sell at a higher price and they would be more willing to take entrepreneurial risks because their housing was secure.[27] New residential compounds that were constructed were based on the idea of "togetherness," with layouts that featured services and housing integrated with open space and leisure space: "The key element is integrating commerce and residential life, to make streets centers for services, lifestyle, and commerce."[28] Renovated housing compounds became even stronger centers for the collective identification of neighbors who perceived themselves as the rightful occupants of these spaces, facilitating collective opposition when the city's plans for these spaces changed in the future.

For example, Yamachang was once the country's largest cotton textile factory, built in the 1950s with Soviet assistance in an industrial cluster in Xiangfang district, southeast of the Harbin city center.[29] In March 1987, a dust

---

[24] *Ha'erbin nianjian, 1987*, 14.   [25] Ibid., 284.
[26] Interview with vice director of the Harbin Society of Urban Planners, October 2007.
[27] Interview with retired senior urban planners, November 2007.
[28] *Ha'erbin nianjian, 1987*, 284.
[29] The cluster was one of 13, out of 156 national-level "key industrial projects," located in Harbin during the First Five-Year Plan. See Ha'erbinshi jingji fazhan diaocha weiyuanhui, *Ha'erbin shi zhi: Chengshi guihua, tudi, shizheng gongyong jianshe*, 12.

FIGURE 5.1. Yamachang Factory, 2008
Source: Photo by author.

explosion during the night shift embroiled most of the main factory compound in a massive fire with workers trapped inside, killing 56 people, injuring 177, and closing down the factory. An official investigation and report on the origins of the fire in highly flammable dust has not entirely dissolved rumors, alive for decades, that the plant was suffering tremendous economic losses and the fire was a convenient way to close the compound.[30] By 1989, the plant all but stopped production, and it was becoming clear that workers would be formally laid off and that the factory lacked the resources necessary for pension payouts. Under these conditions, the Urban Planning Bureau, with financing from the MBIC, undertook renovation of worker housing in the Yamachang compound (see Figures 5.1, 5.2, and 5.3). This renovation work repaired some damage from the explosion but primarily upgraded housing compounds originally built

---

[30] See "Ha'erbin Yamachang Yama fenchen baozha shigu yu jingguo yu chuli" (The Aftermath and Treatment of the Harbin Yamachang Dust Explosion Accident). The investigation, conducted by provincial authorities and the National Safety Committee, concluded that the factory manager and vice manager were to be fired, and various demotions and demerits were to be accorded to the Harbin Municipal Textile Industry Bureau and even the vice mayor of the city, who was in charge of industrial safety.

FIGURE 5.2. Yamachang Housing, 2008
Source: Photo by author.

in the 1950s, some with shared kitchens and dining areas in the style of Great Leap–era communalization.

After the work was completed in 1991, residents were encouraged to buy their homes during the rounds of housing commodification, among which the Yamachang neighborhood was one of the first in Harbin. Residents bought their homes at extremely low prices – one planner recalls an average of about 100 RMB per square meter.[31] The layout of the compound was in the predictable work-unit style of the high socialist period, with apartment blocks facing away from the street and the compound insular in orientation. Residents of the 1970s and 1980s continued to live and work in the neighborhood into the late 2000s. Various streets in the compound became popular small market clusters, selling everything from food items to industrial products and textiles. When the city finally drafted plans to demolish the still-standing factory and to designate the site for an exhibition center to bear the Yamachang name, the Urban Planning Bureau and residents of the neighborhood lobbied to have the surrounding streets declared "cultural protection areas" because of the Soviet and

---

[31] Interview with retired senior Harbin Urban Planning Bureau planner, May 2008.

FIGURE 5.3. Yamachang Markets, 2008
Source: Photo by author.

early Chinese socialist style of construction, with numerous green areas and a layout reminiscent of the "dreams of manufacturing among generations" in Harbin and New China.[32]

The general approach to land and property management was one of decentralization, permitting local neighborhoods and enterprises to draw up and implement their own detailed plans (*xiangxi guihua*, 详细规;划), albeit with the approval of the municipal-level planning department. Typically, this meant that local units, either districts (*shiqu*, 市区), neighborhoods (*jiedao*, 街道), or the enterprises themselves, would contract with planners from the UPB to draw up the plans. At the beginning of 1986, the Harbin Municipal Urban Planning Bureau (under the Municipal Construction Bureau) formally designated that relocation (*banqian*, 搬迁) work should "follow the trend of district-level management," but with clear institutional recourse to higher-level officials should the residents object to local management. By August, each district government had established offices to deal with the relocation and reassignment

---

[32] "Ha'erbin Yamachang yuanzhi fujin Yama bolan zhongxin, baohu jianzhu baoliu" (Harbin to Build Yama Exhibition Center on Site of Yamachang, Leaving Preserved Architecture), *Dongbei wang* (Northeastern Net), March 14, 2009.

of housing as well as with the renovation projects. An essay by a prominent Harbin urban planner, Yu Binyang, explains:

Harbin has had a difficult time incorporating widely accepted standards and national standards of good living environments. For example, average living space per person is much lower than in the rest of the country, but neighborhoods and surroundings are much more convenient. Harbiners do not want to demolish large parts of the old city to build green space, and new space for commerce and tertiary industry has developed somewhat organically in the downtown area without a great deal of demolition and reconstruction.[33]

For these reasons, the essay concludes that decentralized discretion over the built environment is a condition particular to Harbin and one that at times has complicated municipal efforts at spatial transformation. However frustrating, Yu argues that it has ultimately benefited the distinctive quality of Harbin's urban form.

Property Rights and the Emergent Private Sector

Although the location of the "organic development" of commerce to which Yu alludes was predictable, the emergence of Harbin's private and petty entrepreneurial sector was a product of the local political environment and the city's fragmented property-rights regime. During the 1980s and 1990s, as formal-sector workers experienced either layoffs or wage cuts or anticipated their inevitability, many turned to petty commerce, trade, and street-level services as a means of livelihood. Predictably, the spaces where these activities emerged were those that boasted a rich tradition of private (*geti*, 个体) entrepreneurial and commercial activity prior to the nationalization of industry in 1956. Daoli district, home to Harbin's celebrated Central Boulevard (Zhongyang dajie, 中央大街) and the center of the Russian émigré petit bourgeoisie in the 1920s, became the epicenter of commercial and service enterprise development during the reform period. "Daowai" ("老道外" in the parlance of Harbiners), housing the Muslim quarter surrounding the city's largest mosque, had been settled by Chinese railroad laborers in the early twentieth century. Both Daoli and Daowai districts claim a long tradition of vibrant private enterprise and entrepreneurship, and the commercial impulse was quick to return under conditions of political liberalization.[34] Figure 5.4 shows the growth of the private economy from 1978 to 1991.

---

[33] Yu Binyang, "Shuli xiandai chengshi guihua linian, danghao jingying chengshi de 'longtou'" (Create the Concept of Modern Urban Planning and Act as the 'Dragon Head' of City Management), in *21 shiji Ha'erbin chengshi guihua duice yanjiu*, ed. Yu Binyang, 76. This essay was selected by the municipal government as the third most outstanding essay on Harbin to be published in 2002 – a clear sign that Yu's views reflected those of the authorities.

[34] Daowai before 1949 was home to 4,950 self-owned stores and businesses – 63 percent of such businesses citywide. *Ha'erbin shi Daowaiqu shehui jingji fazhan tongji zonghe nianjian, 1978–1987* (Daowai District of Harbin City Social and Economic Development Comprehensive

To be sure, the growth of commercial streets and bourgeois clusters was far from spontaneous. The MBIC was instrumental in fostering an advantageous environment, institutionally and physically, for the burgeoning of small commercial and service-sector endeavors. As early as April 1980, the MBIC encouraged local-level experimentation with private business, and at the end of 1980 it issued instructions to ease the registration process for urban private enterprises. By 1981, the city had registered more than twelve thousand private enterprises, twenty-one times the number registered at the end of 1978.[35] Critically, the onus of encouraging, registering, and approving private enterprises rested with lower-level district governments, which also granted business licenses and spaces for their operations. The blossoming of commercial activity – shoe repairs, craftsmanship, barber shops, food stalls, teahouses, bakeries, and the like – emerged in clusters along streets that traditionally housed these businesses, such as Central Street and Jingyu Road near the Daowai mosque, and under the purview of street offices (*jiedao banshichu*, 街道办事处) that were well integrated with the local communities. The central municipal branch of the MBIC and its local arms acted as advocates for urban private enterprise, designating spaces for operations and refusing to censure these activities when they conflicted with other local governmental goals and policies.[36] The city decentralized the bureaucratic process to encourage these types of economic activities. In 1984, when the Central Committee in Beijing officially encouraged private laborers to register as such and enterprises to employ them, the MBIC also devolved to the district the rights to approve of the joint operation of enterprises between the private sector and the street level.[37]

As early as 1985, Harbin, along with many cities nationwide, began experimenting with leasing out the operation of small state-owned enterprises.[38] By

---

Statistical Yearbook, 1978–1987) (Harbin, 1988), 3. These impulses were not restricted to historically entrepreneurial areas. In fact, small-scale markets emerged without obstacles all over the city – even in Taiping district's industrial parks, established in the 1950s as the heart of public enterprise in a city dominated by such public enterprises. Additionally, the industrial cluster of Sankeshu developed a 1.78-square-kilometer "market area" in which workers clustered to buy and sell refashioned industrial products. *Ha'erbin nianjian, 1987*, 586.

[35] MBIC [1980] Document 195, "Guanyu shidang fazhan chengzhen geti gongshang yehu ruogan wenti de guiding" (Some Regulations on the Problems Related to the Appropriate Development of Urban Private Industrial and Commercial Enterprises), *Heilongjiang minying jingji nianjian, 2004* (Heilongjiang Province Private Enterprise Yearbook, 2004) (Ha'erbin: Heilongjiang renmin chubanshe, 2004), 102.

[36] Interviews with members of the Daowai District Commerce Association, March 2008. Business owners throughout Jingyu market credited the MBIC, chiefly its Daowai district organ, for their survival during the hard times of the 1980s and 1990s.

[37] MBIC, "Guanyu xiafang hezuo jingying qiye (minban qiye) he geti gongshang yehu shenpi quanxian de tongzhi" (Notice on the Devolution of Authority over Registration of Jointly Operated Enterprises and Private Industrial and Commercial Enterprises), *Heilongjiang minying jingji nianjian, 2004*, 103.

[38] For more on this, see Dorothy J. Solinger, *China's Transition from Socialism: Statist Legacies and Market Reforms, 1980–1990* (Armonk, NY: M. E. Sharpe, 1993).

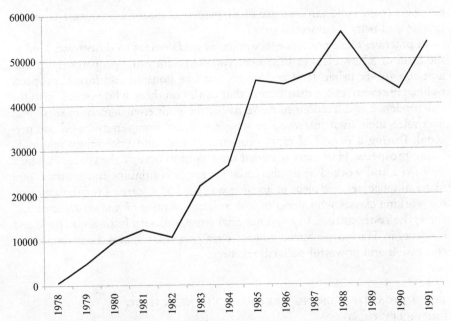

FIGURE 5.4. Private Enterprises in Harbin, 1978–1991
Source: Heilongjiang minying jingji nianjian, 2004 (Heilongjiang Province Private Enterprise Yearbook, 2004) (Ha'erbin: Heilongjiang renmin chubanshe, 2004), 104–5.

1987, 1,001 such units had been leased for private operation, or 31.4 percent of the city's small-sized SOEs.[39] In practice, this meant that ownership and management – especially of small enterprises in the commercial sector – became increasingly privatized, well before this occurred in most cities in China, and certainly before others in the Northeast. These small commercial enterprises were often small stores or service shops, meaning that even in the 1980s, the local state was steadily relinquishing control over the city's commercial space. Importantly, the new economic actors who acquired power and de facto property rights in the 1980s were formally integrated into the city's political fabric. In 1987, the Harbin Commercial Coalition (Ha'erbin shangye lianhehui, 哈尔滨商业联合会) was allowed by the municipal government to elect members not only from large and medium SOEs, but also from foreign-invested enterprises, collectives, and the private sector. The group gained 696 new

---

[39] *Ha'erbin nianjian, 1988* (Harbin Yearbook, 1988) (Ha'erbin: Heilongjiang renmin chubanshe, 1988), 89; 319 of these enterprises were industrial, of which 8 were SOEs and 311 were collectives; 682 were commercial, of which 353 were SOEs and 329 collectives. Thus, a full 54.5 percent of the city's small commercial enterprises were leased out for private management.

members from 1986 (an increase of 21 percent), 306 of whom were from the private and petty commercial sector.[40]

In practice, these policies encouraged new claimants to downtown land in the form of a new class of urban entrepreneurs. Informal property rights and autonomy over urban land and space, just like housing and formal property rights, are resources for distribution that confer on those who possess them the independence and freedom to make use of the built environment in ways that maximize their own interests, be they economic, community-based, or personal. During a period of rapid economic change and uncertainty regarding future prospects, Harbiners regarded their right to occupy the spaces in which they lived and worked as a substantial source of continuity and security. In a material sense, reinvestment in housing was used as a form of redistribution to the working classes who stood to lose in future rounds of market reforms and enterprise restructuring. In a less material sense, officials, business owners, and residents in Harbin perceived control over particular spaces as an important concession and powerful political resource.

THE 1990S: DEEPENING REFORMS, ENTRENCHING PROPERTY CLAIMS

In the late 1980s, as a reaction to both the steady growth of the private sector within Harbin and the ascendance of the southern coastal cities that were eclipsing the old industrial base in economic importance in China, certain groups in Harbin, often linked to large SOEs, became critical of the reforms. The central municipal government in 1988 launched a campaign to "rejuvenate Harbin" (*zhenxing Ha'erbin*, 振兴哈尔滨), which sought to draw together officials from all departments, entrepreneurs, cadres, intellectuals, workers, peasants, and soldiers to eliminate the "old ideology, old ideas, old habits, old practices, and old styles." Mayor Gong Benyan, well connected in the state sector as a former manager of a large SOE in the city, after criticizing those in the city who seemed too "encumbered," exclaimed in a speech to the municipal government and party committee: "We will not be backwards! Harbin must rejuvenate!"[41] Beginning in 1989, the newly established Bureau of Land Planning Management (BLPM) united behind the plan to restrict industrial development in the urban core; renovate residential compounds in Daoli, Nangang, and Daowai districts; and establish two new development zones outside the traditional city center.[42]

---

[40] Ibid., 89.

[41] *Ha'erbin nianjian, 1989* (Harbin Yearbook, 1989) (Ha'erbin: Heilongjiang renmin chubanshe, 1989), 29.

[42] Chengshi guihuaju (Urban Planning Bureau of Harbin Municipality) and Ha'erbinshi chengshi guihua xuehui (Urban Planning Society of Harbin Municipality), *Ha'erbin yinxiang, 1950–2000* (Glance Back at the Old City's Charm, 1950–2000) (Beijing: Zhongguo jianzhu chubanshe, 2005), 178–9; *Ha'erbin nianjian, 1987*, 112.

In 1989, the BLPM set its sights on "illegal construction" downtown – that is, land use for purposes not officially approved by the city authorities. However, it encountered resistance not only from the occupants, who perceived themselves as the rightful de facto occupants of the land that had been redistributed to them, but also from the lower-level bureaucrats who had made these informal pacts with the occupants. Plans to demolish "illegal construction" were the most controversial, as this construction included space carved out for small businesses and petty commerce that was beginning to generate tax revenue for the district governments.

Because of these conflicts, the municipal government established the Property Dispute Arbitration Department in 1989. The department began taking cases in September of that year, and within only four months it had received 541 complaints or appeals.[43] Furthermore, in order to head off complaints from the burgeoning entrepreneurial sector, the municipal government, against the wishes of the BLPM, decreed in November 1989 that all new construction projects, whether industrial or residential, were required to allot a minimum of 7 percent of space to commercial purposes.[44]

This reflected a new strategy of clustering the small-scale private sector in designated areas rather than allowing informal appropriations of space. The municipal government was attempting to allow the burgeoning private sector to flourish, to placate groups that staked claims to urban land, and to assert official control over land use and the allocation of urban property. In 1991, commercial streets were officially designated at Central Boulevard in Daoli district, Fendou Road in Nangang district, and Jingyu Street in Daowai. Central Boulevard boasted 139 independent commercial enterprises by the end of 1991, Fendou Road had more than 300, and Jingyu Street more than 400, most of which were small businesses run by petty entrepreneurs.[45] By 1995, there were thirty additional such designated areas, including seven recognized as having "national-level excellence," and nineteen with provincial recognition. Moreover, the city of Harbin boasted three of the nation's fifty largest industrial product markets.[46] Many of these markets were located in industrial compounds, especially compounds that had undergone rounds of layoffs and privatization. Secondary markets developed for the crafting and sale of

---

[43] *Ha'erbin nianjian, 1990* (Harbin Yearbook, 1990) (Ha'erbin: Heilongjiang renmin chubanshe, 1990), 271.

[44] "Ha'erbin shi shangye wangdian jianshe guanli banfa" (Harbin City Measures on Construction Management of Commercial Space), *Ha'erbin nianjian, 1990*, 597. This section borrows heavily from an interview with two retired senior urban planners, November 2007.

[45] *Ha'erbin nianjian, 1992* (Harbin Yearbook, 1992) (Ha'erbin: Ha'erbin nianjianshe, 1992), 223.

[46] *Ha'erbin nianjian, 1995* (Harbin Yearbook, 1995) (Ha'erbin: Ha'erbin nianjianshe, 1995), 65. The total exchange value of these markets was more than 5.2 billion RMB, an increase of nearly 44 percent from 1994. These markets were the physical spaces where enterprises that produced over the planned quotas could sell their wares and retain the profits, and enterprises on the demand side were permitted to source their own materials at market prices.

industrial tools and materials, as well as for the attendant businesses in the service sector. Such markets were not only substantial sources of income and economic activity for the city, but also major outlets for the reemployment of former public-sector workers. By 1998, the city hosted 621 official locations with nearly 78,000 registered businesses, employing more than 127,000 people, 60 percent of whom were laid-off industrial workers.[47]

Into the 1990s, property rights and the plight of workers became the most politically salient issues in Harbin. According to letters and visits (*xinfang shangfang*, 信访上访) data for 1997, issues related to insurance, pensions, and wages for laid-off or retired workers accounted for 25 percent of all collective visits or letters (that is, group visits and petitions), and city construction, relocation, and planning accounted for another 20 percent.[48] Severe rounds of layoffs and privatization of SOEs precipitated large strike waves in many eastern and northeastern cities in China in 1997, and Harbin was no exception.[49] Management reforms and privatization left workers with insufficient pensions, while workers still employed at many SOEs during these rounds of reforms were owed back wages. Predictably, strikes and unrest (including sit-ins, traffic blockages, and in some cases even holding factory managers hostage) were concentrated in the industrial clusters, mostly in Xiangfang and Dongli districts. One strike in January 1997 involved workers from fifty-six enterprises marching together for back wages and guarantees of pensions and housing after layoffs.[50]

After these layoffs and the subsequent worker unrest, the MBIC and the Municipal Construction Committee again turned to housing renovation and privatization as a way of distributing benefits to the burdened populations and groups that had proven to be politically disruptive. In July 1999, the Municipal Construction Committee launched a campaign called "To Resolve Housing Difficulties, We Will Help You." The campaign assisted 9,860 households to make renovations to their homes, most of which were financed by the city.[51]

---

[47] *Ha'erbin nianjian, 1999* (Harbin Yearbook, 1999) (Ha'erbin: Ha'erbin nianjianshe, 1999), 70.

[48] *Ha'erbin nianjian, 1998* (Harbin Yearbook, 1998) (Ha'erbin: Ha'erbin nianjianshe, 1998), 83. The system of letters and visits is an institutionalized complaint mechanism by which citizens in China can lodge complaints with local governments and all the way up to the central state in Beijing.

[49] See Ching Kwan Lee, "Pathways of Labor Activism," in *Chinese Society: Change, Conflict, and Resistance*, ed. Elizabeth Perry and Mark Selden (3rd ed., New York: Routledge, 2010), 57–79; Lee, *Against the Law*; Hurst, *Chinese Worker after Socialism*; Hurst and O'Brien, "China's Contentious Pensioners."

[50] *Ha'erbin nianjian, 1998*, 124.

[51] *Ha'erbin nianjian, 2000* (Harbin Yearbook, 2000) (Ha'erbin: Ha'erbin nianjianshe, 2000), 205. These were renovations of homes that were simultaneously commodified, i.e., sold to longtime occupants at preferential prices. According to official sources, 5 percent of the funding was from wages, 6 percent from individuals, and 8 to 10 percent from the work units, depending on their solvency.

Importantly, most of these projects benefited the industrial compounds that had experienced strikes and social unrest during the previous two years.[52]

One such example is the Dongli Square and Heping Road neighborhood of Dongli district, a major site of strikes and sit-ins in 1997. After investing more than 5 million RMB in housing linked to factory compounds in the area between 1998 and 2000, the Dongli District Construction Bureau and the Harbin Urban Planning Bureau launched a campaign to widen roads and redirect traffic in the neighborhood, one of the busiest arteries in the city. At the initial stages of the renovation project, the managers of the SOEs in the area were suspicious that officials in the district and the UPB were attempting to snatch up land under the guise of renovations. Many of the medium and large enterprises along Heping Road – which runs through Dongli Square – had laid off workers in the late 1990s, and the area was undergoing the early stages of building commercial enterprises and small businesses.

One small cluster of entrepreneurial activity, mostly by laid-off-workers-turned-petty-businesspeople, was the Kunlun outdoor market. To allay fears that the city would use the project to demolish small businesses, whose structures were largely unapproved and technically illegal, Mayor Shi Zhongxin inspected the area and encouraged the district and the UPB to think beyond the "old city management paradigms" and to solicit the participation of neighborhood residents and enterprises in the planning and execution of renovations. Officials in charge of the project were dispatched to collective markets such as Kunlun and to local enterprises to clarify the intentions of the project and to collect additional proposals and requests for renovations, including street lighting and the upgrading of public space. Enterprises such as Harbin Electronics Limited, one of the city's largest SOEs, which had recently introduced renovations to employees' living quarters and was involved in layoffs, were entreated to contribute funds for the construction of infrastructure in informal markets where many of their former employees were attempting to make a living.[53]

---

[52] In addition to upgrading extant housing stock that was associated with SOEs, the city paid to relocate the laid-off and retired workers to new compounds, both in the city's core and in new residential compounds in Xiangfang and Dongli districts. Chengshi guihuaju and Ha'erbinshi chengshi guihua xuehui, *Ha'erbin yinxiang, 1950–2000*, 198–202; Ha'erbin shi chengshi guihuaju (Urban Planning Bureau of Harbin Municipality) and Ha'erbin shi chengshi guihua sheji yanjiuyuan (Urban Planning and Design Research Institute), *Ha'erbin chengshi guihua zongti guihua (2004–2020): Shuoming shu* (Master Plan of Harbin Municipality [2004–2020]: Manual) (2004), ch. 8.

[53] All information on this project is from Xu Guijun, "Yong jingying chengshi de linian gaohao dengshi lianghua gongcheng dazao pinpai jielu pinpai guangchang" (An Effective Street-Lighting Campaign to Renovate Famous Streets and Squares), in *21 shiji Ha'erbin chengshi guihua duice yanjiu*, ed. Yu Binyang, 157–63. Xu Guijun, as the project manager of the Dongli District Construction Bureau, writes from an insider's perspective. His essay was awarded first prize in 2002 by the Harbin City Urban Planning Bureau and the Bureau of Land Resources Management, indicating that the views expressed in the essay were somewhat representative of the overall view of urban planning in Harbin.

The renovation of the neighborhood, which was completed by March 2002, demonstrates the kind of negotiations among urban bureaucracies, public and private enterprises, and residents that became standard in Harbin. Officials incorporated the interests of public enterprises and private entrepreneurs in the drafting of the plans for renovation and used the projects as a way to redistribute infrastructure and public goods, such as street lighting and parks, to the recent "losers" from the reforms. The neighborhood renovation allowed municipal officials to mediate between recently laid-off-workers-turned-neighbors and the larger enterprises that dominated their environs. The logic of the project, as relayed by one of its chief managers, was more political – aiming to assuage urban interest groups and to maintain social harmony – than related to efficient economic investment or generating income for the local government.[54]

NEIGHBORHOOD HARBIN: LOCAL POLITICS OF DISTRIBUTION AND LEGITIMACY

I have argued that carrying out reforms to the state sector in a climate of resource scarcity created a fragmented municipal government preoccupied primarily with distributing resources, such as land and property control, to minimize political fallout. As a result, some urban constituencies, residing in ecological environments that facilitated collective identity and collective action and unified by moral entitlements to occupancy, proved difficult to dislodge and surprisingly able to constrain the goals of the municipal government. This pattern of local government distribution resulted in the obstruction of its own plans in neighborhoods in the downtown core as Harbin attempted outward expansion. Such stories underscore how land and property-rights policies were formed under conditions of uncertainty and in the absence of any strategic land vision among the local authorities. Land and economic development policies both evolved from piecemeal and ad hoc decisions as officials sought to maintain political stability amid economic reforms.

The Inferno: Old Daowai

The trajectory of Daowai district, one of Harbin's poorest districts, best illustrates how the political logic of property allocation during the first several decades of reform empowered unlikely groups in the city of Harbin. Daowai district is called the "Inferno," not only as a reference to hell but also because of the frequency of conflagrations as residents heat wooden homes with fire in the winter. Daowai typifies the kind of urban blight we associate with post-industrial cities – abandoned buildings, haphazard new construction, few signs

---

[54] Xu Guijun, "Yong jingying chengshi de linian gaohao dengshi lianghua gongcheng dazao pinpai jielu pinpai guangchang," 157–63.

of disposable income, and so forth. Yet, the area is not a hotbed for crime and residents have seemed to be in no hurry to flee their neighborhoods for higher ground. Street-level commerce is visibly vibrant; real estate prices (even for quite old structures) are as high as in other parts of the city; and relations among neighbors appear tenacious and mutually dependent.[55]

Daowai's pre-1949 economy was dominated by private business, both small handicrafts as well as "celebrated businesses" (*shangye zhuming,* 商业著名) run by entrepreneurs of some repute. These enterprises sold oil, alcohol, and grain, but workers were often destitute, leading the district to acquire the reputation of a "poor person's cave" (*pinmin ku,* 贫民窟), and eventually the "Inferno."[56] The high architectural and population densities, not to mention the prospects of very lucrative land for lease on the southern banks of the Songhua River and bordering the wealthier districts of Daoli and Nangang, landed neighborhoods in the area on the slate for renovation and relocation in every master plan drafted during the reform period.[57] Though housing has been renovated and reconstructed in the area, the residents in Daowai are generally the same residents who have lived there for decades. Frequently, the heads of the residents' committees in the 2000s were former factory foremen in enterprises that had been closed down for nearly fifteen years.

Many of these residents remained in the area because their homes were their greatest assets and because their livelihoods were provided by the small-scale private economy that flourished in the neighborhood. The district and its original residents weathered the reform period in part by reviving the kind of entrepreneurial activities, commercial and service-oriented, that the district had been known for before 1949. The local branch of the MBIC supported local commercial endeavors, particularly by workers laid off from public enterprises or by those employed by enterprises that were encountering problems with paying wages and providing social welfare. There were twenty-two new private enterprises established in 1986 alone, with nine commercial streets, eleven collective markets, and one service street – all established clusters of petty commerce and entrepreneurial activity.[58] By 1986, a total of 1,113 workers were reportedly engaged in these kinds of commercial activities, compared to 3,573 working for district-level collectives. The composition of the district's

---

[55] *Ha'erbin ribao* (Harbin Daily), October 31, 2007, reports that rents along Nanerdaojie, a 100-year-old *hutong,* are on par with those of the newly constructed residential neighborhoods in Daoli. This is at least in part because units in the newly constructed neighborhoods are not selling or renting at rates as high as in other large cities. But residents in Daowai also benefit from the neighborhood's charm and popularity and are likely to rent to outsiders at much higher rates.

[56] *Ha'erbin nianjian, 1987,* 578.

[57] "Daowaiqu weifang gaizao guihua" (Planning the Renovation of Slum Housing in Daowai), 2000; Chengshi guihuaju and Ha'erbinshi chengshi guihua xuehui, *Ha'erbin yinxiang, 1950–2000,* 207.

[58] *Ha'erbin nianjian, 1987,* 578.

economy had changed radically in favor of private enterprise and small-scale capitalism within only six years after the onset of the reforms.

In November 1988, the city set out to renovate key streets in Daowai district, planning the renovation of 434 households. The slogan was "Housing and Real Estate Authority Puts into Place a Self-Selected Relocation." All households were given a packet of information about the formal rules and procedures, and four monitors were supplied by the district to act as liaisons between the residents and the developers. Residents, organized by street offices and residents' committees, were very vocal about the relocation following these clearly defined procedures and laws. The city funded the construction of 489 new homes in the exact same area, and former residents had first pick in a lottery to determine the sequence for selecting new apartments.[59] A longtime chief planner of the Harbin Urban Planning Bureau, who had worked directly with the Daowai plans for decades, described the process of planning in Daowai as one of constant negotiation and concessions: "Every project is difficult because you have to agree to do some upkeep that the residents want and to give them some advantages, and only then can you engage in any kind of renovation."[60]

The Huifangli neighborhood is emblematic of the kind of conflict and concessions described by this planner. In 1989, the UPB declared the area to be one of the city's greatest "latent dangers," and thus it set out to relocate 1,026 households and private enterprises, or a total of 3,429 people. Pressured by the local street office and factory managers representing the concerns of the workers and their dependents, municipal officials from the Bureau of Civil Affairs and other departments (that is, outside the Bureau of Land Planning Management) agreed to monitor the compensation, relocation, and construction processes. The city financed the project and in the end negotiated with business managers and residents to reserve twenty-two thousand square meters of space, of a total of sixty-five thousand square meters, for commercial markets as well as for leisure facilities and for emergent service endeavors (restaurants, small repair shops, and so forth).[61] To be clear, the residents were by no means rich, but they weathered the loss of their state-sector jobs through involvement in the private sector. The neighborhood is a commercial destination for residents from all over Harbin, who go there to stroll and shop or eat in the area's famous restaurants and bakeries.

In 1998, the Harbin Municipal Government commissioned a series of surveys and fieldwork-based studies of Daowai by the Heilongjiang Academy

---

[59] *Ha'erbin nianjian,* 1989, 164–5. These projects have been praised for their speed of completion – from renovation to moving back in – by the real estate authority. Typically, residents move into new buildings as they are completed during the phases of the projects, eliminating the need for displacement, however temporary.

[60] Interview, Urban Planning Bureau, April 2008.

[61] *Ha'erbin nianjian,* 1990, 267. This neighborhood had been the locus of conflict that led to the establishment of the Property Dispute Adjudication Office, described previously.

of Social Sciences. At a conference of academics and city officials at which the results were presented, the officials concluded that private and entrepreneurial activity had blossomed in the district because of the legacy of strong businesses with private management and high population and architectural densities that gave rise to small businesses that survived on foot traffic and word of mouth. They also pointed to what they called Daowai's "urban sense of mutual aid" (*chengshi hubu xing*, 城市互补性), or the social closeness of the neighborhoods in the district. The conference concluded that in order to encourage more of the kind of economic activity that thrived in Daowai and had helped to offset the painful retreat of the socialist welfare net, the city should promote the "grassroots economy" and allow space for the spontaneous growth of the private sector.[62]

Contemporary Harbin planners and land management officials report that they shy away from projects in Daowai, both because the residents tend to organize against anything that would drastically change the neighborhood's aesthetic and composition and because the economic success of the private enterprises and the tertiary sector in the area discourages land and property policies that may displace them. As one urban planner described: "Old Harbiners still live there and will organize to protect their neighborhood, businesses, and homes by claiming to protect the old architecture. We can plan many service centers and allot space for commerce, but their experience in Daowai is more spontaneous. If you over-plan, the problem is that it lacks spontaneity."[63]

Development Zone

Harbin's development zone, like many zones nationwide and especially those in the inland cities, was established in 1992. According to city records, the "main reason" for establishing the new zone was, as in Dalian, to "solve the problem of insufficient land available for development" in the downtown core area.[64] In terms of policy, the Harbin Development Zone operated nearly identically to that in Dalian: Investors were offered low-cost land, tax rates at 15 percent instead of 33 percent, and no real estate taxes for the first three years of the investment period.

In 1995, Harbin's zone was ranked nationally in several categories; of forty-nine such "national-level" zones, Harbin's was ranked seventh in total earnings

---

[62] *Ha'erbin nianjian, 1999*, 323.   [63] Interview, Urban Planning Bureau, April 2008.

[64] Ha'erbin jingji jishu kaifaqu guanli weiyuanhui (Harbin Economic and Technology Development Zone Management Committee), Ha'erbin gao xin jishu chanye kaifaqu guanli weiyuanhui (Harbin High Technology Park Management Committee), and Ha'erbin shi chengshi guihua sheji yanjiuyuan (Harbin Urban Planning and Design Institute), "Ha'erbin kaifaqu xinqu zongti guihua zhuanti baogao" (Harbin Development Zone New Area Master Plan Report) (December 2004), 1.

from industry and trade, sixth in the gross value of GVIO, eighth in tax earnings, and sixth in the value of exports. [65] During the Ninth Five-Year Plan, however, from 1996 to 2000, growth in the development zone lurched to a near-stop, with earnings and growth falling behind the national average and further and further behind the other development zones nationally, with which Harbin ceased to be competitive. [66] By 2001, average Harbiners were beginning to refer to the new zone as "Corruption Street" (*fubai yitiao jie*, 腐败一条街), home to the city's most expensive and exclusive restaurants and the largest golf course in the province.

Why did the Harbin Development Zone initially succeed and then fall prey to corruption and economic decline? In many ways, its trajectory illustrates in a microcosm the argument that I make about the city of Harbin as a whole. As early as 1994, official documents report that the development zone was suffering from "governance problems," chiefly related to the management of taxes, finances, and land. [67] Soon after the establishment of the zone, land parcels were distributed to individual factories and organizations that had autonomy over the development of the land. Instead of relocating factories from the downtown areas to the development zone, the way that the process was carried out in Dalian, major factories in Harbin were given land in the new zone without requiring that they move there. Early development zone documents indicate that the Harbin authorities wanted to apply the "grafting on" method of linking enterprise reform with foreign direct investment (FDI), but clearly they failed to execute such a plan. [68] Land either was used for nonproductive purposes, or, when it went to productive purposes, there was no investment in infrastructure that would have made the zone a more general success. The result was a development zone nominally managed by a single committee, but in reality controlled by various groups that lacked incentives to invest in the kinds of housing, infrastructure, or public-use development that would have enhanced the zone's competitiveness.

What is now called the Harbin Development Zone (*kaifaqu*,开发区) began as two separate development zones (Harbin Economic and Technology Development Zone and Harbin High Technology Park) and three industrial clusters (Nangang Cluster, Haping Road, and Yingbin Road). Nangang cluster, which is in Nangang district, was the first of the clusters, and for nearly ten years it

---

[65] Ibid., 2.   [66] Ibid., 2.

[67] Fang Cunzhong, "Liangge kaifaqu cunzai de wenti he jianyi" (Problems in Two Zones and Suggestions), in *Ha'erbin kaifaqu wenxian, 1991–1994* (Documents on the Harbin Development Zone, 1991–1994), ed. Ha'erbin kaifaqu guanli weihui (Management Committee of the Harbin Development Zone), HMA F129.935/1-53, 32–3. Fang was a member of the management committee of the development zone.

[68] Wang Shouchuan, "Kaifaqu yu qiye yidi banqian gaizao yanjiu" (Research on Offsite Relocation of Enterprises in the Development Zone), in *Ha'erbin kaifaqu wenxian, 1991–1994*, HMA F129.935/1-53, 92. Wang was the head of the research unit of the management committee of the development zone.

had only basic infrastructure in its six square kilometers before the construction problems were resolved. Some of these problems were as basic as whether and where to locate a management headquarters and a technology center; problems related to commercial and residential real estate generated even more contention. There were two main axes of conflict: first, between the two development zone management boards and, second, between the management boards and the Nangang District Government. From 1993 until the formal unification of the two boards into a single development zone in 2001, the embryonic district was under the jurisdiction of both the Harbin Economic and Technology Development Zone (*jingkaiqu*, 经开区) and the Harbin High Technology Park (*gaokaiqu*, 高开区). The resulting conflict over which board was to assign and oversee land development crippled the district.[69]

Moreover, both boards found themselves at odds with the Nangang District Government, which provided basic infrastructure for the new zone (that is, water treatment for industrial projects, gas, and road maintenance), with the understanding that some tax revenue, as well as a percentage of the land-lease fees, would accrue to the district government. However, the Nangang part of the zone failed to attract enterprises that would pay taxes, and most of the land was allocated to extant SOEs, without collecting lease fees. Therefore, in 1998, officials from the district government appealed to the BLPM to be granted the right to approve real estate development projects and to lease land on their own. The BLPM, frustrated with the infighting among the management committees and much more dependent on cooperation with Nangang officials than with officials from the underperforming development zones, granted the district about 1.5 square kilometers of land for its own developmental plans. The heart of this area, Hongxiang and Hanshui Roads, is precisely where a taxi driver would drop a patron who asked, matter-of-factly as Harbiners often do, to be driven to Corruption Street.

The Haping cluster is the industrial heart of the development zone as well as the source of most of its economic productivity. The cluster houses the zone's automobile manufacturing, foodstuffs plants, and pharmaceuticals plants, which together make up 72.7 percent of the zone's GVIO.[70] The Haping Road area encapsulates a neighborhood in Pingfang district called "South Factory," one of Harbin's oldest industrial clusters and home to two of its largest public enterprises – the Hafei Auto Manufacturing Company and the Harbin Dong'an Engine Factory. The area, under the control of the Harbin Economic and Technology Zone Management Committee, won bids for both a Coca-Cola bottling plant and an instant noodle factory in the mid-1990s. In the late 1990s

[69] Ha'erbin jingji jishu kaifaqu guanli weiyuanhui, Ha'erbin gao xin jishu chanye kaifaqu guanli weiyuanhui, and Ha'erbin shi chengshi guihua sheji yanjiuyuan, "Ha'erbin kaifaqu xinqu zongti guihua zhuanti baogao," 1, 5.

[70] My own calculations based on data from ibid., 1, 72.

the Harbin Pharmaceutical Company (HaYao) was also granted land intended for relocation to Haping.[71]

Despite being the major engine for economic growth and industrial production in the development zone area, Haping still struggles with a lack of foreign investment, and the management committee lacks a capacity to anchor projects in land that is still under the control of individual factories. The October 2001 master plan, drafted for the area by the management committee and the Urban Planning Bureau, leaves most of the area unplanned and designated for "extant enterprise use."[72] In the late 2000s, this land was occupied neither by productive uses, attendant worker housing, nor welfare buildings. In 2008, most of the lots were vacant. Some were occupied by dilapidated basketball courts, others consisted of constructed fields, and some were hidden behind large walls, which in one case stretched continuously to connect the unconstructed areas to a housing complex for Hafei workers.[73]

Officials of both the management committee of the development zone and the BLPM attribute the decline of the development zone to land and property-rights policy: "The policy style of handing over small plots of land to industrial clusters gradually reduced the speed of growth."[74] As of 2002, the price of land in the development zone (7.5 RMB per square meter) was lower than the average in national development zones, as was the density of land use (a measure of the clustering of economic activity), meaning that the local government was neither successfully attracting productive activity nor capitalizing on the leasing of land. The development zone management committee and the Harbin Urban Planning and Design Institute issued a special report intended to attract the help of the BLPM.

The report tracks the decline of the Harbin Development Zone as compared to similar zones in other cities; in the 2002 national rankings of development zone competitiveness (in which Harbin ranked eighteenth of thirty-two), Harbin was tied for top ranking with Guangzhou and Tianjin in the "investment environment" category and for eighth place in "operational costs," but

[71] Ibid., 2–3.

[72] "Ha'erbin jingji jishu kaifaqu zongti guihua" (Master Plan of Harbin Economic and Technology Development Zone) (Ha'erbin: Ha'erbin shi chengshi guihua guanliju, 1984); Yu Binyang, ed., *Ha'erbin xin shiji chu chengshi guihua zuopin xuanji* (Selected Works on Harbin City Planning at the Beginning of the New Century) (Ha'erbin: Ha'erbin chubanshe, 2002), 143.

[73] My own inquiries about plans for the land on official visits (when I was accompanied by a member of the Urban Planning Bureau in one case or by officials from the management committee in another case) and unofficial (solo) visits were met with unsurprising silence. Officials responded with comments like "Still don't know," or "It is complicated." At other times, however, officials from the management committee would complain that the SOEs in their zone, naming Hafei and Dong'an directly, were protective of their land and were not supportive of the zone's "overall development" (April 2008 visit).

[74] Ha'erbin jingji jishu kaifaqu guanli weiyuanhui, Ha'erbin gao xin jishu chanye kaifaqu guanli weiyuanhui, and Ha'erbin shi chengshi guihua sheji yanjiuyuan, "Ha'erbin kaifaqu xinqu zongti guihua zhuanti baogao," 2.

twenty-fourth place in terms of both "infrastructure capability" and "social and environmental conditions," evidence for the authors' conclusion that the zone's stagnation was due to fragmented control over land.[75] They concluded that the management committee, with the assistance of the Bureau of Urban Planning, should "exercise greater management control over urban planning and urban construction," meaning all construction plans should be routed through that office and enterprises and industrial compounds should no longer have autonomy over land-use allocations.[76] Even when firms were given land in the development zone for relocation, they retained control over the land parcels they occupied downtown. The idea was to encourage firms to move, allowing them to generate income by releasing originally occupied space. Firms would then pay only real estate and value-added land taxes on the original space, while they would pay lower industrial taxes in the development zone.[77] Therefore, development zone land policies impeded municipal control over not only the zone itself, but also downtown land and property.

CONCLUSION: THE MAKING OF POSTSOCIALIST PROPERTY

Yu Binyang, a longtime Harbin urban planner and chief documentarian of Harbin city planning, ends his edited volume on city planning in Harbin by reflecting on some of the city's most obvious problems. After citing, as I have, the failed attempts at urban expansion, as well as the lack of large-scale urban public works projects such as those we see in Dalian or farther afield in Shanghai and Beijing, Yu concludes that perhaps these ostensible "problems" in fact make the city more livable. He argues that all cities proclaim the goal of "putting people first" (*yiren weizhu*, 以人为主), but in Harbin you can see this in practice. Yu concludes simply:

Traditionally, the renovation of Harbin's city center has come first, which has created problems for projects to make use of new areas and zones. Small planning is key, like the neighborhoods in Daowai and Daoli. Harbin should become nationally famous for making a larger city environment from small environments.[78]

---

[75] Ibid., 11. The categories "investment environment" and "operational costs" include more traditional variables that economists would associate with incentivizing investment: ease of investment approval, labor costs, price of industrial land use, and proximity to major transport centers. "Infrastructural capability" and "social and environmental conditions" include variables that measure the cohesion and extent of local government: fixed-asset investments, technological investments, public goods provision (electricity, gas, and water), education and social welfare expenditures, and environmental regulation compliance. The data and the categorizations are from the Ministry of Commerce.

[76] Ha'erbin jingji jishu kaifaqu guanli weiyuanhui, Ha'erbin gao xin jishu chanye kaifaqu guanli weiyuanhui, and Ha'erbin shi chengshi guihua sheji yanjiuyuan, "Ha'erbin kaifaqu xinqu zongti guihua zhuanti baogao," 146–7.

[77] Wang Shouchuan, "Kaifaqu yu qiye yidi banqian gaizao yanjiu," 92.

[78] Yu Binyang, ed., *21 shiji Ha'erbin chengshi guihua duice yanjiu*, 11–12.

In Yu's view, the city's property-rights regime has prevented city authorities – including his own Urban Planning Bureau – from carrying out a vision for urban transformation, but it has made Harbin's urban environment morally legitimate because residents feel connected to their communities and local authorities respond to their needs.

These neighborhoods and the more general pattern of fragmented land control have evolved in Harbin through the fragmented politics of decentralization and distribution. City officials, mostly at the very lowest levels, have pursued housing and neighborhood renovation, spatial autonomy for newly emergent private and entrepreneurial clusters, and land acquisition by state-owned enterprises as a way to advance the goals of economic reform and growth while maintaining social stability. As territorial claims have evolved, they have taken on a moral content as well. In the absence of land deeds and formal property rights, claimants invoke their earlier pacts with the local state – in the form of public enterprises or municipal officials at all levels – as evidence of their rights to occupy and make use of urban land. The longer these groups of claimants live or work together in a shared occupation of territory, the stronger their collective identification becomes and the more difficult it will be for municipal officials to dislodge them.

Harbin, lacking the wealth or foreign capital of its neighbors, is a local state where more diverse urban interests have been incorporated into the city's planning and transformation. Harbin's municipal power is dispersed and fragmented among arms of the local state, and groups within society have managed to carve out space – both physical and metaphorical – for autonomy and the articulation of their interests. It is not a coastal city exposed to foreign capital and influence and further along on a path to market reform and economic wealth that boasts an active and capacious "pluralistic" society, but rather the city that has yet to "overcome its socialist past."[79] Ironically, it is precisely the lingering elements of Harbin's socialist past that empowered, both politically and morally, what appears to be very much like private, indeed capitalist, claims to urban land and property.

[79] Woetzel et al., *Preparing for China's Urban Billion*, 226.

6

Changchun Motor City

The Politics of Compromise in an Industrial Town

> We are a late-comer.
>
> Changchun Deputy Mayor Yin Wen on the city's development zone efforts[1]

> Cities have special national functions, especially those designated as key industrial bases. We cannot take all functions, such as tourism, foreign opening, industry, and culture, to be the nature of any single city, or the nature will have no meaning and we will have no guide for planning work. Changchun is principally an auto city.
>
> Mu Yinghua, urban planner, Changchun City[2]

Of the cities in this study, the capital of Jilin province, Changchun, may be the most recognizable analog to a Western "rust belt" city. Home to China's first automobile manufacturing plant established in the 1950s, First Automobile Works (FAW) (*yiqi*, 一汽), the city prior to the reforms had an economy that was dominated, by state-owned heavy industry and was organized around that single sector. City officials and residents alike have embraced the city's monikers – Motor City (*qiche chengshi*, 汽车城市) or China's Detroit. As in Detroit, the city of Changchun and the auto industry seem to possess a shared fate, depending on each other for survival and prosperity. Yet, the city's relationship with its principal industry has not always been congenial, and Changchun's leadership has struggled continuously during the reform period to lay a foundation for the city's success independent of its largest and most famous constituent. That the city began the reform era chained to a socialist industrial

---

[1] Quoted in Renee Lai, "City Aspires to Be Chinese Detroit," *South China Morning Post*, July 7, 1994, 7.

[2] Mu Yinghua, "Lüelun chengshi de xingzhi: Yi Changchun shi wei lie" (Brief Discussion on the Nature of the City: Changchun as an Example), *Dongbei shifan daxue xuebao* (*Ziran kexue ban*) (Northeast Normal University Journal [Natural Science Edition]) no. 2 (1983): 73.

behemoth provided both a constraint on its attempts at growth and urban transformation as well as a motivation to overcome its socialist past.

THE ARGUMENT IN BRIEF

Like Harbin, Changchun was laden with loss-making SOEs that politic-ally difficult reforms under conditions of grave capital shortages, and the city's leaders turned to housing reform and entrepreneurship as a way of assuaging the losses to some caused by the economic reforms in the state sector. As the epigraph to this chapter suggests, the city's leadership was aware that it was a "late-comer" in opening to the global economy, but this awareness, coupled with the city's special relationship with the auto sector, united them behind a drive to expand the city and its economy in the 1990s. As in Dalian, the establishment of economic development zones featured prominently in Chang-chun's economic and spatial expansion and transformation. But unlike in Dalian, the development zones in Changchun were deeply integrated into the city's larger economy and provided specific industries spaces for clustering and experimentation. The development zones were not tools for bypassing the old industrial base to gain new sources of wealth, but rather they provided spatial policies that simultaneously appeased their constituencies and asserted municipal government control over the industrial clusters surrounding the city center. Changchun's municipal leaders were united in a search for wealth outside the auto sector, leading them to make property and land decisions in the 1980s and 1990s that in later periods would aid the city's growth and consolidate the local government's regulatory authority over property.

The ambitions of the local government to consolidate authority over land and property were evident from the outset. Even prior to the commodification of land in 1988, Changchun's authorities, chiefly the Land Management Bureau (LMB), played an active role in taking stock of land use in the city. The bureau initiated major efforts to survey land use and property rights over buildings, to create official records of use and ownership, and to contrast official records with actual practices and either update records or punish viola-tors. Administrative power over land and property allocations was articulated by the municipal LMB beginning in the 1980s and remained concentrated there even as the rules that governed markets in land and property changed in the 1990s. Changchun authorities articulated rules about the allocation, use, and transfer of land that differed for various urban groups, but, unlike in Harbin, those rules were enforced in a unified and coherent way. Changchun's property-rights regime was pluralistic, with multiple legitimate claimants to urban property in a way that left the various parties satisfied but the municipal leadership with sole regulatory authority.

Changchun's property-rights regime emerged as the local government bar-gained with powerful groups in a climate of capital scarcity. These groups included the potentially politically disruptive laid-off workers and the budding entrepreneurial sector, as in Harbin, but they also included the firms that composed the city's powerful auto sector. The political bargains struck with these various groups are reflected in their different claims to urban property rights. Powerful firms were granted autonomy over the land and property they occupied, and, as in Harbin, the authorities extended preferential property-rights arrangements to potential losers from the reforms to head off political conflict. The ideological positioning of land as a resource shared some commonalities with that in Harbin, namely, in the lingering power of property rights as moral entitlements for the losers from the reforms. In contrast to conditions in Harbin, however, a sense of dependence on the automobile industry produced bureaucratic coherence in Changchun. The Changchun Municipal Government articulated its regulatory or administrative power over land and property markets as necessary in a local economy that was vulnerable to an industry it could not control.

STAGNATION BEFORE OPENING: GROWTH IN CHANGCHUN

During the period of high state socialism and central planning under Mao, Changchun was designated a center of the command economy and a locus of crash industrialization, as were its neighbors in the Northeast. Also like its neighbors, the city of Changchun had already experienced previous periods of infrastructure creation and industrialization during the eras of railway growth and Japanese colonization.[3] According to official statistics, Changchun had more than 10,271 industrial and commercial firms in 1949, all but 76 of which were privately owned and operated.[4] These enterprises were nationalized during the nationwide socialization campaign in 1954–7, and Changchun was established as a base of heavy industry, focusing on automobiles, heavy machinery, and agricultural processing. At the onset of the reforms, Changchun's economy was one of those most heavily dominated by SOEs and heavy industry in the country. In 1980, the city boasted 5,016 industrial enterprises, and 68 percent of the industrial workforce was employed at SOEs.[5]

Changchun's growth trajectory after the initiation of market reforms in late 1978 underscores the importance of the distribution of preferential policies from Beijing. Municipal officials were eager to embark on reforms and opening to the global economy, but they were resignedly aware that Changchun lacked

[3] On urban planning and industrialization in Changchun during the South Manchurian Railway and Manchukuo periods, see David D. Buck. "Railway City and National Capital: Two Faces of the Modern in Changchun," in *Remaking the Chinese City: Modernity and National Identity, 1900–1950*, ed. Joseph Esherick (Honolulu: University of Hawaii Press, 2000), 65–89.
[4] *Changchun shi zhi: Gongshang xingzheng guanli zhi* (Changchun Industrial and Commercial Management Gazetteer) (Changchun: Changchun shi difangzhi bianzuan weiyuanhui, 2006), 3.
[5] Ibid., 19. These data reference only industrial enterprises and exclude firms and enterprises in commerce and services.

preferential policies that would attract foreign investment and much-needed capital for the city's enterprises. First Party Secretary Wu Yixia (serving from 1986 to 1988) stated in his 1988 annual speech to the city's CCP: "According to the national coastal development strategy, coastal cities get rich first and inland cities are staged for development. For our city, this is an opportunity as well as a challenge: the circumstances are pressing."[6] Changchun made significant strides toward enterprise reform and private sector growth in the 1980s – detailed later – but it was not until the introduction of preferential policies in 1992 that the economy experienced a takeoff. After 1992, Changchun's year-on-year growth rate remained steady, at between 10 and 20 percent, through 2004.[7]

The greatest challenge for local officials was the overwhelming reliance of the city's economy on the automobile sector. Changchun's rebirth as a motor city began with the 1956 construction of the FAW, an enormous automobile manufacturing SOE whose Liberation brand trucks and Red Flag limousines were once the pride of the city and the country.[8] In the early PRC years (and in the reform era), domestic automobile manufacturing was a symbol of the country's capacity for modern industrial production and self-reliance. Contemporary visitors to Changchun often tour the FAW "homeland" (*jiayuan*, 家园) facilities to see the massive auto complex where Jiang Zemin once served as a manager and to stroll in the "automobile sculpture gardens" that house socialist realist monuments to worker solidarity as well as modernist renderings of sedans that look like smiling human faces.

The FAW facilities, which in 2012 occupied a tract of land large enough to merit several zip codes, lie about four kilometers southwest of the Changchun city center at People's Square. In addition to more than one square kilometer of factory space, the FAW compound includes more than one thousand apartment buildings, twenty-six schools, ten nurseries, and the massive Auto Workers Leisure and Cultural Center, which occupies three urban blocks along Xi'an

---

[6] Wu Yixia, "Jiefang sixiang, shenhua gaige, wei zhenxing Changchun nuli fendou (zhai yao): Zai Zhongguo gongchandang Changchun shi di qici daibiao dahuishang de baogao." (Liberate Thoughts and Deepen Reforms to Revitalize the Struggling Changchun City [Excerpts]: Report to the Seventh Meeting of Delegates of the Communist Party of Changchun Municipality), April 28, 1988. In *Changchun nianjian, 1988* (Changchun Yearbook, 1988) (Changchun: Changchun chubanshe, 1988), 4.

[7] Data from 1996 to 2010 are all from China Data Center, University of Michigan, via China Data Online, accessed September 2012. Data from 1990 to 1996 are from *Xin Zhongguo chengshi wushinian, 1949–1998* (Fifty Years of Cities in New China, 1949–1998) (Beijing: Xinhua chubanshe, 1999), 353–88, 317–22, 377–82, 407–12. FAI data from NBS via CEIC. Pre-1990 data are from *Changchun tongji nianjian* (Changchun Statistical Yearbook) (Beijing: Zhongguo tongji chubanshe), various years.

[8] Sources indicate that Changchun was selected as the site of China's first auto manufacturing plant because of its well-developed rail networks and strategic location close to the Soviet Union but far from the eastern coast; with the onset of the Korean War in 1950, central planners were beginning to consider protecting industry from the more militarily vulnerable coastline. *Changchun keche chang zhi, 1954–1990* (Changchun Coach Company Gazetteer, 1954–1990) (Changchun: Jilin renmin chubanshe, 1997), 14–15.

Road. Adjacent to the FAW compounds farther down Xi'an Road are large research and development facilities and the offices of the Changchun Automobile Research Center, comprising nine large office buildings and research facilities. In 1980, even before the FAW entered into joint-venture cooperation agreements (with Volkswagen) and expanded its facilities, the enterprise owned and operated more than twenty-two square kilometers of floor space for nonproductive purposes, that is, worker housing and ancillary facilities.[9] In 2010, the FAW employed more than 120,000 workers in Changchun and shouldered responsibilities for an estimated 100,000 to 150,000 dependents.[10]

That the State Planning Commission (SPC) decided to locate China's first domestic auto manufacturer in Changchun was a boon to the city during the Maoist period, entitling Changchun to high levels of state investment in its enterprises and urban infrastructure to facilitate growth in a flagship industry. During the reform period, however, the Changchun local government has had a more ambivalent attitude toward the industry, and to the FAW in particular, viewing the latter as an albatross as well as an opportunity. Critically, the FAW has always been a centrally owned and operated SOE, meaning that control rights over the enterprise and access to profits all belong to the central state in Beijing rather than to the local government. In this sense, the city's fortunes are linked to a large enterprise over which it has little or no control. Eric Thun explains Changchun's eroding share of the Chinese domestic market relative to producers in Shanghai and Guangzhou in the 1990s by looking at this institutional gap between the local government and its largest enterprise. Changchun municipal authorities had little influence over the FAW or its eventual joint-venture partners since decisions over supply sourcing and pricing were made at the central level, and both the FAW and its joint-venture partners were unlikely to invest in start-up local suppliers. Thun finds that, even six years after production began in the new FAW–VW joint venture and despite contractual agreements stipulating that 28 percent of the VW Jetta's components would be supplied by FAW firms, only 15 percent actually were.[11] Even when the auto industry in Changchun made significant gains in the late 1990s and early 2000s, it was not necessarily local suppliers – those paying taxes in Changchun and absorbing the Changchun local workforce – who were benefiting.

[9] *Changchun qiche yanjiusuo zhi, 1950–1985* (Changchun Auto Research Institute Gazetteer, 1950–1985) (Beijing: Changchun qiche yanjiusuo, 1987), 26.

[10] *Changchun nianjian, 2011* (Changchun City Yearbook, 2011) (Changchun: Jilin renmin chubanshe, 2011), 189.

[11] Ibid., 175. The FAW–VW joint venture was established in 1991, with an initial 8.9 billion RMB in investment, and 60 percent FAW control and 40 percent VW control. Thun reports that VW did not necessarily invest in the FAW because it thought Changchun was the best place for sedan manufacturing, but rather because it gave it greater control over the Chinese domestic market, and competitors would have cooperated with the FAW had it passed. Eric Thun, *Changing Lanes in China: Foreign Direct Investment, Local Governments, and Auto Sector Development* (Cambridge: Cambridge University Press, 2006).

Many cities in China are home to centrally controlled SOEs, of which there were 112 in 2015.[12] These cities face similar challenges as major employers and economic agents are appointed by and accountable to the central level, and therefore their priorities can be far removed from those of the local governments. Politically, the president of the FAW, appointed by the Central Party Organization Department in Beijing, holds a higher rank in the CCP than does the mayor of Changchun.[13] Yet, the large workforces employed by these enterprises reside locally and constitute significant urban constituencies with which the local governments must contend. When central SOEs downsize, face wage arrears, or seek to reduce their social welfare burdens in terms of social insurance, housing, and pensions, displaced and potentially contentious workers become the problems of the local governments. These massive enterprises also control large tracts of urban land, setting the stage for conflicts between the SOEs that stand to gain from liquidating land holdings and the local governments that seek the same financial gains and are also charged with urban spatial transformation projects.

In addition to the FAW, Changchun was home to three other large central SOEs – the Changchun Coach Company, the Changchun Tractor Factory, and the Changchun Railway Car Company – as well as dozens of motorcycle and auto suppliers.[14] Although these other large factories did not survive the reform period intact or exercise as much influence over Changchun's politics as did the FAW, they established Changchun not only as home to the country's flagship auto manufacturer, but also as the base for the larger transportation manufacturing industry.[15] Much like Detroit, Changchun had an economy dependent on one sector and the continued viability of a few large firms.

CAPITAL SHORTAGES, URBAN REFORM, AND LOCAL ADMINISTRATIVE POWER

> Stability is China's greatest strength; stability trumps everything.
>
> Feng Ximing, Changchun first party secretary, December 23, 1990[16]

---

[12] "State-Owned Assets Supervision and Administrative Commission of the State Council (SASAC), "List of Central SOEs," February 9, 2015, at www.sasac.gov.cn/n86114/n86137/c1725422/content.html, accessed March 6, 2015.

[13] Thun, *Changing Lanes in China*, 181.

[14] *Changchun nianjian, 1988* (Changchun City Yearbook, 1988) (Changchun: Jilin renmin chubanshe, 1988), 286.

[15] The Changchun Tractor Factory underwent substantial management reforms in 1991 and was eventually split up and privatized, with its main production absorbed by the FAW. Changchun Coach and Railway Car companies are now limited liability companies (*youxian gongsi*, 有限公司), subsidiaries of the China National Rail Corporation Ltd. (CNR), a large central SOE headquartered in Beijing.

[16] Feng Ximing, "Jianchi yi jingji wei zhongxin, qieshi jiaqiang dangde jianshe, ba shehuizhuyi xiandaihua shiye jixu tuixiang qianjin: 1990 nian 12 yue 23 ri zai Zhonggong Changchun shiwei

Changchun in the 1980s, like many cities in China, faced both dire capital shortages and pressing needs for investments in urban infrastructure and technological renovation. Throughout the decade, Changchun municipal officials eagerly embraced the reform atmosphere to encourage the growth of an embryonic private and commercial sector. As in Harbin, the emergence of petty laborers and small-scale entrepreneurs began in specific parts of the city, some heirs to historical commercial traditions and others simply located near concentrations of idle workers with unmet commercial needs. Also similar to the conditions in Harbin, these small firms and individual laborers benefited from their informal appropriation of property, with tacit and sometimes explicit approval from the Changchun urban authorities.

In dealings with urban planning, property rights, and land markets, Changchun's policies demonstrate a distinct political logic of targeting public investment in potentially unstable communities. At the beginning of the 1980s, housing renovation was concentrated in the city's poorest and most overcrowded areas and in those neighborhoods most likely to absorb returnees from the countryside. Toward the end of the decade, efforts turned to work units undergoing reforms or facing wage arrears. The critical difference between Changchun and Harbin, however, was the high level of coordination among bureaucratic units in Changchun, as opposed to the decentralized and embedded nature of the Harbin bureaucracy.

The Restoration of Entrepreneurship and the Private Economy

Changchun's urban workforce in the early 1980s was overwhelmingly composed of employees at public enterprises in both the industrial and commercial sectors. In 1980, labor statistics indicate that Changchun was home to 649,849 workers at SOEs, of whom 24 percent were employed at central-level SOEs, 18 percent at provincial SOEs, 35 percent at municipal SOEs, and the remaining 23 percent at the county level or below.[17] Of the citywide total of 950,785 workers, 59 percent were employed in the industrial sector.[18] By the early 1980s, the city's public sector was already in crisis, and unemployment loomed large in the fears of local officials. Official statistics indicate that in 1980, 119,200 people in the city were "awaiting assignment" (*dai fenpei*, 待分配) and that number was

qijie liuci quantishang de baogao (zhaiyao)" (Adhere to the Economy as the Center of Building to Strengthen the Party, Continue to Push Forward the Cause of Socialist Modernization: Speech to the Sixth Session of the Seventh Plenum of the Changchun CCP, December 23, 1990 [excerpt]), in *Changchun nianjian, 1991*(Changchun Yearbook, 1991) (Changchun: Jilin renmin chubanshe, 1991), 1.

[17] *Changchun shi zhi: Laodong zhi* (Changchun Labor Gazetteer) (Changchun: Changchun shi difangzhi bianzuan weiyuanhui, 2006), 53.

[18] Ibid., 54; 2.2 percent were in the primary or agricultural sector and the remaining 35 percent in the tertiary or services sector. These data only include workers in Changchun's five urban districts (*shiqu*, 市区) at the time.

expected to reach 155,000 by 1985. The unemployed consisted mostly of youth returned from the countryside, recent graduates, or employees linked to public enterprises that could not absorb or pay them.[19]

Officials from the Municipal Bureau of Industry and Commerce (MBIC) and the Labor Bureau concluded that it would be necessary to eliminate the "iron rice bowl" mentality, which had led urban residents to expect employment in public enterprises and birth-to-death social welfare. In addition to rehabilitating the public sector, these bureaus encouraged growth outside the public sector. The bureaus produced decisions that stressed that "efforts should be made to encourage individuals voluntarily to organize co-operatives and co-operative business groups by raising funds themselves." They affirmed that it was "necessary to allow individual laborers (*geti hu*, 个体户) to earn a living on their own if the laws permit and others are not exploited." Practically, the bureaus concluded that "people who engage in individual businesses must be given a green light and allowed to bring their children and one or two apprentices [into their businesses]." To demonstrate support for the private sector, the city exempted newly established small businesses from enterprise or operations taxes for one year.[20] By 1985, the MBIC had officially registered 26,183 such shops or laborers, a roster that employed more than 30,000 people and used more than 215 million RMB in operating capital, all privately generated.[21]

Support for the embryonic private sector included property policies that allocated specific places for new firms and workers, some of which had been prerevolutionary commercial areas and others that surrounded large factory compounds and could service densely populated areas. In the area surrounding People's Square (the symbolic city center) and the train station, small commercial clusters emerged near major transportation arteries.[22] These architecturally dense and highly populated areas had prerevolutionary architecture that left the streets with accessible building façades and high foot traffic, conditions conducive to repair shops, food stores, and commercial activities. A survey conducted by the MBIC estimated that by 1986 these areas

---

[19] *Changchun ribao* (Changchun Daily), October 18, 1980. Labor statistics in Changchun estimate a total of 248,440 "intellectuals and youth" were sent down to the countryside or went down voluntarily between 1961 and 1981 as part of the "Up to the Mountains and Down to the Villages" (*shangshan xiaxiang*, 上山下乡) campaign. In Harbin, the numbers are comparable (relative to Harbin's larger population): 316,347 such people between 1968 and 1979. Data from *Changchun shi zhi: Laodong zhi*, 95–7; *Ha'erbin shi zhi: Laodong, renshi, dang'an* (Harbin Labor, Personnel, and Archives Gazetteer) (Ha'erbin: Heilongjiang renmin chubanshe, 1997), 42.

[20] "Other Reports on Unemployment: Changchun Employment Conference," Jilin Radio, in BBC Summary of World Broadcasts, November 7, 1980. The directives specifically mentioned employment opportunities for youth returning from the countryside.

[21] *Changchun shi zhi: Gongshang xingzheng guanli zhi*, 80.

[22] For example, Changjiang, Dama, Chongqing, and Guiyang Roads.

were the most developed commercial centers in the city, each with a concentration of more than two hundred small firms and more than 500 workers. Moreover, the areas were becoming markets that reached well beyond neighborhood needs; the MBIC estimated that these areas saw total traffic of 100,000 to 200,000 people per day, many from outside the city, making the nascent commercial centers important to the provincial economy as well as to the city itself.[23] Secondary markets also emerged around the large industrial compounds. The same MBIC survey shows smaller clusters of one hundred to two hundred firms and 150–500 workers lying outside the city's core and overlapping with the large industrial clusters developed during the early PRC period, particularly surrounding the FAW compound to the southwest of the city center and the Changchun Coach and Railway Car factories to the west and northwest.[24]

In the early 1980s, Changchun drafted its first urban master plan of the reform period and its second in the city's postrevolutionary history. Like Harbin, Changchun acquired no new urban land in the 1980s, so the plan focused exclusively on development in the existing city areas.[25] As the MBIC was encouraging the growth of local commercial and private enterprise clusters in the early 1980s, the Urban Planning Office of the Municipal Construction Bureau was conducting investigations of land and building usage in these areas. On the basis of large-scale field investigations in 1983 and 1984 in consultation with the MBIC, the 1985 urban plan designated spaces that housed these clusters for commercial development. The plan also set aside building space for commercial activity around the industrial compounds to the city's south and east, as well as building space surrounding the major residential areas. As the Changchun 1985 Master Plan states in a section explicating its "guiding philosophy," "urban planning during reform and opening should maximize the potential of experience and flexibility" rather than overplanning and "use the energies of the grassroots" to unite urban plans and economic reform efforts.[26] In other words, local government policies regarding land and property use would follow economic activity as it developed and would support forms of use as necessary rather than directing it from above.

The 1985 plan was remarkably vague about land-use and construction goals, particularly in the city center. Yet, urban planning and construction

---

[23] Li Zhenquan, Li Chenggu, and Zhou Jianwu, "Shilun Changchun shi shangye diyu jiegou" (On the Structure of the Commercial District in Changchun), *Dili kexue* (Scientia Geographica Sinica), no. 2 (1989): 133–41.

[24] Ibid.   [25] Interview, Urban Planning Department (roundtable), June 28, 2012.

[26] Changchun shi chengshi guihuaju (Changchun City Urban Planning Bureau), "Changchun shi 1985 chengshi zongti guihua fang'an shuoming shu" (Changchun City 1985 Draft Master Plan Explanation Book) (1986), 3–4. The Urban Planning Bureau (*chengshi guihuaju*, 城市规划局) was formally established out of the Planning Office of the Ministry of Construction in 1989.

continued unabated throughout the 1980s and 1990s in response to the conditions in the city. As one urban planner put it, "[during the 1980s] the city's development direction was unsettled. Urban planning work was best carried out to give full play to experience and to coordinate with society and other bureaus to develop economically and to undertake reforms." He continued; "The road of reform is never obvious. At that time, we just knew one system, but that system would not be suitable for reform, so we conducted urban planning work in a soft [*ruan*, 软] rather than hard [*ying*, 硬] way."[27] In this sense, the urban planner conceived of the work he did in the 1980s as responding to trends developing on the ground rather than rigid implementation of preconceived land-use designations according to a state plan.

This approach to the appropriation of space and flexibility in urban planning and land use continued throughout the 1980s and into the 1990s. As in Harbin, Changchun authorities would eventually formalize spatial practices that emerged somewhat organically from the encouragement of municipal officials. A 1993 report on city construction captures the thinking about street markets with the slogan "Out of the streets and into the buildings" (*tuilu jin suo, tuilu jin yuan*, 退路进所,退路进院), remarking that commercial enterprises, which enlivened the streets, should not be treated as illegal or be "blindly demolished." Instead, buildings should make space on the first floors for the permanent development of commercial activities and storefronts.[28]

As of 2012, Changchun's economy included a relatively thriving private sector; the tertiary (services) sector had seen remarkable growth in the city and unemployment remained substantially lower than that in Harbin or Dalian. A 2010 survey of entrepreneurs' attitudes toward the private sector in Changchun gauges their perceptions of the institutional, social, and political environment of the city. The authors found that Changchun's entrepreneurs rated the city's institutional and policy environment relatively high, and that negative opinions primarily focused on industrial policies that favored large firms, although the respondents "showed knowledge that this is national policy."[29] Changchun was given relatively high scores in the following areas: government services, particularly infrastructure provision in entrepreneurial

[27] Interview, retired Changchun senior urban planner, July 19, 2009.
[28] Changchunshi tigaiwei (Changchun Municipal Restructuring Committee), "Woshi shichang tixi jianshe qude fengshuo chengguo" (Results of Building a Fruitful Market System in Our City), 1993, in *Changchun nianjian, 1993* (Changchun Yearbook, 1993) (Changchun: Jilin renmin chubanshe, 1993), 49–52.
[29] Li Xueling, Wang Lijun, and Yao Yiwei, "Chengshi chuangye zhidu huanjing manyi de pingjia yanjiu: Yi Changchun shi wei lie" (Evaluation Research on the Satisfaction of Urban Entrepreneurs with the Institutional Environment: Changchun City as an Example), *Chengshi fazhan yanjiu* (Urban Studies), no. 10 (2010): 4.

clusters; the cultural environment, as entrepreneurs in the city enjoyed a high status and "good relationships with local officials" because many entrepreneurial clusters grew out of "dead spots during the 1980s"; and, finally, property-rights protection, which achieved close to a perfect score in the survey.[30]

In explaining the growth of the private sector in China during the first two decades of reform, Kellee Tsai has argued that "informal and adaptive strategies by entrepreneurs have both reflected and foreshadowed far-reaching changes in the formal policy environment governing the private sector since the Chinese Communist Party consolidated its power on the mainland."[31] The experiences of Changchun and Harbin show the ways in which local states were adaptive to change and complicit in the emergence of the private sector. In Changchun, the MBIC saw the burgeoning entrepreneurial sector as a way to absorb excess labor from the public sector as well as returnees from the countryside, stabilizing employment in the city and simultaneously opening an avenue for growth outside the moribund heavy industrial base. Indeed, local officials adopted proactive policies to encourage the growth of the private sector, even if the classic formal institutions we associate with the private economy – private property rights, labor contract enforcement, and so forth – were absent. Moreover, this encouragement and adaptation extended to the realm of land use and physical property use; local officials permitted the informal appropriation of urban buildings and land for the emerging private sector, and these informal but tacitly approved practices were later formalized in urban plans. In this sense, urban planning practices in Changchun during the early reform period sought to maximize flexibility regarding the use of urban land and space in the course of an uncertain economic transition.

Housing and Redistribution: The Politics of Stability

The major work of urban construction in Changchun in the 1980s and early 1990s showcases the nature of political bargaining to ensure political stability

---

[30] Ibid., 5–7. The term "property-rights protection" (*chanquan baohu*, 产权保护) refers to rights to space and land as well as firm resources and intellectual property.
[31] Kellee S. Tsai, *Capitalism without Democracy: The Private Sector in Contemporary* China (Ithaca, NY: Cornell University Press, 2007), 45. For similar perspectives, see also Bruce J. Dickson, *Red Capitalists in China: The Party, Private Entrepreneurs, and Prospects for Political Change* (Cambridge: Cambridge University Press, 2003), 72; Susan Young, *Private Business and Economic Reform in China* (Armonk, NY: M. E. Sharpe, 1995). On entrepreneurs, see David L. Wank, *Commodifying Communism: Business, Trust, and Politics in a Chinese City* (Cambridge: Cambridge University Press, 1999); Doug Guthrie, *Dragon in a Three-Piece Suit: The Emergence of Capitalism in China* (Princeton, NJ: Princeton University Press, 1999); Margaret M. Pearson, *China's New Business Elite: The Political Consequences of Economic Reform* (Berkeley: University of California Press, 1997).

and maximize future potential for growth. The decade began with massive housing investment concentrated in the city's heart, aimed at renovating Changchun's most visible "slums" (*penghuqu*, 棚户区, or *weifang*, 危房), and construction of new residential neighborhoods to absorb the returnees from the countryside. As Changchun began implementing piecemeal reforms to public enterprises in the middle of the decade, housing investment and ownership reforms were undertaken in ways that both targeted potential losers of the reforms and reasserted the municipal government's administrative control over urban land.

The early 1980s featured a national push for housing construction in all of China's major cities, necessitated by the collapse of urban construction during the Cultural Revolution and the ongoing return of urban residents from the countryside after 1978. In 1980, 62.2 percent of fixed-asset investment (FAI) in Changchun was devoted to housing and infrastructure construction (as opposed to capital construction or technological upgrading in SOEs).[32] Also in 1980, the city completed 1.145 million square meters of housing construction, a 58.7 percent increase over that in 1979.[33]

Many of the first targets were areas around the Yitong River to the city's east, commonly called the "old city" because it was the first area to be settled in Changchun. One of the first major projects in the 1980s was the large-scale renovation of Peach Blossom Road (Taoyuan Lu) on the western bank of the river, an area with architecture dating back to the 1930s. This area, which was little more than two square hectares yet was home to more than twenty-five hundred people in 1980, had been managed by the Municipal Housing Department since 1949. As in many of the city's designated "slums," households commonly lacked running water, indoor plumbing, and kitchens; single-room homes typically housed multigenerational families. According to a senior urban planner at the time, the guiding philosophy of the project was to "expand the scope of land use, protect the return rights of the original residents, and give every household 45 square meters." The first floors of each of the ninety-two new buildings were reserved for commercial space: "Because residents in the area face difficulties from the economic reforms, we must preserve space for expansion of employment into the service industries."[34] The project involved 5 million RMB in investment from the national level and some investment from the city level. The city's contributions were dispersed primarily to returnees from the countryside through a subsidization

[32] Xinhua, April 15, 1981. Through most of the 1970s, this number hovered around 30 percent of FAI in urban infrastructure and 60 percent in SOEs. *Jilin tongji nianjian, 1987* (Jilin Statistical Yearbook, 1987) (Beijing: Zhongguo tongji chubanshe, 1987).

[33] Xinhua, April 15, 1981.

[34] Yu Chunlin, "Changchun shi Taoyuan lu penghuqu gaijian guihua" (Renovation Plan for the Peach Blossom Road Slums in Changchun City), *Zhuzhai keji* (Housing Science) no. 8 (1986): 29–31. Yu Chunlin was the vice director of the housing office at the time.

scheme that entitled returnees to homes on the basis of the length of time that they were out of the city and their marital status.[35]

The funding schemes for these renovation projects differed significantly from those in Harbin, where work units that possessed land-use rights commodified housing on their own terms with the consent of the municipal authorities, but without their participation. In Harbin, this pattern resulted in stagnation and conflict in later years, when residents organized to resist relocation and to fight the municipal government's claim to land. In Changchun, however, projects early in the 1980s and throughout the decade involved coordination among bureaucratic units under the assertive control of what would become the city's LMB. In one such project, also located in the old city on the banks of the Yitong River, some of the "slum" buildings subject to renovation belonged to work units in the area. In 1982, renovations began in Quan'an Square in Nanguan district, to place eight hundred families, mostly multigenerational households with countryside returnees, in new homes. The financing arrangement was considered experimental (*shidian*, 试点) for its combination of funding from the Housing Bureau and from the residents themselves, a model closer to homeownership than was typical of housing institutions at the time. The project used approximately 80,000 RMB from the Housing Bureau and 4,000 RMB of the residents' own contributions.[36] The first phase was completed within two years and received high praise; Liu Zhiming, the vice director of the Changchun Housing Bureau at the time, waxed poetic about the degree of harmony among residents, urban planners, and architects, who debated several proposals and together decided on the ultimate plan.[37]

The second phase enlarged the project not only physically but also in political importance and bureaucratic scope. It involved more than 41 million RMB in investment, three-quarters of it from the city construction fund and the remaining quarter from the national level and from the residents. During this

---

[35] *Changchun shi zhi: Laodong zhi*, 108–9. It is not surprising that many of the returnees from the countryside had family connections in the more downtrodden parts of town and resettled in the most crowded areas. Thomas Bernstein's study of the origins of the movement reveal that it was at least in part a response to unemployment pressures in the city, and therefore many youths who originally departed for the countryside were those unable to continue their educations or to find work in the cities. See Thomas P. Bernstein, *Up to the Mountains and Down to the Villages: The Transfer of Youth from Urban to Rural China* (New Haven, CT: Yale University Press, 1977), 33–44, and ch. 6 on early problems of resettlement even before Mao's death and the initiation of reforms.

[36] The burden fell primarily to the bureau, but after all these were mostly impoverished or returnee households.

[37] Liu Zhiming, "Jiucheng gaizao guihua yu shixian: Changchun shi Quan'an guangchang jiu zhuzhaiqu gaizao gaikuang" (Planning and Implementation in Renovating the Old City: Renovation of Changchun City's Quan'an Square), *Zhuzhai keji* (Housing Science) no. 10 (1983): 6–7, 26.

phase, the Housing Bureau engaged with enterprises to renovate the housing under their purview. According to Liu, this stage was less harmonious, stirring up debates about who should maintain the complexes after completion, the Housing Bureau or the work units whose employees occupied the buildings. In the end, a compromise was reached, whereby the Housing Bureau and the work units would split management responsibilities (and de facto ownership) equally. Although various work units would continue to manage one-half of the new building space, the Housing Bureau actually gained net assets from renovations funded by the city's enterprises.[38] For the public facilities and infrastructure that surrounded the new compounds, responsibilities were shared in a system called the "big platform" (*da pingtai*, 大平台), in which multiple municipal bureaucracies shouldered financial and administrative responsibilities for different portions of a project under the leadership of the Housing Bureau. In this case, for example, road widening and renovations fell to the Ministry of Construction (MoC), but in return all road-use fees would accrue to the MoC after completion. Water and heat facilities were the burden of the Public Utilities Bureau, but they gained from the usage fees. Commercial space was the responsibility of the MBIC, which would benefit from the taxes paid by the commercial users.[39]

This pattern by which the Housing Bureau consolidated administrative authority over urban construction, renovation, and management continued as Changchun commenced reforms of public enterprises and their attendant facilities in the 1980s.[40] As in Harbin, Changchun's municipal authorities gradually began to undertake a variety of politically difficult enterprise reforms without the benefit of large influxes of foreign capital. Enterprise reforms first focused on the ownership structure and the internal structure. Ownership reforms, as in Harbin and even Dalian, initially involved contracting management responsibility and devolving control over enterprise operations to managers who would encourage firms to produce above-plan quotas for the market.[41]

[38] The structure of the "city construction fund" (*chengjian zijin*, 城建资金) fluctuated year to year, but it was primarily composed of enterprise and operations taxes as well as public utility and road fees, which were paid by the enterprises rather than by the residents.
[39] Liu Zhiming, "Jiucheng gaizao guihua yu shixian," 6–9.
[40] The exact same method of utilizing the city construction fund for renovation and the "big platform" for ancillary goods provision was followed in at least nine other projects between 1986 and 1988, totaling more than 120,000 square meters of space. In these cases, work units and enterprises that contributed substantial amounts to the construction fund received preferential pricing from state-owned construction companies for renovation of their own facilities. *Changchun nianjian, 1988* (Changchun Yearbook, 1988) (Changchun: Jilin renmin chubanshe, 1988), 229.
[41] Wu Yixia, "Jiefang sixiang, shenhua gaige, wei zhenxing Changchun nuli fendou (zhai yao)," 5–6.

Reforms to ownership and responsibility at the top of the enterprises were less controversial than the internal policies that retracted social welfare provisions and introduced wage reforms. Whereas in some places the devolution of authority over wages and bonuses resulted in enterprise managers' increasing payments to their workers (even at the expense of the firms' already sagging bottom lines), many Changchun enterprises were in such dire straits that they accumulated wage arrears.[42] These reforms, especially in the midst of macroeconomic instability and inflation in 1988 and 1989, generated no small amount of unrest. First Party Secretary Feng Ximing reflected in 1990 that "instability at factories and work units has been the primary obstacle to implementing reforms." Similarly, reports from the research office of the Changchun Party Committee state that production levels at many of the city's enterprises were reduced to half or production stopped altogether.[43] An economics professor recalled the period as one of many "contradictions": "To be productive, enterprises had to enact reforms, but workers would stage many protests and the enterprises could not implement the reforms."[44] He continued that the city was in a state of anxiety. Changchun residents were aware that other parts of the country were becoming wealthy, while they were anticipating impending unemployment and shortages and were focused on potential ways in

[42] This was apparently especially the case at some larger SOEs, such as the tractor, bicycle, and washing machine factories, some of the first factories to face bankruptcy in the early 1990s. For reports of unrest at these enterprises caused by nonpayment of wages, see *Changchun nianjian, 1989* (Changchun Yearbook, 1989) (Changchun: Jilin renmin chubanshe, 1989), 51; *Changchun ribao*, May 3, 1988; May 5, 1988. Changchun's workers were also active in the spring of 1989. At least sixteen "ringleaders" were arrested at the FAW for initiating strikes and protests all over the city. They supposedly had organized at least one year prior to June 1989 and were waiting for the proper time. Mayor Shang Zhanling also cited groups of workers rushing factory floors to recruit workers and to stage strikes as well as to block intersections. See "Counter-Revolutionary Clique Arrested in Changchun," Jilin Provincial Service, July 8, 1989, in BBC Summary of World Broadcasts: The Far East, FE/0507/B2/1, July 13, 1989; "Mayor of Changchun Urges Protesters to Act 'Reasonably,'" BBC Summary of World Broadcasts, June 8, 1989. On devolution and increased wages, see Edward Steinfeld, *Forging Reform in China: The Fate of State-Owned Industry* (Cambridge: Cambridge University Press, 1998), 86, 112, who examines the case of Anshan Iron and Steel.

[43] Feng Ximing, "Jianchi yi jingji wei zhongxin, qieshi jiaqiang dangde jianshe ba shehuizhuyi xiandaihua shiye jixu tui xiang qianjin," 3, 41. In 1988, 1,088 of the 6,474 "letters and visits" complaints to government offices concerned nonpayment of wages. *Changchun nianjian, 1989*, 144.

[44] Moreover, inflation hit Changchun particularly hard in the late 1980s. Relative to the rest of the country, prices were low in Changchun prior to August 1988, when the costs of daily commodities increased 25.6 percent within one month, much higher than the national average. *Changchun nianjian, 1989*, 61. One reporter even states that people in Beijing referred to residents of Changchun as "northeastern tigers" during the 1980s because the low inflation made their purchasing power higher than that of Beijingers. Li Xia, "The Changchun Economic and Technological Development Zone: Trying to Turn China's Northeast Around," *China Today* (December 1996): 25–7.

which the local government was failing the city: "It was very clear that Changchun was backward."[45]

In this climate, the Real Estate Bureau undertook large-scale housing commodification as a way to liquidate some enterprise assets and to placate workers by redistributing assets.[46] Housing commodification and the outright sale (transfer of full ownership) of public housing did not occur in most of China until 1998, when the State Council issued a landmark decree ending public housing and encouraging commodification.[47] Changchun also initiated massive housing reform and commodification in the late 1990s and early 2000s, but its methods had their roots in reforms initiated out of necessity more than a decade earlier. In 1988, city officials had made the case that enterprises lacked the capital to maintain the housing compounds and their ancillary facilities: "Nurseries have insufficient rooms inside or play-space outside. Public green areas are trampled and constructed upon; some have become office space, some have become residential areas, and some have become spontaneous markets."[48]

Establishing Administrative Power over Land and Property

Changchun municipal authorities projected administrative power by systematically routinizing the management of land and property markets. Unlike in Dalian, they did not pursue their own monopoly over land control, but rather they sought to bureaucratize the process of land and property exchange in a way that positioned these activities under the exclusive regulatory authority of the urban government. The Urban Planning Bureau (UPB) was established in 1989 to facilitate rehabilitation of the urban landscape by "having one office in charge of urban planning and urban management."[49] In the same year, the LMB initiated sweeping citywide campaigns to conduct building censuses and to register occupancy claims with the municipal government. Furthermore, in September 1989, the city also established the REB, which was charged with managing property rights over land.

From its inception, the UPB, newly independent of the MoC, had marching orders to work closely with the LMB and the REB. This alliance set the stage for concentrated regulatory authority over land politics that would facilitate enforcement of Changchun's rules about land and property. In the parlance of the city's own annals, the administrative changes signaled a "new stage for the management

---

[45] Interview, July 15, 2009.

[46] The Real Estate Bureau was the product of a consolidation of the Housing Bureau and the Real Estate Management Office (later the Real Estate Management Bureau) of the City Construction Committee. I refer to it simply as the Real Estate Bureau (REB).

[47] State Council Document [1998] 23, "Guowuyuan guanyu jinyibu shenhua chengzhen zhufang zhidu gaige jiakuai zhufang jianshe de tongzhi" (Notice on Further Deepening Reform in the Urban Housing System and Accelerating Housing Construction), at www.ggj.gov.cn/vfggw/qtfg/200806/t20080610_262964.htm, accessed February 9, 2015.

[48] *Changchun nianjian*, 1989, 56.   [49] Changchun City Document 45 (1988).

of land assets in Changchun."[50] The division of labor among the agencies was relatively clear: The LMB was the accountant and owner-manager of urban land, the real estate authorities were charged with leasing out land to generate capital, and those at the UPB were the strategic planners and enforcers of the city's plans for the urban landscape. Whereas in Harbin policies in the 1980s decentralized and fragmented authority over urban land, pitting the UPB against the MBIC and the housing authorities, in Changchun personnel staffing in these agencies frequently moved back and forth, and flexibility in urban plans allowed them to maximize growth, control over land, and political stability. According to interviewees who worked in the UPB in the early 1990s, there were few conflicts among the agencies, and the key motivation was the perceived crisis in city revenue in the late 1980s and the readily visible dilapidation of the urban environment. One former official remarked that "all of the offices in charge of land understood that in order for the problems [in the city's economy] to be solved, we had to solve the problems of the city's layout, and the only way to have money to do that would be to use the land."[51]

By 1989, the LMB and the Real Estate Office circulated no fewer than seven directives clarifying the rights to control, generate income from, and transfer urban land.[52] None of the regulations appropriated control of SOE-controlled land – and work-unit–controlled land constituted an estimated 82 percent of the city's five core urban districts in 1989[53] – but the introduction of extensive regulations on the exchange of use and occupancy rights moved land and property transactions firmly into the realm of municipal monitoring and administration rather than leaving them entirely to owner units (i.e., enterprises) and beyond the reach of the municipal authorities. The registration drive for property rights over urban housing, for example, was rationalized as follows:

The reason for this policy of real estate registration was the confusion over property rights and records as a result of the legacy of private and work-unit certificate diversity. Many work units owned and managed the real estate and state-owned land that they used. Because organizations have changed, property rights have changed many times, and land-use rights have changed several times, but many records have not been transferred over a long period after undergoing these procedures; because many buildings have been privatized but not gone through sale procedures, the records are incomplete.[54]

[50] *Changchun nianjian*, 1989, 302–3.
[51] Interview, former vice director of the UPB and presently professor of urban planning and architecture, Jilin University, July 14, 2009.
[52] These included the Changchun City Real Estate and Building Management Guidelines, the Changchun City Supplemental Directive for Managing the Transfer of Real Estate, the Notice on Imposing a Private-Use Fee for State Land, the Regulations on Several Issues Regarding Registration Fees for Land Use, the Changchun City Residential Area Post-Construction Management Regulations on Fees for the Exchange of Land Holdings, the Regulations and Standards for Compensation in Surrounding Areas during Renovation and Demolition Projects, and the Regulations for Registration and Approval of Land-Use Plans.
[53] *Changchun nianjian*, 1989, 302.
[54] *Changchun shi zhi: Tudi zhi* (Changchun City Land Gazetteer) (Changchun: Jilin renmin chubanshe, 1998), 178.

The campaign required the issuance of new certificates and centralized dispute resolution at the county or district level, but nonetheless it respected the autonomy of the large work units within the city limits: These "land-owners" would investigate actual practices on their properties with their own records and modify certificates of ownership and use accordingly.[55] In 1989 the LMB alone handed out 4,697 deeds to work units and 3,925 deeds to private actors, all working within strict guidelines under the slogan "Without hastily approving one inch of land, without issuing one incorrect certificate."[56] The Real Estate Office, now possessing extensive records of ownership, immediately began to lease out land. Revenue in 1989 from land-use fees exceeded 2.12 million RMB, and the office oversaw 1,792 real estate development or exchange contracts worth more than 13.87 million RMB during the first three months of the Real Estate Office's existence (September through December 1989), generating 463,000 RMB in taxes and 342,000 RMB in fees.[57] Table 6.1 displays data on the growth of the real estate industry in Changchun from 1991 through 1996. The industry generated hundreds of millions of RMB in capital each year through land conveyances (*churang,* 出让), some of which accrued directly to the municipal government but all of which produced municipal revenue in fees and taxes.

TABLE 6.1. *Real Estate Development in Changchun, 1991–1996*

	1991	1992	1993	1994	1995	1996
Land developed (sq. km)		19.94	12.92	4.94	9.27	
Land reclaimed from waste (sq. km)		1.18	1.31	4.49	.19	
Land registrations (#)				719,766	24,860	
Land transfer fees (million RMB)		17.38	21.66	57.01	67.99	47
Construction land (sq. km)	5.96	7.26	9.81	6.92	3.72	
Illegal construction cases solved (#)	110	69	326	417	322	814
Real estate firms (#)	121	133	125	183		
Real estate firm employees (#)	11,986	14,731	14,684	15,392		

Source: Changchun nianjian (Changchun Yearbooks), various years.[58]

[55] Ibid., 179.   [56] *Changchun nianjian, 1989,* 303.   [57] Ibid., 303.
[58] Ideally, the yearbooks would provide longitudinal data for each category, but unfortunately this is not the case.

Throughout the late 1980s and the 1990s, considerably ahead of national large-scale housing privatization, Changchun's LMB and REB worked together and in tandem with enterprise reforms to liquidate land assets and to maximize the municipal government's involvement in housing construction, privatization, and distribution as well as its administrative control over the SOE land-conversion process. Whereas enterprises and work units in many cities were leasing and allocating land without municipal involvement or approval, Changchun authorities made great efforts to bureaucratize and regulate land transactions, allowing enterprises to capitalize on their land holdings – but not without paying the fees and taxes that accrued to municipal coffers.[59] Housing and property rights were used as a form of redistribution in Changchun, but under the firm bureaucratic control of the UPB, LMB, and REB. I provide a summary of their notable administrative activities and the major housing reforms in Tables 6.2 and 6.3.

Though the three agencies were established in 1989 with 82 percent of urban land under the control of work units, the ratio had changed substantially by 1995, with 20 percent of urban land for construction under the control of central SOEs, 40 percent under the control of collectives and local SOEs, and 40 percent under private control (with rents accruing to the municipal government).[60] By 1999, when the rest of the country was also undergoing major housing reforms, the Changchun REB was a "national outstanding" office for the "scientific" management of property rights and urban land assets.[61] The REB administered the preferential pricing of housing privatization for work units to prevent enterprises from inflating prices to resolve their own debts: "Anything else is a violation of the workers' rights."[62] For many factories whose housing facilities were dilapidated and insufficient, the REB worked

[59] In addition to the previous chapter on Harbin, see You-tien Hsing, *The Great Urban Transformation: Politics of Land and Property in China* (Oxford: Oxford University Press, 2010). See also idem, "Land and Territorial Politics in Urban China," *China Quarterly* no. 187 (2006): 575–91; Peter Ho, "Who Owns China's Land? Policies, Property Rights, and Deliberate Institutional Ambiguity," *China Quarterly*, no. 166 (2001): 394–421.

[60] Calculations are my own based on yearbook data. These estimates are conservative since the 1996 yearbook displays data on urban land for construction throughout the city's jurisdiction, rather than only the five core districts referenced in the 1989 data. Therefore, much of the 40 percent of urban construction land for collectives was rural land controlled by TVEs; that means that the actual proportion of land leased out was likely to be much higher than 40 percent. *Changchun nianjian, 1996* (Changchun Yearbook, 1996) (Changchun: Jilin renmin chubanshe, 1996), 143.

[61] Li Shu, "Zhengfu gongzuo baogao" (Report on the Work of the Government), 2000, in *Changchun nianjian, 2001* (Changchun Yearbook, 2001) (Changchun: Changchun chubanshe, 2001), 4.

[62] Hui Chen and Li Lin, "Shenhua zhufang zhidu gaige tuijin zhufang fenpei huobihua" (Deepening Reforms in Housing Distribution and Commodification), in *Changchun nianjian, 2002* (Changchun Yearbook, 2002) (Changchun: Changchun chubanshe, 2002), 13.

TABLE 6.2. *Administrative Land Activities in Changchun, 1990–1998*

Year	Administrative activities
1990	Campaign to produce, record, map, deed, and photocopy every property registration; Changchun one of the national leaders in property-rights management
1991	Selected as one of the fourteen best cities in terms of property-rights management
1992	Drafted preferential regulations for the leasing of land to foreign holders in the development zones
1993	Commercial area construction financed through land conveyances; decisions regarding preferential commercial leases for extant occupants in commercial areas
1994	Decision on using the city construction fund, composed in part of fees and taxes collected by the REB, for resettling residents and for renovations
1995	Strengthened regulation over land conveyance fees, generating 3 million RMB in fees and taxes from these transactions; media campaign to heighten awareness of proper land use, including 14 TV appearances, 5 public meetings, 7 art projects, 213 consulting stations, and 198 posted notices
1996	Two decisions regarding land prices to exercise municipal control over SOE leasing
1997	Land-rights adjudication the focus of the LMB; SOEs required to register land-usage rights with the LMB before the leasing of land; citywide campaign to register SOE land holdings
1998	Dealt with the reallocation of the land of 63 enterprises, generating 800 million RMB in income from the value of the land

with the enterprises and the workers to establish a "housing distribution fund." Under this funding arrangement, the REB leased land to private developers for the construction of new, economic worker housing, while the LMB and REB contributed to the construction by waiving conveyance fees and real estate taxes, directing the forgone capital back into construction. The result was a boost in worker morale and some resolution to the social welfare problems. According to the REB:

Workers at the Eastern Water Pump and the 793 Factory could not believe their eyes when construction [on new housing] began and a housing complex appeared from the ground. It was not until they began moving in that people finally believed what was in front of them. One worker said, "Our factory is troubled, but the officials could still use 100 percent of their heart and blood to build us housing, so we also want to use 100 percent of our strength to work for 100 percent quality and to make 100 percent of a contribution."[63]

---

[63] Quoted in ibid., 14–15.

TABLE 6.3. *Housing Reforms in Changchun, 1990–1999*

Year	Housing reform efforts
1990	Jiemin Road renovation project, involving 119 buildings and 3,407 people, all of whom were resettled; construction assumed by the REB 34 work-unit housing compounds relocated, only 12 returned to work-unit control
1991	All new housing administered by the REB and built by the REB-owned construction company 40 work units facing capital shortages undertake reforms using leasing methods
1992	3 major housing renovation projects moved residents back to their original housing and capitalized on the saved space for leasing
1993	Changchun Housing Institution Reform Proposal allows leasing and preferential sales for housing reform; promotes liquidation of work-unit-owned housing by preferential pricing for occupants
1994	Experimentation with preferential pricing sales begins with workers at struggling SOEs (railway car factory, subway car factory, and grounds of the old motorcycle factory)
1995	329 investigations of SOEs for unapproved construction, levied fines, and ending of construction
1996	Designated as national experimentation city for social welfare reform; sold off 2.2 million square meters of housing* for as low as 100 RMB per square meter
1997	Major housing privatization; initial participating work units: municipal government, city party committee, FAW, Jilin Tech, and research groups
1998	Economic housing (*jingji zhufang*, 经济住房) priority for poor households; designated 2.7 million square meters of economic housing; by year end REB had renovated and returned 8,921 households
1999	Major housing reforms create "craze" (*fanggai re*, 房改热); through September alone, REB and LMB assisted city and central-level units in selling more than 10 million square meters of space, generating 133 million RMB in income for the city

*Especially at the 28 annexed and 18 bankrupt work units
Source: Compiled from *Changchun nianjian* (Changchun Yearbook), various years.

The model of encouraging moribund enterprises to dispose of (*chuzhi*, 处置) land holdings through leasing, assisted by the REB and LMB,[64] continued for the next several years under the policy of "using land reform to encourage enterprise reform" (*yi digai cu qigai*, 以地改促企改). Changchun land and real estate officials insisted on their involvement in the land-transfer process, even

[64] The LMB merged with the Mineral Resources Bureau in 2000 to form the Land Resources Bureau under the National Ministry of Land Resources. *Changchun nianjian*, 2002, 161.

when SOEs were undergoing ownership restructuring or privatization. It was argued that because of the poor understanding of the value of land of these enterprises and because of their weak positions, land would be undervalued absent the intervention of the municipal authorities. The solution was not, as in Dalian, to have the state dispose of SOE land holdings on its own, but rather to ensure that the process was procedurally thorough – to have the state administer the leases and to turn over the lease revenue to the SOEs.[65]

The year 1998 saw the most bankruptcies, firm closures, and layoffs (79,000 in one year alone) in the city's history. Reforms were induced through mergers and acquisitions, privatization, and leasing, as well as outright firm closures. At least twenty-six enterprises accepted closure, laying off a cumulative 15,628 workers, less than one-third of whom were eligible for support from old-age insurance institutions. City officials set explicit goals of giving workers optimal housing prices and then reclaiming and "capitalizing" (*zibenhua*, 资本化) the land of the former firm to finance the social welfare burdens that persisted even after the enterprises were closed.[66]

Officials in Changchun's Urban Planning, Land Management, and Real Estate Management bureaus were far ahead of the national curve in exploiting land under their control to generate funds for development. Administrative and bureaucratic coordination among these agencies allowed the Changchun Municipal Government to consolidate its regulatory authority over, but not necessarily ownership of, urban land throughout the late 1980s and 1990s. This coordination was the product of a municipal government squeezed by its dependence on a single sector for its economic survival, fears of instability in reforming the defunct state sector, and knowledge that preferential policies and access to FDI were not immediately en route to rescue the local economy. The same bureaucratic agencies would employ similar land policies to attract foreign investment and undertake reforms when the city was allowed to open to the global economy in the 1990s.

GLOBAL OPENING AND URBAN EXPANSION

Changchun opened to the global economy in 1992 with the State Council's approval of the city's first development zone, an economic and technology development zone (ETDZ) established to the east of the Yitong River and

---

[65] Here, Changchun authorities learned from a neighboring city, Siping, that some land bureaus could help SOEs hide land assets to protect the enterprises. On the basis of those experiences, Changchun authorities argued that city officials should act as intermediaries. See Pei Fuxiang, "Panhuo qiye tudi zichan, cujin qiye shunli zhuanzhi" (Liquidate Land Assets, Promote a Smooth Restructuring of Enterprises), in *Tudi de nahan* (Crying Out about Land), ed. Pei Fuxiang (Changchun: Jilin renmin chubanshe, 1996).

[66] *Changchun nianjian, 1999* (Changchun Yearbook, 1999) (Changchun: Jilin renmin chubanshe, 1996), 43. UPB officials rationalized and publicized this process in a 1998 campaign.

TABLE 6.4. *Changchun Land Area and Urban Area, 1985–2000 (Square Kilometers)*

	Total land area	Urban area	Urban built-up area
1985	18,881	1,116	105
1986	18,881	1,116	105
1987	18,881	1,116	105
1988	18,881	1,116	108
1990	18,881	1,116	114
1991	18,881	1,116	114
1992	18,881	1,116	114
1994	18,881	1,116	117
1995	18,881	3,116	124
1996	18,881	3,116	145
1997	18,881	3,116	145
1998	18,881	3,116	145
1999	18,881	3,116	154
2000	20,571	3,603	159

Sources: Zhongguo guotu ziyuan nianjian (Ministry of Land and Resources Yearbook), various years.

southeast of the city center in an initial space of ten kilometers that expanded to thirty kilometers by 1994 (see Table 6.4).[67] The policies for the new zone were similar to those at most of the national-level ETDZs,[68] including short-term preferential tax structures and waived administrative fees. Changchun also waived land-use fees for ten years for FIEs in the automobile, agricultural processing, high technology, and petrochemical industries.

The scarcity of capital and the abysmal conditions in the city's enterprises, as well as the increasing pressures for employment and social welfare, led the city's leaders to court foreign capital with great zeal. Mi Fengjun, Changchun's mayor and party secretary during the 1990s, declared in an English-language article that Changchun was "casting off the yoke of the traditional planned

[67] *Changchun jingji jishu kaifaqu zhi, 1992–2004* (Changchun Economic and Technology Development Zone Gazetteer, 1992–2004) (Changchun: Jilin renmin chubanshe, 2008), 33–4. As in Dalian, the area had primarily been farmland prior to the designation of the ETDZ. The acquisition process, according to official reports, involved payouts of 8,000 RMB to occupants between eighteen and thirty-five years of age and 16,000 RMB to those above the age of thirty-five, in addition to the national standard for peasants losing land for agricultural production (three times their annual income plus predetermined prices per meter for various crops).

[68] The policies were 1) 15 percent industrial tax for the first two years (as opposed to 33 percent outside the zone); 2) no enterprise management (operations) tax for the first two years and only one-half for the third through the fifth years; 3) all FIEs established before the year 2000 entitled to waived land-acquisition fees; 4) no land-use fees for ten years for targeted industries; and 5) no real estate tax for newly opened enterprises during the period while the ETDZ was awaiting national approval. *Changchun nianjian*, 1994, 453.

economic system while increasing the role of the market" and announced that the city had obtained the same economic administrative status as a province and therefore could negotiate its own investment terms.[69] The young director of the ETDZ, Yu Deman, in a widely cited article on the governing philosophy of the Changchun ETDZ, explained that "although the Changchun development zone lags seven or eight years behind the coastal city development zones," the zone would become a success "by giving full play to the 'catch-up effect' (*hou fa xiaoying,* 后发效应) to achieve 'leaping' development."[70]

Establishing a development zone in an area that was previously farmland required remarkable amounts of investment – capital the Changchun authorities did not have in 1992 and 1993. The area southeast of the Yitong River lacked even a rudimentary road system, much less high-volume transport links with national highways and capacious public goods and infrastructure.[71] The city government provided 600,000 RMB (a quarter of the city's total FAI in that year) in initial investment for transport, telecommunications, land acquisition, and office space, but that was still insufficient to attract FIEs to establish production bases in Changchun. The ETDZ Management Committee borrowed 30 million RMB from the China Development Bank, issued provincial-level bonds to raise an additional 37 million RMB, and established the Changchun Development Zone Construction Limited Liability Group for an additional 970 million RMB.[72]

The initial investments made the zone ready for the establishment of FIEs, but because preferential policies mitigated tax and fee income during the first few years, the authorities depended on capital from land leasing to fund further development. Figure 6.1 shows data on the composition of the ETDZ finances between 1993 and 2004. During the first several years of the zone, the leasing of land was critical to financing further infrastructure construction. In keeping with established patterns regarding land control inside the city's core, the development zone authorities set up an ETDZ branch office of the LMB to coordinate with the UPB. All land transactions and usage rights would go through the LMB, which worked under the direction of the ETDZ Management Committee.[73] The zone's LMB branch, after initial years of work leasing out land to FIEs, began to work with the MBIC to initiate what Yu Deman called a "dual track" reform process for enterprises experiencing losses in the city center: "On the one hand, we constructed a modern industrial open zone

[69] Mi Fengjun, "Mayor's Message," *Zhongwai fangdichan shibao* (China International Real Estate Times), no. 13 (1994): 8.
[70] Yu Deman, "Jiakuai kaifaqu jianshe, tansuo chengshi jingying jingyan" (Boosting Construction of Development Zones as a Way of Running Cities), *Chengshi fazhan yanjiu* (Urban Studies) no. S1 (2001): 23–6. Yu mentions the seven- to eight-year gap between the founding of the Changchun ETDZ and those in the coastal cities three times in his three-page article.
[71] Li Xia, "The Changchun Economic and Technological Development Zone," 25–7.
[72] Yu Deman, " Jiakuai kaifaqu jianshe, tansuo chengshi jingying jingyan," 23–6.
[73] *Changchun jingji jishu kaifaqu zhi, 1992–2004,* 33.

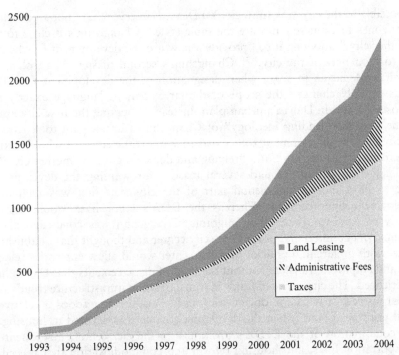

FIGURE 6.1. Revenue Composition of the Changchun Development Zone
(Million RMB)
Source: Changchun jingji jishu kaifaqu zhi, 1992–2004, 183.

and, on the other, we reformed SOEs by allowing them to move to the
development zone, vacating valuable land [in the city center] for development.
They took the capital they raised through real estate transactions to build new
and better facilities in the development zone," after which the ETDZ authorities
would help "graft on" (*jiajie*, 嫁接) foreign capital.[74] Forty SOEs underwent
such a process in the 1990s, and the introduction of foreign capital and
ownership reforms helped induce further competitiveness in these enterprises.[75]

This process was similar to the one that occurred in Dalian during the
"enterprise relocation" campaign in the 1990s, but the differences in the
development zones themselves were of great importance for the level of integration between the development zones and their host cities. In contrast to
Dalian's DDA, Changchun's ETDZ is only five kilometers from the city's
symbolic center at People's Square, a distance residents can walk in less than
one hour, and at least six bus routes serve the areas between the ETDZ's
nominal center at Century Square. The decision to locate the new zone as close

[74] Yu Deman, "Jiakuai kaifaqu jianshe, tansuo chengshi jingying jingyan," 23–6.   [75] Ibid.

as possible to the city was strategic. Yu Deman observes that "not all development zones in Chinese cities are the same style"; Changchun's is close to the "mother city," allowing it to "provide a new area of development for the city but to be a part of the city."[76] Changchun's second master urban plan, on which work began in 1993 when designation of the development zone had fundamentally changed the scope of the city, contains language exactly the opposite of that in Dalian's urban plan. Instead of "taking the new city area" as the key, the "leading ideology" of Changchun's urban plan took care to specify that the development zone exists to support the city as a whole, taking "the main city as the key" and "relying and depending on the mother city."[77]

Changchun authorities had several reasons for wanting the development zone to be a more fundamental part of the city. The first was related to employment opportunities. Whereas the DDA's labor base would consist mostly of rural-to-urban labor migrants, Changchun was concerned about unemployment and social order in the city center and thought that establishing a base with preferential policies near the center would allow enterprise relocation and employee transfers without the kind of displacements that Dalian had experienced. The city invested funds in transportation infrastructure (roads and buses) instead of workers' dormitories, and even into the 2000s a relatively small portion of land use in the development zone was devoted to housing.[78] The combination of the ETDZ's proximity to the city center, investment in transportation links, and housing reform and commodification that preceded the relocation of many SOEs to the development zone explains in part why Changchun experienced remarkably little suburbanization compared to other large Chinese cities.[79] Planners also hoped that the close proximity of the development zone would help ideas about "modern" management and market competition diffuse more easily throughout the city and contribute to breaking

---

[76] Ibid.

[77] *Changchun shi chengshi zongti guihua, 1996–2020: Shuoming shu* (Changchun Urban Master Plan, 1996–2020: Explanatory Book) (1997), 3.

[78] In the 1996 plan, 12.8 percent of land use was devoted to housing. In terms of overall land-use composition citywide (for urban construction land), the proportion for housing remained between 27.43 percent and 29.72 percent throughout the 1990s. Zhang Hongbo and Xu Zhenwen, "Changchun jingji jishu kaifaqu gongye buju yanjiu" (Research on the Industrial Layout in Changchun Economic and Technology Development Zone), *Changchun shifan xueyuan xuebao* (Journal of Changchun Teachers' College) no. 2 (March 2000): 70–7; Lu Shichao, Qi Yong, and Li Bingxin, "Changchun shi chengshi jianshe yongdi jiegou yanbian ji qidongli fenxi" (Study on the Evolution and Driving Force of the Urban Construction Land Structure in Changchun City), *Jilin jianzhu gongcheng xueyuan xuebao* (Journal of the Jilin Institute of Architecture and Civil Engineering) 27, no. 5 (October 2010): 46.

[79] Geographers rank Changchun's level of suburbanization as extremely low among the forty largest Chinese cities according to population. The built area of the city has remained essentially within a ten-square-kilometer area since the onset of the reforms. See Wang Qichun, Li Chenggu, and Ding Wanjun, "Changchun shi chengshi diyu jiegou tixi yanjiu" (Study on the Urban Area Structure of Changchun City), *Dili kexue* (Scientia Geographica Sinica) 21, no. 1 (February 2001): 81–8.

the "iron rice bowl" mentality that plagued attempts to reform the SOEs. One Changchun urban planner remarked, "The theory of selecting sites for development zones to the southeast, west, and northeast was to encircle (*baowei*, 包围) the large enterprises." If they were surrounded by competitors, especially in the same industries, they would be forced to become more efficient or would be induced to undergo reforms.[80]

CONCLUSION: REGULATION AND POLITICAL COMPROMISE

> I went to Detroit and I saw the Mayor and I told him that we are turning Changchun into another Detroit, making this our own Motor City. Although the one difference is that in Changchun we have good social order, whereas in Detroit, you don't dare go out at night.
>
> Vice Mayor Yin Wen, 1995[81]

Changchun is still very much a Motor City. The auto industry accounted for an astonishing 78.2 percent of industrial output in 2003, up from 35.2 percent in 1989.[82] In 2007, Changchun ranked eighth in the world in terms of automobile production (after Detroit, Toyota, Stuttgart, Turin, Wolfsburg, Tokyo, and Paris), and the city produced 80 percent of the subway cars used in Chinese urban metro systems, a promising avenue for growth given the explosion of metro construction.[83] Eric Thun's early 2000s assessment of Changchun's potential to foster the growth of local auto firms concluded with a bleak outlook; the FAW and its affiliates were plagued by the multiple pathologies of SOEs and the city government lacked the financial and political capital to nurture local suppliers who would benefit from linkages with the major manufacturers.[84] Yet, by 2010, more than half of the parts in the FAW and in FAW–VW production were supplied locally.[85]

---

[80] Interview, planner at the Changchun Urban Planning Bureau, May 2008. The planner is referring to the city's original three main economic zones: the ETDZ, a high-tech zone that had provincial status before the ETDZ, and the Auto Trade Zone. The high-tech zone, located to the northeast, merged administratively with the ETDZ in the late 1990s. Changchun has a third designated "development" zone, the Jingyuetan Open Zone, devoted to attracting tourism and recreation to the lake and forest area southeast of the city.

[81] Quoted in Patrick E. Tyler, "Changchun Journal: Motor City Keeps Communism in the Driver's Seat," *New York Times*, May 22, 1995, A4, at www.nytimes.com/1995/05/22/world/changchun-journal-motor-city-keeps-communism-in-the-driver-s-seat.html, accessed February 8, 2015.

[82] *Changchun nianjian, 2004* (Changchun Yearbook, 2004) (Changchun: Jilin renmin chubanshe, 2004), 183.

[83] Liu Mingtai, "Changchun, a City of Many Wonders," *China Daily*, November 15, 2007.

[84] Thun, *Changing Lanes in China*.

[85] Han Tianyang and Liu Mingtai, "Changchun Special: Changchun Auto Industry Growing," *China Daily*, October 19, 2010, at www.chinadaily.com/cn/cndy/2010-10/19/content_11426410.htm, accessed March 5, 2015.

In addition to these changes in the manufacturing sector, the Changchun economy has shown progress toward service transition and growth of the private sector. As early as 2004, the ratio of earnings in the public economy to the private economy in Changchun was 40:60.[86] Twenty-five years after the reforms began, this "firm-dominated" old socialist industrial base city had produced a thriving private economy. Strides toward competitiveness in the investment environment were also substantial. In 2003, a World Bank assessment ranked Changchun as seventh among medium and big cities in terms of its investment environment; the city was ranked sixth by *Forbes* among China's most hospitable cities in which to open a factory; and the Chinese government ranked Changchun thirteenth nationally in terms of its economic competitiveness.[87]

The municipal government, through bureaucratic coordination among the Urban Planning, Real Estate, and Land Management Bureaus, established itself as the sole regulator of rights to use, generate income from, and transfer urban property. Like Harbin, Changchun undertook difficult reforms to public enterprises before opening to foreign capital. In a climate of capital scarcity, the city was pressured to redistribute to residents and to upgrade urban infrastructure and, at the same time, to carry out politically contentious reforms to the city's economy. The growth of the private sector in the 1980s was the product of municipal encouragement. Officials simultaneously provided explicit support for the small-scale private sector and allowed the informal appropriation of space downtown and the surrounding industrial clusters. Once the private sector proved to be a promising avenue for reemployment and began to generate tax revenue, support for these commercial clusters became formal policy.

Housing construction and commodification served as a way to ensure stability when enterprises downsized or social welfare provisions retrenched. The difference between this process in Harbin and that in Changchun is in the concentration of regulatory authority. In Harbin, extensive decentralization to lower levels of administration and enterprises led these embedded authorities to conduct housing commodification on their own terms and to distribute control over urban space as political resources.

In Changchun, these resources were just as valuable politically, but the bureaucratic agencies involved in the control of land and property were coordinated with one another, were hierarchically controlled, and were heavily involved in the regulation of urban property. To be clear, this did not mean that the Changchun authorities always controlled urban property or were

---

[86] *Changchun nianjian, 2003* (Changchun Yearbook, 2003) (Changchun: Jilin renmin chubanshe, 2003), 37. This is a measure of GDP.

[87] "Changchun a City of Opportunity," *China Daily*, May 30, 2006, at http://topic.chinadaily. com.cn/index/cache/collection/cbsweb/source/title/changchun%3A+A+city+of+opportunity? aid=5351085, accessed March 13, 2015.

themselves the sole owners of urban land. But the administrative and regulatory roles established by these bureaucracies legitimized the municipal government as the sole allocator of the right to control, generate income from, and transfer urban property. In fact, municipal publications, including land and real estate statistics, land violation cases, and handbooks, share a strikingly consistent emphasis on process rather than outcome.

This administrative cohesion and regulatory capacity, I have suggested, result from the city's simultaneous dependence on and alienation from its largest economic constituent, the FAW and its affiliates, whose social and political burdens the city bears without enjoying the bulk of its economic fruits. Changchun's local leaders were eager to find ways to finance necessary upgrades and construction and used the control of land to generate income for the city itself and for its starved enterprises. In essence, a more concentrated capital base created a more concentrated urban bureaucracy.

In Changchun's three postreform urban plans (1985, 1996, and 2004) and in regulations governing urban space, the state (i.e., the city government) articulates a strong regulatory capacity, but it does not put forward transformative visions of Changchun's social or urban landscape. Whereas Dalian embarked on massive modernization campaigns and aspired to be the "Hong Kong of the North," Changchun aspired to be a Motor City, or China's Detroit, an identity it could have just as fittingly claimed in 1960. As the epigraphs to this chapter illustrate, Changchun's leaders and urban planners had a definite sense of what kind of city Changchun was and had limited ambitions to overhaul it. Planners' and officials' discussions of the 2004 plan contain explicit statements about the function of urban planning and the nature of urban governance. Three urban planners write in a discussion of the 2004 plan that different areas have different "essential factors" and so should receive different "spatial governance methods." They explain that the 2004 master plan was the result of extensive investigation and analysis of the "essential factors" that identify different areas and their different needs, and they warn against "blind planning" that ignores local conditions.[88] In this sense, land planning in Changchun can be seen as a technical response to the practical needs of economic change as it occurs, rather than as either a modernist vision of an entrepreneurial municipal government, like Dalian's, or as a hostage of contentious residents and uncooperative economic actors, like Harbin.

Ideologically, municipal authorities in Changchun articulated a role for the local government that primarily was not to capture or deploy economic resources, but rather to act as a reliable administrator and economic intermediary. Some of the moral economic arguments that proved powerful in

---

[88] Han Shouqing, Li Chenggu, and Zheng Wensheng, "Changchun shi chengzhen tixi de kongjian guanzhi guihua yanjiu" (Study of the Spatial Governance Plan of Changchun), *Chengshi guihua* (Urban Planning) no. 9 (2004): 81-4.

Harbin – about the state's obligation to protect the erstwhile builders of socialism from the vulnerabilities they faced under market competition – were powerful forces that shaped the use of land in Changchun. The different elements of the city's economic and social base – a large SOE, workers, collectives, and emerging entrepreneurs – were able to negotiate with the local government different rules about land control. But the dominant narrative about what Changchun's authorities owed their city emerged from the city's status of being squeezed between a very large firm not subject to local control and the requirements of reform. In this sense, real estate and land markets proved to be an ideal arena of administrative management onto which the local government could project its authority and control, promoting both a new path of economic growth as well as a new source of political authority.

7

Conclusions

Some have suggested that the entire process of economic reform in China can be viewed as a reassignment of property rights. Property rights – over firms, firm assets, land, and so forth – have changed hands between central and local levels of the state, among different intrastate agencies, and between the state and various elements of the private sector.[1] The speed and direction of this process have been dynamic, tortuous, and politically contingent rather than proceeding steadily from plan to market or toward private-property rights. Decisions about who controls land and property have been at the center of political contests for power and for recognition, in which a variety of players both inside and outside the Chinese state have staked claims. The chapters in this book have examined this "reassignment of property rights" at the national and subnational levels. Doing so has revealed a process of political bargaining over land control that contains theoretical lessons about the nature of property-rights change and empirical lessons about the role of land and property in Chinese capitalism. In this concluding chapter, I review the theoretical and empirical findings of the book, explore the argument about property rights as political bargains in comparative perspective, and finally turn to the present and future of land and capitalism in China.

THE POLITICS OF PROPERTY RIGHTS

In the first chapter of this book, I outlined a theoretical approach that positions political choice and bargaining at the center of property-rights changes. Such changes, during the modern era, are rarely imposed on societies or economies

---

[1] Jean C. Oi and Andrew G. Walder, eds., *Property Rights and Economic Reform in China* (Stanford, CA: Stanford University Press, 1999), 6.

by some exogenous forces; rather they emerge through political processes in which actors consciously seek to implement changes to property-rights arrangements. Whereas classical approaches envisage that changes in value – of land, labor, goods, and so forth – stimulate changes in the arrangements of control over property, this political approach sees value as endogenous to the political process.[2] Property assumes greater or lesser value as the result of political decisions that assign value.

Political decisions that assign or change value and property rights are the products of political bargaining and moral argument, both of which occur under conditions of uncertainty. Social and economic actors bargain over property rights as they do over the distribution of any other power resource. However, actors do not adopt positions on property rights with exclusive attention to the expected distributional gains.[3] Instead, changes in property rights typically occur amid more seismic, general transformations in the political economy, during which groups are as uncertain about the distributional gains as they are about their larger fate. State agents and social actors adopt positions on property rights as they bargain over political power and economic status in this larger and more uncertain context. Specific property-rights arrangements are not necessarily reflections of the relative power of various groups – that is, the stronger group secures more extensive property rights – but instead they may sometimes be concessions granted to groups that stand to lose power or status as a result of general social and economic change.

In such larger contexts of social transformation, ideological and moral debates about the value of property and to whom that value ought to accrue matter as much as any material interests. Fundamentally, a property right is a claim on property that is regarded as legitimate. In all societies, even those in which legal structures establish and adjudicate property-rights claims, groups and individuals attempt to persuade one another of the moral correctness or of the fairness of specific property-rights arrangements. In contemporary Western societies, these debates may involve discussions about the nature and limits to the "public good" and the status of individual and group challenges.[4] In

---

[2] For example, see David Weimer, "The Political Economy of Property Rights," in *The Political Economy of Property Rights*, ed. David Weimer (Cambridge: Cambridge University Press, 1997), 1–19. Weimer argues that property-rights systems can be treated as exogenous institutions when we view their impacts on political and economic developments, but we must analyze the emergence of property-rights systems as endogenous.

[3] Approaches to property-rights change from the rational choice institutionalist perspective look exclusively at the expected distributional gains and the relative bargaining power of the various groups. For a review, see ibid., 10–11.

[4] In the United States these issues have surfaced most recently with regard to the state's power of eminent domain. In *Kelo v. New London*, the Supreme Court upheld the city of New London's right to invoke eminent domain for private use, generating a great deal of controversy in legal and economic circles as well as in public debate. President George W. Bush even issued an executive order attempting to prevent federal takings for economic-growth purposes. Jane B. Baron,

particular, in the contexts of general social transformation when the systems of control and distribution of resources are undergoing uncertain reorganization, changes in property-rights arrangements are accompanied by processes of ideological and moral suasion. At times, these processes are dominated by state agents seeking to legitimize the new property arrangements through moral arguments. At other times, social groups stake effective claims against the state by drawing on moral arguments. In any case, the moral content of property-rights claims can be an effective constraint. When property claims are granted moral legitimacy, they become entitlements that are difficult to revoke.

The period during which contemporary China experienced its first foray into land markets illustrates the endogeneity of property rights to the political process. In Chapter 2, I tracked how national debates about the value of land changed during the 1980s – from viewing land primarily as an input to production to considering land as a source of capital accumulation. When use rights were separated from ownership rights in 1988 and markets were introduced for the exchange of use rights, state agents in Beijing and elsewhere ventured into the growth of real estate through experimentation under conditions of great uncertainty. During the period between 1988 and the end of the real-estate bubble in 1994, property and land markets were liberalized and stimulated to generate economic growth, and in particular to provide a new source of revenue for urban governments in the form of real-estate and land-use taxes. A lack of clarity regarding state ownership and decentralization of the financial system created low barriers to entry as groups both inside and outside the state attempted to "make money by developing land" (yitu shengcai, 以土生财). This rapid commodification of land and property coalesced in a real-estate bubble. In the aftermath, the CCP rearranged property rights over land yet again, but this time assigning the right to lease land and to generate capital from land markets exclusively to local governments. The decision to allow land to generate capital value – commodification – and the later decision to assign that value exclusively to local governments – fiscalization – were both political decisions that emerged from episodes of crisis and learning.

Differing systems of property-rights management emerged in the cities of Dalian, Harbin, and Changchun as a result of their different contexts of political bargaining and moral suasion. Municipal authorities in Dalian initiated land markets to enrich the local government, which enjoyed a monopoly over urban land well before local governments were designated by Beijing as the owners of state-owned land. Other potential claimants, such as firms and residents, relinquished their claims to urban land and property because of their dependence on the municipal government during the process of the reforms. In Harbin and Changchun, the municipal governments distributed control over land and property to firms and residents as part of a political strategy to secure their compliance with the economic reforms. In Harbin, such a distribution occurred haphazardly as the city authorities decentralized control over firms and neighborhoods in a climate of uncertainty and municipal crisis. In Changchun, specific parts of the urban municipal bureaucracy – the Real Estate, Land Management, and Urban Planning Bureaus – established administrative and regulatory dominance over the process of land and property exchange.

In all three cities, moral debates about the rightful claimants to urban land empowered some actors and constrained others. In Dalian, the city's monopoly over urban property – which entailed the dislocation of firms, workers, and residents – was facilitated by ideological campaigns stressing that transformation of the built environment was necessary for collective prosperity. Individual claims or noncompliance was portrayed as exactly the sort of cultural and economic backwardness that would cause Dalian to lose investment to the more forward-thinking cities in the south. Ironically, state control over urban land was depicted as a requisite for market competition.

In Harbin and Changchun, urban firms and workers sought to legitimize their claims to land and property by repurposing the moral economic discourse of the Maoist state-socialist period. The dismantling of the institutions of collective consumption, production, and ownership rapidly reversed the fates of urban state-sector workers from a privileged class of nation builders to destitute victims of the market reforms. The "lingering validity" of the socialist system of organization and the vaunted status of urban workers proved to be powerful ammunition in the struggle for urban land claims.[5] Moreover, the distribution of urban land and property in the process of the economic reforms further amplified these moral claims. Urban workers had been stripped of their jobs and their social welfare guarantees, but they were left with rights to their homes and with autonomy over the built environment. When the urban authorities later sought to dislocate such groups, they faced resistance from organized entities with perceived moral entitlements.

PROPERTY RIGHTS AND CHINA'S DEVELOPMENT STRATEGY

The reassignment of property rights over land has been central to the strategies of economic development at the national and local levels in China. Varying approaches to political and economic control of land have produced different strategies to pursue wealth during the reform era and different regimes of

[5] Ching Kwan Lee, *Against the Law: Labor Protests in China's Rustbelt and Sunbelt* (Berkeley: University of California Press, 2007), 12–13.

capital accumulation. Continued state dominance over landownership, particularly after the 1990s real-estate bubble, has enabled the Chinese Communist Party (CCP) to reconfigure its development strategy from decentralized growth to state-dominated "land-centered accumulation" to, more recently, massive urbanization engineered from above.[6]

Local property-rights regimes were developed as various subnational governments fashioned strategies for post-Mao prosperity and survival. Social groups and local governments pursued both economic growth and a reconfiguration of property rights simultaneously as the national reform priorities unfolded in the 1980s and the 1990s. Local approaches to property rights and land management were constructed to accompany different development strategies, and, in some cases, they were frequently revised through experimentation and change as the local authorities devised new approaches to accompany the new priorities.

In Dalian, the state monopoly of land and property rights was integral to the local state's dominance of the economy. Land policies enabled the local state to direct investments to specific industries and areas of the city, playing the role of arbiter between local firms and workers and pressures from the global economy. Dalian established a development zone that reconfigured the city's economic and political center of gravity through its pursuit of land expansion and land leasing. In turn, such a reconfiguration of Dalian's political economy facilitated the state's reclamation of downtown land in the 1990s in pursuit of service-sector growth. Dalian's post-Mao strategy to achieve prosperity privileged the interventionist role of the urban state; land-based revenue generation and foreign capital liberated the local state from its dependence on local firms; control of physical space thus emboldened the urban state as "planner."

In Harbin, property rights were distributed to firms and residents as part of a strategy of decentralized accumulation – encouraging groups within the local economy to pursue growth opportunities beyond the direction of the local government. Control over urban land and property was decentralized to firms as a political strategy but also in the hope that enterprises would diversify their economic activities and use land in entrepreneurial ways. Workers were expected to use their homes as a form of security as they ventured into the uncertain territory of the private sector. Formal approvals of informal appropriations of urban property for entrepreneurial activities – in the form of urban plans that designated such space and renovations that upgraded facilities without displacing the occupants – were extended as the municipal authorities pursued the growth of the private sector as a way to resolve the stagnation in the public sector. I do not mean to overstate the intentionality of Harbin's fragmented property-rights regime, but instead I wish to emphasize how

---

[6] On "land-centered accumulation," see You-tien Hsing, *The Great Urban Transformation: Politics of Land and Property in China* (Oxford: Oxford University Press, 2010).

strategies of economic growth and property management evolved simultaneously and in an ad hoc fashion.

Municipal authorities in Changchun pursued growth in real-estate and land markets as an economic strategy of growth outside the automobile sector. The city government, unlike that in Dalian, did not pursue its own monopoly over urban land and property. Instead, Changchun authorities encouraged real-estate markets that would stimulate economic growth and allow the local governments to benefit indirectly through the collection of taxes and fees but also politically from their administrative control over a new and important sector.

A key finding in this book is that at the national level the reassignment of property rights over land has not, contrary to some expectations, progressed linearly from state dominance to private control. As detailed in Chapter 2, land was commodified in the late 1980s and early 1990s, when land and property circulated more liberally and with less state dominance than would be the case thereafter. The impetus for commodification was both to generate funds for urban governments – indirectly through the collection of real-estate taxes and land-use fees and directly by leasing land in development zones – and to stimulate systemic economic growth through the creation of a new real-estate sector. Land reforms during this early period were what Huang has described as "directionally liberal" – well short of clear institutions that secure property rights and constrain the state, but nonetheless constituting sufficient marginal changes to allow for changes in economic behavior at the grass roots.[7] Just like the rural reforms that Huang argues were reversed in the 1990s, the directionally liberal land reforms were reversed as well. Land was "fiscalized" in the wake of the first experience with commodification; urban governments were granted exclusive ownership rights over urban land, and therefore they were designated as the recipients of land-use fees. At the same time, control over tax-related revenue streams and the national financial system were recentralized, leaving land-related revenue as one of the few sources of funds that local governments could actually manipulate and control. Property rights over land have been rearranged several times during the reform era in China, and the goal of each rearrangement has been to serve local and national strategies of economic development and capital accumulation.

PROPERTY RIGHTS AS POLITICAL BARGAINS: CHINA
IN COMPARATIVE PERSPECTIVE

Adopting a political theory of property rights has implications for debates within political science and related fields on both the nature of institutional change and the effects of various property arrangements on political and

---

[7] Yasheng Huang, *Capitalism with Chinese Characteristics: Entrepreneurship and the State* (Cambridge: Cambridge University Press, 2008), 34–5.

economic behavior. In general, when we depart from envisaging property-rights changes as the results of exogenous forces and begin to see them as embedded in state–society relations, questions about what types of arrangements are most economically efficient or legally ideal cannot be isolated from questions about which patterns of state–society interactions initially produce property relations.

Increasingly, research in comparative politics is becoming as attentive to institutional strength as it has been to institutional design. Recognizing that institutions can only affect incentives and behavior if social and political actors expect that the laws on the books will be enforced and cannot be easily changed, this body of research aims to understand variation in institutional strength, particularly in new democracies and in the developing world.[8] In the case of property-rights institutions, I suggest that they only acquire strength when they share affinities with other important social and political institutions, such as fiscal rules and central political mandates. In the Chinese case, for example, it is difficult to imagine a change in property-rights institutions that would provide an effective check on state power in the absence of fiscal reforms that would provide local governments with sources of funds outside land revenues.

In cases outside China we also see property-rights practices explained by examining a much wider range of political imperatives than attention to property-rights institutions alone would permit. In some of these cases, we see the state exercising more restraint than that to which it is legally bound, whereas in others, we see how property-rights laws on the books fail to shape behavior or to restrain state agents. What these cases have in common – with each other and with the Chinese cases in this book – is that property-rights regimes emerge as politically ad hoc, rather than as economically strategic, bargains between political elites and the social groups upon whom they depend.

Collier begins his study of elite–mass relations in Peru with the following question: "How is it possible that in a country that has been as oligarchic and authoritarian as Peru there can be such a massive growth of squatter settlements around the nation's capital?"[9] In addition to the tenacity of the squatters, Collier credits elite support as a driving force behind the initiation of land seizures and the persistence of informal settlements. Authoritarian rule in Peru has been punctuated, Collier argues, by political crises that produce coalitions between the elites and the urban poor that in turn shape policy toward the settlements. In essence, informal (and sometimes formal) property rights for the urban poor have been the results of policies of political bargaining and incorporation. Similarly, more recent work examines the politics of forbearance – the

[8] See Steven Levitsky and María Victoria Murillo, "Variation in Institutional Strength," *Annual Review of Political Science* 12, no. 1 (2009): 115–33.
[9] David Collier, *Squatters and Oligarchs: Authoritarian Rule and Policy Change in Peru* (Baltimore: Johns Hopkins University Press, 1976), 3.

intentional nonenforcement of the law – as a form of redistribution and an electoral strategy. Holland finds that Colombian politicians intentionally refrain from enforcing laws, such as those licensing street vendors, in order to "provide informal social welfare and to signal their commitment to poor voters."[10]

Further examples abound in post-Communist Eastern Europe, a region that underwent not only massive property-rights reassignments but large-scale privatization of ownership, precisely as China did not. The gap between the expected socioeconomic effects of privatization and other institutional changes – that they would generate market incentives, efficient behavior, and greater generalized well-being – and the realities of impoverishment, kleptocracy, breakdown of social order, and depressed incentives for production have dominated a generation of social-science research on Eastern Europe. On the specific question of land privatization, scholars have focused on the profound lack of connection between formal institutions adopted on the basis of recommendations of global liberal institutions and local practices and political imperatives. According to Verdery, it was the uncertainty of the generalized transition that produced local creative action to subvert institutional change:

In postsocialist contexts, [market-based institutional relationships] often made life ever less predictable, increasing rather than mitigating uncertainty and risk … people had to figure out their own ways of either avoiding or domesticating the uncertainties they encountered with financial institutions (banks), courts, retailers of inputs of markets for crops, land commissions, and so on. … Daily life rested on constant improvisation, generating routines and networks that could at length produce their own social infrastructure, which would then shape outcomes at the top at least as much as the other way around.[11]

This outcome is not at all unique to the village that is at the center of Verdery's research or to the Transylvanian region more generally. Allina-Pisano argues that postsocialist land systems are a case of convergence:

Whatever the variety in experience among individual members of farming communities in post-Soviet space, and however the allocation of property rights may differ across regions and states, there remains for rural people a common outcome: knowing that they are legally entitled to a set of rights, and experiencing significant limitations on using those rights.[12]

Allina-Pisano explains this disjuncture not by crediting weak institutional environments or rent-seeking local actors, but rather by paying attention to

---

[10] Alisha C. Holland, "The Distributive Politics of Enforcement," *American Journal of Political Science*. 59, no. 2 (April 2015): 357–371.

[11] Katherine Verdery, *The Vanishing Hectare: Property and Value in Postsocialist Transylvania* (Ithaca, NY: Cornell University Press, 2003), 27.

[12] Jessica Allina-Pisano, *The Post-Soviet Potemkin Village: Politics and Property Rights in the Black Earth* (Cambridge: Cambridge University Press, 2008), 16.

what she calls "sub rosa resistance," by which local state actors assume a façade of compliance with central policy while subverting those policies that they judge to be more advantageous for themselves and, sometimes, the communities they serve in favor of the status quo.[13] As in the case of the erstwhile working classes in Harbin and Changchun, it is difficult to make sense of these systems of property rights when one examines them exclusively from the distributional or strategic bargaining perspective. Instead, we must view decisions on property rights in the context of the larger contexts of economic, political, and social change to understand how property-rights arrangements reflect actors' political interests but not necessarily their economic interests.

Boone's masterful study of rural land-tenure regimes and state building in rural Africa places patterns of land control at the center of African politics. Examining national and subnational variation in the rules governing access to and authority over land, Boone details how different regimes – statist versus "neocustomary," in which land access and tenure are governed indirectly through the authority of traditional leaders – produce different electoral dynamics, patterns of political violence, redistributive politics, ethnic competition, and so on. Although Boone's focus is on the institutional effects of land-tenure regimes (i.e., they are the independent rather than the dependent variables in her book), she acknowledges that the tenure regimes are products of contingent choices made by elites under political pressure. Changes in property-rights institutions in rural Africa are driven by, and sometimes prevented by, political choices and conflicts rather than by efficiency concerns or strategic bargaining.[14] Under both regimes, Boone shows how the allocation of land follows a political logic; whether governed directly by agents of the state or indirectly by traditional authorities, land in rural Africa has been "a political as much as an economic asset" in postcolonial national leaders' attempts to "secure rural acquiescence, elicit compliance, and maintain social order in the rural areas."[15]

The arguments in the present volume have focused on how and why specific forms of property rights over land have emerged in China at the national and subnational levels, that is, taking the property-rights regime as the dependent variable. This research is generally not about which forms of property rights are the most secure, fair, or optimal for economic development and growth. That being said, adopting an approach that views property rights as endogenous to the political process does speak to debates about the relationship between property-rights institutions and economic and political behavior.

---

[13] Jessica Allina-Pisano, "Sub Rosa Resistance and the Politics of Economic Reform: Land Redistribution in Post-Soviet Ukraine," *World Politics* 56, no. 4 (2004): 555–6.

[14] Catherine Boone, *Property and Political Order in Africa: Land Rights and the Structure of Politics* (Cambridge: Cambridge University Press, 2014), esp. 52–63.

[15] Ibid., 45–6.

For decades, social scientists have wrestled with the uncomfortable fit between the Chinese experience of economic dynamism and political stability and classical expectations about the necessity of secure private property rights. Clearly, investment and growth were proceeding apace in China during the 1980s and 1990s, even in the absence of property-rights institutions that would meet most scholars' baseline standards for being secure and clear, much less private. Efforts to reconcile social science theory and Chinese practice inspired a generation of research on the Chinese political economy that, in essence, proposed various alternatives to legal individualism that nonetheless delivered a degree of security, including "market-preserving federalism," "local state corporatism," and provincial power.[16] Most of these alternatives focus on the role of political and fiscal decentralization; it is argued that devolving power and resources to lower levels of government creates both a constituency for reforms and sufficient incentives to encourage growth-generating behavior.

Yet, in the years after most of these approaches were developed, many elements of decentralization have been reversed and levels of investment and growth have only risen. Chapter 2 describes this process of recentralization of fiscal and financial resources from local governments to the center. To be sure, we do observe greater conflicts between state and society over land and property control, but these conflicts are nearly always a result of local governments' behaving in opportunistic and, indeed, predatory ways. This outcome is the opposite of the pernicious effects of recentralization that were hypothesized by some scholars. For example, at the onset of the 1994 fiscal recentralization Huang writes:

Centralizing both political and fiscal controls is a highly risky strategy as it places an inordinate requirement on the honesty and rationality of the central government. China's recent history shows the hazards of concentrating too much political power in the hands of the central government, and in this regard, fiscal decentralization can be viewed as equivalent to purchasing an insurance policy against such hazards.[17]

The centralization of fiscal and political controls has not, however, produced an unrestrained central government. Rather, it has broken the links among local states and societies that tied the fates of local officials with the populations that they governed.

---

[16] Jean Oi, *Rural China Takes Off: Institutional Foundations of Economic Reform* (Berkeley: University of California Press, 1999); Gabriella Montinola, Yingyi Qian, and Barry R. Weingast, "Federalism, Chinese Style: The Political Basis for Economic Success in China," *World Politics* 48, no. 1 (1995): 50–81; Susan L. Shirk, *The Political Logic of Economic Reform in China* (Berkeley: University of California Press, 1993); Donald C. Clarke, "Economic Development and the Rights Hypothesis: The China Problem," *American Journal of Comparative Law* 51, no. 1 (2003): 89–111.

[17] Yasheng Huang, *Inflation and Investment Controls in China: The Political Economy of Central–Local Relations during the Reform Era* (Cambridge: Cambridge University Press, 1996), 328.

We saw in the case chapters how, regardless of the ambiguity and the institutional prerogatives for local governments to claim property rights over land, some local governments nonetheless refrained from predation and instead established property-rights regimes that empowered local political and social groups and incorporated their interests. As local governments became decidedly less reliant on the local population for revenue, they adopted a more predatory approach toward land and property rights, pursuing expansion and acquisition to meet budgetary obligations and to promote economic growth through land-based investments.

Property-rights institutions are not static, formal arrangements, delivered from on high and capable of effectively restraining potential violators no matter how predatory their intentions and incentives may be. Property relations are reflections of relationships between states and societies, and the institutions that govern property relations change when these relationships change. I have argued that a mutual dependence between state and society – for political stability, economic prosperity, or even simply the necessary revenue to provide effective goods and services – is conducive to property relations that protect a wider variety of social and political interests. Conversely, when local governments rely on a narrow base of economic or political support – foreign capital in the case of Dalian and more generally land revenue in the case of urban China in the late 1990s and 2000s – property relations are construed in a way that emboldens the power of the local state over society. At the core is the degree to which local states and social groups enjoy a shared fate.

LAND AND CHINESE CAPITALISM: A POSTSCRIPT ON FISCALIZATION

With the abolition of the agricultural tax in 2006 on the heels of decades of protests and conflicts over the "peasant burdens," local governments were subject to the elimination of yet another significant source of fiscal revenue.[18] State–society relations in rural and periurban China have become no less contentious than they were in the years of the tax protests, but the locus of the conflicts has shifted from taxes and fees to control of land. In the years since

---

[18] On the "peasant burden" and state–society conflict in the 1990s, see Thomas P. Bernstein and Xiaobo Lü, *Taxation without Representation in Contemporary Rural China* (Cambridge: Cambridge University Press, 2003); Kevin J. O'Brien and Lianjiang Li, *Rightful Resistance in Rural China* (Cambridge: Cambridge University Press, 2006). On the abolition of the agricultural tax and the "rural tax and fee reform," see Linda Chelan Li, *Rural Tax Reform in China: Policy Processes and Institutional Change* (London: Routledge, 2011); John James Kennedy, "From the Tax-for-Fee Reform to the Abolition of Agricultural Taxes: The Impact on Township Governments in North-West China," *China Quarterly* no. 189 (2007): 43–59; Christian Göbel, "Uneven Policy Implementation in Rural China," *China Journal* no. 65 (2011): 53–76.

the 1990s the story of land politics in China has become one of increasing battles between state and society and among state agents for control of rural and urban land. Local governments, in search of both economic growth and fiscal revenue, pursue greater levels of expansion and territorial conquest, driving the enlargement of Chinese urban areas and the dramatic reduction in arable farmland and making land conflicts the primary source of state–society conflicts in rural China.[19] The fiscal dependence of Chinese cities on land and the negative consequences generated by such a dependence have become abundantly clear, especially since the global financial crisis of 2008 and the Chinese economic stimulus program of 2009, which intensified local government investments driven by land revenue.[20]

In this climate, local property-rights regimes, such as those described in Chapters 4 through 6, have partially given way to a nationwide convergence on a more predatory politics of land and property. In Dalian, state dominance of land control and the urban built environment was the original model of land commodification and property-rights management. In Harbin and Changchun, many urban communities, emboldened by a sense of moral entitlement, remained tenacious in the face of local state initiatives to reclaim urban land. Although the political and moral bargains of the previous era may remain steadfast in the downtown cores of these cities, all of the case cities – and indeed most cities in China – have undertaken massive efforts of urban expansion to stimulate growth and to finance local government activities (see Table 7.1). Expansionary efforts are particularly serious during times of economic downturn, when government revenues shrink and local governments attempt to stimulate growth by land development.

---

[19] Hsing, *The Great Urban Transformation*; Sally Sargeson, "Villains, Victims and Aspiring Proprietors: Framing 'Land-Losing Villagers' in China's Strategies of Accumulation," *Journal of Contemporary China* 21, no. 77 (2012): 757–77; Jiangnan Zhu, "The Shadow of the Skyscrapers: Real Estate Corruption in China," *Journal of Contemporary China* 21, no. 74 (2012): 243–60; Chiew Ping Yew, "Pseudo-Urbanization? Competitive Government Behavior and Urban Sprawl in China," *Journal of Contemporary China* 21, no. 74 (2012): 281–98; Yu Jianrong, "Dangqian Zhongguo quntixing shijian zhuyao leixing jiqi jiben tezheng" (Major Types and Basic Characteristics of Mass Incidents in Today's China), *Zhongguo zhengfa daxue xuebao* (Journal of China University of Political Science and Law) no. 6 (2009): 114–29. World Bank and PRC Development Research Center of the State Council, *Urban China: Toward Efficient, Inclusive, and Sustainable Urbanization* (Washington, DC: World Bank Group, 2014).

[20] For example, this is recognized in ibid., 267. See also Christine Wong, "Paying for Urbanization in China: Challenges of Municipal Finance in the Twenty-First Century," in *Financing Metropolitan Governments in Developing Countries*, ed. Roy W. Bahl, Johannes F. Linn, and Deborah Wetzel (Cambridge, MA: Lincoln Institute of Land Policy, 2013), 273–308; Yew, "Pseudo-Urbanization?" Le Yin and Alfred Muluan Wu, "Urbanization, Land Development, and Land Financing: Evidence from Chinese Cities," *Journal of Urban Affairs* 36, no. S1 (2014): 354–68.

TABLE 7.1. *Urban Areas and Built-Up Areas, 2001–2010 (Square Kilometers)*

	Dalian		Harbin		Changchun	
	Urban area	Urban built-up area	Urban area	Urban built-up area	Urban area	Urban built-up area
2001	2,415	234	1,660	211	3,583	164
2002	2,415	248	1,660	214	3,603	169
2003	2,415	248	1,660	225	3,603	171
2004	2,415	248	4,272	293	3,603	193
2005	2,415	248	4,275	302	3,603	231
2006	2,415	258	4,275	331	3,583	267
2007	2,415	258	7,086	336	4,789	285
2008	2,415	258	7,086	340	4,789	328
2009	2,415	258	7,086	345	4,789	365
2010	2,415	390	7,086	359	4,789	394

Source: Zhongguo guotu ziyuan nianjian (Ministry of Land and Resources Yearbook), various years.

Dalian

Predictably, Dalian's land-driven urban expansion continued into the late 1990s and 2000s and accelerated precisely when the municipal government needed revenue and sought to generate economic growth. The expansion of the DDA illustrates this logic. The original mid-1980s plans for the DDA proposed an eventual expansion to 220 km^2. By the beginning of 2000 it had expanded from 10 km^2 to 50 km^2.[21] These data reflect the area of land under the DDA's administrative control, that is, land that the DDA converted from collectively owned farmland to land for urban construction to obtain lease revenue, which would accrue directly to the Dalian Municipal Government. By 2009, the land area of the DDA totaled 400 km^2; but it was between 2009 and 2012 that the zone grew exponentially.

Dalian, like many Chinese coastal cities with export-oriented economies, proved to be extraordinarily vulnerable during the global economic contraction that began in 2008. Wholly foreign-owned businesses, the vast majority of which produced for export, constituted more than one-half of Dalian's economic and employment base. Therefore, contraction in foreign demand brought about a dramatic contraction in the regional economy and, by extension, the local tax base; between 2008 and 2009 alone, the value of exports declined by 25 percent.[22] In 2009, Mayor Xia Deren, reluctant to preside over a contraction in the region

[21] *Dalian shi zhi: Waijing waimao zhi* (Dalian City Foreign Trade and Opening Gazetteer) (Beijing: Fangzhi chubanshe, 2004), 518.
[22] *Dalian Jinzhou xin fazhan baogao 2011* (Dalian Jinzhou New Area Development Report 2011), 12.

and eager to respond to Beijing's call to invest in local development projects to stimulate the economy and to prevent a recession, proposed an expansion of the DDA from 400 km² to 1,040 km² by merging the DDA with Jinzhou district to form the "Dalian Jinzhou New Area," subsuming a massive swath of the northern part of the city under the direct control of the municipal government in one fell swoop.

Interestingly, the merger was not popular with either DDA officials or district officials in Jinzhou. Even though Jinzhou officials were happy to receive the open area designation and to be subject to preferential policies (e.g., lower tax rates) that would attract more firms to the area, they saw the merger primarily as a land grab and they were unhappy about turning most of their administrative attention to negotiating with village leaders over land compensation when in fact they would no longer benefit from the land revenue at all.[23] DDA authorities, in contrast, felt that although the DDA had needed the land several years earlier, they should now be less focused on expanding physically and should pay more attention to retaining firms that could easily move elsewhere in China or Asia in search of cheaper labor. But, more importantly, the new designation removed the DDA's administrative independence and put DDA authorities – and DDA land and revenue – directly under the hierarchy of the municipal government. In other words, whereas the initial creation of the DDA involved separating it from the former administrative structure, the expansion removed its autonomy. DDA authorities also viewed the merger as a land grab by a local government that was desperate for both revenue and economic expansion during the downturn.

Harbin

Many parts of the urban centers in Harbin and Changchun look the same as they did in the mid-1990s, with large SOEs and ancillary compounds occupying prime downtown space, even when those factories have not been in production for years. Both cities, however, particularly in the 2000s, have adopted predatory and expansionist policies outside the traditional city centers. In both Harbin and Changchun, dislodging periurban and rural dwellers has proven to be more politically feasible and economically desirable than pursuing a consolidation of property rights over the urban core.

It is no exaggeration to say that Harbin has pursued territorial expansion projects in nearly every direction; Harbiners joke that every mayoral change-over produces a new "direction of development" (*fazhan fangxiang*, 发展方向) to the city, accompanied by massive infrastructure development, land sales, and real-estate development. Since 1996, Harbin's periurban development has

---

[23] Dalian interviews, June 20, 2012–July 2, 2012. Indeed, in the summer of 2012, at least two villages mounted substantial protests against land conversions.

Conclusions

185

pushed north, beyond the Songhua River into Hulan district. The so-called Songbei New Area is not a development zone with preferential policies similar to the DDA, but rather a new part of the city to which the local government has attempted to attract businesses, residents, and educational institutions. In the original 1996 plans for the area, the city government designated much of the land for industrial enterprise relocations from downtown, similar to the process in Dalian. However, it was unable to force these relocations, and by the mid-2000s it turned its attention to developing the area as an upscale residential and commercial area.[24] Though the city government relocated its offices to Songbei in an attempt to redirect investments, Harbiners in the 2000s referred to the area as a "ghost town," since many of the high-end apartments had been purchased as investment properties and the area seemed to have everything except residents and commercial activity.

Yet, the experience in Songbei did not prevent the city government – under new rounds of leadership – from expanding similarly in other directions. South of the Songhua area but west of the city center there are two major expansion projects: Qunli New Area, built on former farmland and reclaimed wetlands surrounding the Songhua River, is Harbin's major urban planning showcase of the last ten years: an enormous residential area planned for "economic housing," preferentially priced apartment units for low- and middle-income urban residents that are owned and developed by the municipal government. The Qunli New Area became the focus of major municipal investment during the 2008 and 2009 economic downturn, when local government revenue declined but exhortations to stimulate economic growth were at a new high. The municipal government financed the construction of economic housing with land revenue from an adjacent potentially desirable riverside area with commercial and residential developments. As of summer 2012, investment totaled US $1.5 billion, and the area was projected to absorb at least 320,000 new residents.[25] Also in 2010, Harbin municipal officials launched an expansion drive even farther westward, placing them in direct conflict with villagers in the western suburbs. The area was to be called "Haxi" (Harbin West), and the municipal officials sought to make it a "new center" of the city. The center of the area, and the main signal of the local government's intentions for the area, is a new high-speed rail station. Official figures for revenue generated from land leasing for these projects are unavailable, but interviewees from the project offices in each area have suggested that lease revenue from these areas exceeded the city government's entire budgetary revenue for 2008.[26]

[24] Ha'erbin shi chengshi guihuaju (Harbin Urban Planning Bureau), "Ha'erbin shi Songbei xinqu zongti guihua fang'an, 2010–2020" (Harbin City Songbei New Area Master Plan Draft, 2010–2020), in Ha'erbin xin shiji chu chengshi guihua zuopin xuanji (Selected Works of Harbin City Planning at the Beginning of the New Century), ed. Yu Binyang (Ha'erbin: Ha'erbin chubanshe, 2002), 144–5.
[25] Harbin interviews, July 3, 2012.   [26] Ibid.

Changchun

Changchun's expansionary policies, particularly during the last ten years, have been equally dramatic. The city's original development zone expansion project is located only about five kilometers south of the city center. By the mid-2000s it had expanded to include about 100 km². Beginning in 2005, municipal authorities, pleading that the original development zone was too dense and was insufficient for the new large-scale industrial projects, established two additional development zones: one to the northwest, in Chengde, and another directly north of the city, called the "high-tech new zone" (*gao xinqu*, 高新区). These new zones, for which land requisitions from village collectives occurred in 2008 and 2009, cover 390 km². In 2009, when the central government and the MLR sought to arrest post–financial crisis land grabs by banning the declaration of new development zones, Changchun did what many other cities did: It unified multiple, noncontiguous development zones into a single zone governed by a single committee, but it nonetheless continued to expand the land area.[27] By the end of 2009, all of the land requisitioned in 2008 and 2009 had been leased to developers. Again, official revenue figures are unavailable, but one well-placed Changchun official stated:

The new area is much richer than the entire Changchun city government put together. They want to move people out of downtown and raze the old houses, but they cannot afford it. Out here in the countryside where the new zone is located, they pay maybe 100 or 200 RMB per square meter, whereas they pay more than 10,000 RMB per square meter in the city. So it is easier to build out here.[28]

The countryside in Jilin province is often referred to as "China's breadbasket" because of its high levels of corn and grain production; provincial land resource documents invariably begin by urging caution in land use, since China's food sustainability depends on agriculture in the region. As a result, converting 390 km² of cropland to land for urban construction and municipal leasing required that the city contend with five main village collectives in a single county. Compensation for the villagers ranged from 1 million RMB to 10 million or even 20 million RMB, with holdouts receiving even more for their acquiescence.[29] Dislocated villagers were given new apartments in urban-style apartment communities (*xiaoqu*, 小区) in the new zone, and some villagers were given jobs (mostly in construction). Most villagers, however, found themselves with relatively large lump sums of money, but without work. Many felt they had no choice but to accept the state compensation, and although they lamented their loss of land and their former lifestyles, they

[27] Changchun interview, June 26, 2012.   [28] Ibid.
[29] Holdouts took the form of "nail houses" – villagers who simply refused to sign over the land of their living quarters – rather than collective action. Changchun interview, June 26, 2012.

were relatively pleased with their living conditions and felt that they now had a lot more leisure time.[30]

Plans for the new zone were under way in 2012, though construction had just begun and was not expected to be completed by 2020. The plans included thousands of apartment buildings, several industrial clusters focusing on five pillar industries (foodstuffs, biomedical supplies, telecommunications, LED and lighting technology, and nanotechnology), at least four ancillary university campuses, a large sculpture park, and an "Olympic Park" with five stadiums, tennis courts, and a cultural district with a small replica of Beijing's Forbidden City. Investment for construction in 2012 amounted to 35.2 million RMB, 4.2 times that of all other city development zones in 2008.[31]

A conventional narrative of property-rights institutions would interpret the rapid urban expansion, the rise of predatory land politics, and the endemic conflicts over land as inevitable consequences of an unclear or inefficient property-rights regime. Yet, as the empirical chapters in this volume demonstrate, although land rules have been vague since the 1980s, many local governments – for example, Harbin and Changchun – built property-rights regimes in which the local states were quite restrained in terms of their interventions in local land markets and in their monopolization of property rights. Therefore, the turn toward predation and expansion must be understood in the context of more seismic changes in the Chinese political economy, namely, the reorganization of the fiscal and financial systems that rendered local governments less politically and economically dependent on local tax revenue and on local populations and more dependent on land. Since such reorganization in the 1990s, land has become the primary state input to generate economic growth and land institutions have become the key to state intervention in the economy.

LAND BARGAINS AND THE FUTURE OF CHINA

What is the future of property-rights arrangements governing land in urban and rural China? Land has been at the heart of the changes in the political economy that have brought China this far in the more than three decades since the onset of the market reforms; in the future, land control will continue to be central to changes in China's macroeconomic and institutional arrangements. As I have argued, changes in property rights over land have not all been in the direction

[30] Changchun interviews, June 28, 2012. On similar projects to condense villagers elsewhere, see Kristen Looney, "China's Campaign to Build a New Socialist Countryside: Village Modernization, Peasant Councils, and the Ganzhou Model of Rural Development," *China Quarterly* no. 224 (December 2015). Lynette H. Ong, "State-Led Urbanization in China: Skyscrapers, Land Revenue and 'Concentrated Villages,'" *China Quarterly* no. 217 (2014): 162–79; Christian Sorace, "China's Vision for Developing Sichuan's Post-Earthquake Countryside: Turning Unruly Peasants into Grateful Urban Citizens," *China Quarterly* no. 218 (2014): 404–27. Note that the Changchun villagers were neither angry nor expressly happy about their new, periurban lives.
[31] Cited at Exhibition Hall, Changchun City High-Tech Zone. Visited June 26, 2012.

from state ownership toward privatization. An examination of urbanization policy and the priorities of the "fifth generation" of Chinese leaders does not suggest many reasons to think that this direction will change. On the contrary, the persistence of state and collective ownership of land is an underlying reality that has allowed the CCP to pivot its strategies to meet new developmental needs as it maintains stewardship of social and political change.[32]

When Xi Jinping ascended to a preeminent position in the CCP's fifth-generation leadership in 2012, many, if not most, of the sources of social conflict and economic imbalances in China were linked to the control of land. In addition to direct conflicts over the appropriation of collective land for urbanization, rising housing prices were perceived to be a distinct threat to social stability and support for the urban middle class, dwindling farmland was a threat to food security, increasing reports of "ghost towns" were evidence of poor investments, and so forth.[33] Most importantly, after the 2008 global financial crisis exposed the extent of China's dependence on global export markets, the CCP began a search for new strategies to sustain economic growth. Chinese domestic consumption has long been suppressed and household savings have been incredibly high, making economic growth dependent on global demand and (mostly state-driven) investment.[34] The success of any strategy will depend on its ability to stimulate domestic demand.

Urbanization – meaning both the massive construction and expansion of urban centers and the creation of hundreds of millions of new urbanites – constitutes just such a strategy. Unifying a decade of rural policies that sought to transform the physical appearance of the Chinese countryside into the realities of land-based urban expansion, the central authorities in 2012 settled on a plan to urbanize 200 million new urban residents by the year 2020: 100 million of these new urbanites will be relocated farmers, and 100 million will be rural-to-urban labor migrants who are currently residing in the cities but, because of migration restrictions, are denied access to urban social welfare and public services.[35] The theory behind the strategy, articulated most clearly in

---

[32] Liu Shouying, *Zhimian Zhongguo tudi wenti* (Land Issues and Transitional China (Beijing: Zhongguo fazhan chubanshe, 2014).

[33] Public attention in the West became fixed on China's "ghost cities" after a CBS *60 Minutes* report that aired on March 3, 2013. See www.cbsnews.com/news/china-real-estate-bubble-lesley-stahl-60-minutes/, accessed January 29, 2015.

[34] See Barry Naughton, "China's Economy: Complacency, Crisis and the Challenge of Reform," *Daedalus* 143, no. 2 (2014): 14–25.

[35] See Ian Johnson. "China Releases Plan to Incorporate Farmers into Cities," *New York Times*, March 17, 2014, at www.nytimes.com/2014/03/18/world/asia/china-releases-plan-to-integrate-farmers-in-cities.html?_r=0, accessed March 3, 2015. See also idem, "China's Great Uprooting: Moving 250 Million into Cities," *New York Times*, June 15, 2013, at www.nytimes.com/2013/06/16/world/asia/chinas-great-uprooting-moving-250-million-into-cities.html, accessed March 3, 2015. On rural policies, urbanization, and domestic demand, see Looney. "China's Campaign to Build a New Socialist Countryside"; Ong, "State-Led Urbanization in China"; Sorace, "China's Vision for Developing Sichuan's Post-Earthquake Countryside."

TABLE 7.2. *Urbanization Scenarios Envisioned by the Development Research Center of the State Council*

	Year 2010	Year 2030 baseline projections	Year 2030 projections with reforms
Urbanization rate (%)	52	66	70
Share of the labor force in agriculture (%)	38	17.1	11.6
GDP growth (average annual growth during the past five years)	8.5	4.9	5.2
Consumption as a share of GDP (%)	46.5	62.0	66.5
Investment as a share of GDP (%)	48.8	35.5	30.9

Source: Adapted from World Bank and Development Research Center, *Urban China*, 35.

a report issued jointly by the World Bank and the Development Research Center (DRC) of the State Council, builds on the relationships among construction, urbanization, and economic growth (see Table 7.2).[36] Demand has been suppressed in both urban and rural China as migrants face insecurities and therefore underconsume, and China remains "underurbanized" relative to other countries at the same level of per capita income. Drawing millions of rural Chinese into urban and, more likely, periurban newly constructed areas in both new and existing cities will stimulate construction demand related to homeownership, and, more indirectly, will result in the creation of a large urban middle class. In addition to the massive infrastructure investments required to achieve such a scale of urbanization within a matter of years, the central government is aggressively pursuing the expansion of affordable housing programs for both new and existing urban residents.[37]

To be sure, such a massive project of urbanization requires some rearrangement of land and property systems, principally the institution of collective landownership that has heretofore prevented rural residents from being allowed to transfer individual or household land rights. Parallel reforms in citizenship institutions – namely, the *hukou* system – will supposedly enable greater freedom of movement for rural and urban citizens and will allow rural

[36] World Bank and Development Research Center of the State Council, *Urban China*.

[37] See Youqin Huang, "Low-Income Housing in Chinese Cities: Policies and Practices," *China Quarterly* no. 212 (2012): 941–64; Ya Ping Wang, "Recent Housing Reform Practice in Chinese Cities: Social and Spatial Implications," in *China's Housing Reform and Outcomes*, ed. Joyce Yanyuan Man (Cambridge, MA: Lincoln Institute for Land Policy, 2011), 19–44.

citizens access to urban social services. Indeed, the World Bank/DRC report calls for extensive reforms to China's land institutions: strengthening property rights for farmers, making land use more efficient and compensation for land takings more fair, reforming the *hukou* system such that every citizen will have equal access to social and public services regardless of location, reforming public finance to reduce reliance on land revenue, and so forth. Some detailed policy ideas are suggested to achieve these goals, such as levying a capital gains tax for newly marketed construction land, centralizing the burdens of public services, and clarifying the "public interest" and its limits in land takings, among others. In general, this direction of land reforms seems to be quite similar to the reforms in Chongqing, Chengdu, and elsewhere that have enabled rural residents to exchange land rights for urban citizenship; urban governments either facilitated the purchase of, or purchased themselves, development rights for rural land plots, providing farmers with both cash compensation and access to urban social welfare benefits and services.[38]

As of the time of this writing, the plan to achieve these goals remains vague, to say the least. Wallace, writing about the possibilities for reform of China's *hukou* system and the urban bias, describes constant refrains for reform as a sort of "Chinese Groundhog Day, the continual endless repetition of the same story with no real changes actually occurring or even on the horizon."[39] There is perhaps reason to be slightly more sanguine about land reforms, but the research in these chapters makes at least two points abundantly clear. First, institutional changes to "strengthen property rights" or to "clarify the public interest" will have little impact on the realities of land expropriations and urban expansion without commensurate reforms of public finance. The World Bank/DRC report reveals that the authorities in Beijing are well aware of this problem, but public finance reforms may prove to be even more difficult politically than the property-rights reforms. To resolve the mismatch between

---

[38] See Meina Cai, "Land for Welfare in China," Working Paper, 2012. See also Su Wei, Yang Fan, and Liu Shiwen, *Chongqing moshi* (The Chongqing Model) (Beijing: Zhongguo jingji chubanshe, 2010).The exchange of development rights permits local governments or developers to develop for urban construction a land plot of equal size, while the physical homestead of the former rural resident is converted into arable land. This allows urban governments to lease more land for urban construction while not exceeding the quotas of urban construction land or dipping below the designated "red lines" for arable land. Liu Shouying, *Zhimian Zhongguo tudi wenti*; Ong, "State-Led Urbanization in China"; Hui Wang et al., "Farmland Preservation and Land Development Rights Trading in Zhejiang, China," *Habitat International* 34, no. 4 (2010): 454–63. The recent World Bank/DRC urbanization report discourages the model that trades land rights for social welfare and instead proposes both to compensate rural citizens for land and to delink land rights from social welfare, more closely following the model in periurban Beijing. World Bank and Development Research Center of the State Council, *Urban China*, 326–7.

[39] Jeremy L. Wallace, *Cities and Stability: Urbanization, Redistribution, and Regime Survival in China* (Oxford: Oxford University Press, 2014), 217. "Groundhog Day" is a reference to the Bill Murray movie, during which the main character wakes up on February 2 over and over again.

massive local government expenditure burdens and minimal local revenue streams (outside land revenue), the CCP faces choices that involve either decentralizing revenue or centralizing burdens. The former seems to require a level of trust in and disciplinary control over local governments that presently eludes the CCP.[40] The latter, the likely path under current Minister of Finance Lou Jiwei, will require colossal bureaucratic coordination efforts if central bureaucracies are to provide social welfare and services of equal quality for China's 1.4 billion citizens regardless of place of residence.[41]

Second, we should not expect land reforms in China to be in the direction of the privatization of property, even in a piecemeal fashion. Liu Shouying, the foremost authority on land in China and an author of the DRC report, writes: "One [of two major constraints to land reform and change] is the institutional constraint. A fundamental characteristic of China's land institutions is public ownership: rural land is owned by the collective and urban land is owned by the state. From the perspective of reform policy making, no matter how land institutions will be reformed, the effects of alternative arrangements on public ownership are of utmost importance." Liu goes on to explain that public ownership is integral to the ruling party, to the meaning of "socialism with Chinese characteristics," and to the fundamental character of China's economic institutions: "These conditions fundamentally decide which choices are available and which choices are unavailable in the process of land reform."[42] We may expect institutional reforms within public ownership, but not the complete abandonment of public ownership.

The prospect of a massive rural-to-urban transition – one even grander in scale and more compressed in time than has already occurred in China during the last thirty years – and dramatic change in rural land holdings has prompted comparisons to the enclosure movement in England, during which institutions of collective ownership over rural lands ("the commons") were replaced by private institutions guaranteeing exclusive use. In the process of this massive land privatization, millions of rural dwellers were dispossessed of access to land and pushed into the urban areas, where they eventually became, depending on one's view of history, the urban working class or the underclass whose labor enabled industrialization and the rise of modern capitalism.[43]

---

[40] Joseph Fewsmith, *The Logic and Limits of Political Reform in China* (Cambridge: Cambridge University Press, 2013); Minxin Pei, *China's Trapped Transition: The Limits of Developmental Autocracy* (Cambridge, MA: Harvard University Press, 2006).

[41] Jiwei Lou, "The Reform of Intergovernmental Fiscal Relations in China: Lessons Learned," in *Public Finance in China: Reform and Growth for a Harmonious Society*, ed. Jiwei Lou and Shuilin Wang (Washington, DC: World Bank, 2008), 155–69.

[42] Liu Shouying, *Zhimian Zhongguo tudi wenti*, 2.

[43] E. P. Thompson, *Whigs and Hunters: The Origin of the Black Act* (New York: Pantheon Books, 1975); Barrington Moore Jr., *Social Origins of Dictatorship and Democracy: Lord and Peasant in the Making of the Modern World* (Boston: Beacon Press, 1966); Douglass C. North, John

Although sixteenth-century England and contemporary China may both be the scenes of dramatic rural-to-urban dislocations and the transformation of communal or collective land tenure to exclusive uses, interpreting China's past, present, or future urbanization and property-rights transformations as another episode in a seemingly familiar social science history would be a grave misreading. The social and political outcomes of the enclosures – uncontrolled urban migration, engorged cities, social agitation, violent conflicts over rural land, and so forth – are exactly the urban transformations that the CCP has thus far avoided and hopes to avoid in perpetuity.[44] The retention of state ownership over land, which enables the state to manage the pace and spatial distribution of urbanization as well as consolidation and direct control over China's precious rural arable land, is precisely the mechanism by which it aims to avoid such transformations. In this sense, the new drive toward urbanization and land-rights change appears less like a mass movement toward privatization and more like a reconstitution of state control over both urban and rural land. Whatever the future of Chinese capitalism, bargains over land control will figure as prominently in its generation as they have in the economic and political orders of the past and present.

Joseph Wallis, and Barry R. Weingast, *Violence and Social Orders: A Conceptual Framework for Interpreting Recorded Human History* (Cambridge: Cambridge University Press, 2009).
[44] On this, see Wallace, *Cities and Stability*.

Bibliography

ENGLISH-LANGUAGE SOURCES

Abdelal, Rawi, Mark Blythe, and Craig Parsons. "Introduction." In *Constructing the International Economy*, ed. Rawi Abdelal, Mark Blyth, and Craig Parsons, 1–19. Ithaca, NY: Cornell University Press, 2010.

Agrarian Reform Law of the People's Republic of China: Together with Other Relevant Documents. Peking: Foreign Languages Press, 1950.

Alford, William P. *To Steal a Book Is an Elegant Offense: Intellectual Property Law in Chinese Civilization*. Stanford, CA: Stanford University Press, 1995.

Allina-Pisano, Jessica. *The Post-Soviet Potemkin Village: Politics and Property Rights in the Black Earth*. Cambridge: Cambridge University Press, 2008.

"Sub Rosa Resistance and the Politics of Economic Reform: Land Redistribution in Post-Soviet Ukraine." *World Politics* 56, no. 4 (2004): 554–81.

Altshuler, Alan A. and David Luberoff. *Mega-Projects: The Changing Politics of Urban Public Investment*. Washington, DC: Brookings Institution Press, and Cambridge, MA: Lincoln Institute of Land Policy, 2003.

Associated Press. "Bush Limits Eminent-Domain Seizures." *Washington Post*, June 24, 2006, at www.washingtonpost.com/wp-dyn/content/article/2006/06/23/AR2006062301722.html, accessed April 11, 2014.

Baron, Jane B. "Winding toward the Heart of the Takings Muddle: Kelo, Lingle, and Public Discourse about Private Property," *Fordham Urban Law Journal* 34, no. 2 (2006): 613–55.

Bernstein, Thomas P. *Up to the Mountains and Down to the Villages: The Transfer of Youth from Urban to Rural China*. New Haven, CT: Yale University Press, 1977.

Bernstein, Thomas P. and Xiaobo Lü. *Taxation without Representation in Contemporary Rural China*. Cambridge: Cambridge University Press, 2003.

Blomquist, William Blomquist. "A Political Analysis of Property Rights." In *Property in Land and Other Resources*, ed. Daniel H. Cole and Elinor Ostrom, 369–84. Cambridge, MA: Lincoln Institute of Land Policy, 2012.

"Bo Xilai," at www.chinavitae.com/biography/72, accessed September 29, 2010.

Boone, Catherine. "Electoral Populism Where Property Rights Are Weak: Land Politics in Contemporary Sub-Saharan Africa." *Comparative Politics* 41, no. 2 (January 2009): 183–201.

    Property and Political Order in Africa: Land Rights and the Structure of Politics. Cambridge: Cambridge University Press, 2014.

Bramall, Chris. "Chinese Land Reform in Long-Run Perspective and in the Wider East Asian Context." *Journal of Agrarian Change* 4, nos. 1–2 (2004): 107–41.

Brandt, Loren et al. "Land Rights in Rural China: Facts, Fictions and Issues." *China Journal*, no. 47 (January 2002): 67–97.

Brandt, Loren, and Xiaodong Zhu. "Redistribution in a Decentralized Economy: Growth and Inflation in China under Reform." *Journal of Political Economy* 108, no. 2 (2000): 422–39.

Bray, Francesca. *The Rice Economies: Technology and Development in Asian Societies.* Oxford: Blackwell, 1986.

Buck, David D. "Railway City and National Capital: Two Faces of the Modern in Changchun." In *Remaking the Chinese City: Modernity and National Identity, 1900–1950*, ed. Joseph Esherick, 65–89. Honolulu: University of Hawai'i Press, 2000.

Cai, Hongbin and Daniel Treisman. "Did Government Decentralization Cause China's Economic Miracle?" *World Politics* 58, no. 4 (2006): 505–35.

Cai, Meina. "Land for Welfare in China." Working Paper, 2012.

    "Land-Locked Development: The Local Political Economy of Institutional Change in China." PhD diss., University of Wisconsin/Madison, 2012.

Cai, Yongshun. *Collective Resistance in China: Why Popular Protests Succeed or Fail.* Stanford, CA: Stanford University Press, 2010.

    State and Laid-Off Workers in Reform China: The Silence and Collective Action of the Retrenched. London: Routledge, 2006.

Cao, Yuanzheng, Yingyi Qian, and Barry R. Weingast. "From Federalism, Chinese Style to Privatization, Chinese Style." *Economics of Transition* 7, no. 1 (1999): 103–31.

    "Changchun a City of Opportunity." *China Daily*, May 30, 2006, at http://topic. chinadaily.com.cn/index/cache/collection/cbsweb/source/title/changchun%3A+A +city+of+opportunity?aid=5351085, accessed March 13, 2015.

Chen, Feng. "Industrial Restructuring and Workers' Resistance in China." *Modern China* 29, no. 2 (2003): 237–62.

    "Chinese Agency Profiles Politburo Standing Committee Member Bo Xilai." Xinhua (New China News Agency), October 22, 2007, in BBC Monitoring Asia Pacific: Political, October 22, 2007.

Cho, Mun Young. *The Specter of "the People": Urban Poverty in Northeast China.* Ithaca, NY: Cornell University Press, 2013.

Chovanec, Patrick. "China's Real Estate Bubble May Have Just Popped." *Foreign Affairs*, December 18, 2011, at www.foreignaffairs.com/articles/136963/patrick-chovanec/chinas-real-estate-bubble-may-have-just-popped, accessed January 27, 2015.

Chung, Jae Ho. "Preferential Policies, Municipal Leadership, and Development Strategies: A Comparative Analysis of Qingdao and Dalian." In *Cities in China: Recipes for Economic Development in the Reform Era*, ed. Jae Ho Chung, 103–38. New York: Routledge, 1999.

    ed. *Cities in China: Recipes for Economic Development in the Reform Era.* London: Routledge, 1999.

Clarke, Donald C. "Economic Development and the Rights Hypothesis: The China Problem." *American Journal of Comparative Law* 51, no. 1 (2003): 89–111.

Cody, Edward. "Striving to Be 'Spiritual': Chinese Campaign Seeks to Combat Western Values." *Washington Post*, January 30, 1997, A13.

Cole, Daniel H., and Elinor Ostrom, eds. *Property in Land and Other Resources.* Cambridge, MA: Lincoln Institute of Land Policy, 2012.

Collier, David. *Squatters and Oligarchs: Authoritarian Rule and Policy Change in Peru.* Baltimore: Johns Hopkins University Press, 1976.

"Counter-Revolutionary Clique Arrested in Changchun." Jilin Provincial Service, July 8, 1989. BBC Summary of World Broadcasts: The Far East, FE/0507/B2/1, July 13, 1989.

Cui, Zhiyuan. "Partial Intimations of the Coming Whole: The Chongqing Experiment in Light of the Theories of Henry George, James Meade, and Antonio Gramsci." *Modern China* 37, no. 6 (2011): 646–60.

Dahl, Robert A. *Who Governs? Democracy and Power in an American City.* New Haven, CT: Yale University Press, 1961.

Demsetz, Harold. "Toward a Theory of Property Rights." *American Economic Review* 57, no. 2 (May 1967): 347–59.

Dickson, Bruce J. *Red Capitalists in China: The Party, Private Entrepreneurs, and Prospects for Political Change.* Cambridge: Cambridge University Press, 2003.

Dikötter, Frank. *The Tragedy of Liberation: A History of the Chinese Revolution, 1945–1957.* New York: Bloomsbury, 2013.

Dimitrov, Martin K. *Piracy and the State: The Politics of Intellectual Property Rights in China.* Cambridge: Cambridge University Press, 2009.

Dong, Xiao-Yuan. "Two-Tier Land Tenure System and Sustained Economic Growth in Post-1978 Rural China." *World Development* 24, no. 5 (1996): 915–28.

Engerman, Stanley L., and Jacob Metzer, eds. *Land Rights, Ethno-Nationality, and Sovereignty in History.* London: Routledge, 2004.

Evans, Peter. "The Eclipse of the State? Reflections on Stateness in an Era of Globalization." *World Politics* 50, no. 1 (1997): 62–87.

Ewing, Kent. "The Coolest Nail House in History." *Asia Times*, March 31, 2007.

Falleti, Tulia G. and Julia F. Lynch. "Context and Causal Mechanisms in Political Analysis." *Comparative Political Studies* 42, no. 9 (2009): 1143–66.

Fan, C. Cindy. "Uneven Development and Beyond: Regional Development Theory in Post-Mao China." *International Journal of Urban and Regional Research* 21, no. 4 (1997): 620–39.

Fewsmith, Joseph. *Dilemmas of Reform in China: Political Conflict and Economic Debate.* Armonk, NY: M. E. Sharpe, 1994.

The Logic and Limits of Political Reform in China. Cambridge: Cambridge University Press, 2013.

Field, Erica. "Entitled to Work: Urban Tenure Security and Labor Supply in Peru." *Quarterly Journal of Economics* 122, no. 4 (2007): 1561–1602.

Field, Erica and Maximo Torero. "Do Property Titles Increase Credit Access among the Urban Poor? Evidence from a Nationwide Titling Program." Unpublished paper, 2010.

French, Howard. "In China, Fight over Development Creates a Star." *New York Times*, March 26, 2007, at www.nytimes.com/2007/03/26/world/asia/26cnd-china.html, accessed January 26, 2015.

Friedman, Thomas. "Doha and Dalian." *New York Times*, September 19, 2007, at www.nytimes.com/2007/09/19/opinion/19friedman.html?pagewanted=print&_r=0, accessed February 6, 2015.

Frye, Timothy. "Credible Commitment and Property Rights: Evidence from Russia." *American Political Science Review* 98, no. 3 (2004): 453–66.

"Original Sin, Good Works, and Property Rights in Russia." *World Politics* 58, no. 4 (2006): 479–504.

Gallagher, Mary Elizabeth. *Contagious Capitalism: Globalization and the Politics of Labor in China*. Princeton, NJ: Princeton University Press, 2005.

Göbel, Christian. "Uneven Policy Implementation in Rural China." *China Journal* no. 65 (2011): 53–76.

Grzymala-Busse, Anna. "The Best Laid Plans: The Impact of Informal Rules on Formal Institutions in Transitional Regimes." *Studies in Comparative and International Development* 45, no. 3 (2010): 311–33.

Guo, Xiaolin. "Land Expropriation and Rural Conflicts in China." *China Quarterly* no. 166 (2001): 422–39.

Guthrie, Doug. *Dragon in a Three-Piece Suit: The Emergence of Capitalism in China*. Princeton, NJ: Princeton University Press, 1999.

Haber, Stephen H., Noel Maurer, and Armando Razo. *The Politics of Property Rights: Political Instability, Credible Commitments, and Economic Growth in Mexico, 1876–1929*. Cambridge: Cambridge University Press, 2003.

Hall, Peter. *Cities of Tomorrow: An Intellectual History of Urban Planning and Design in the Twentieth Century*. Oxford: Blackwell, rev. ed., 1996.

Han Tianyang and Liu Mingtai. "Changchun Special: Changchun Auto Industry Growing." *China Daily*, October 19, 2010, at www.chinadaily.com/cn/cndy/2010-10/19/content_11426410.htm, accessed March 5, 2015.

Harvey, David. "Labor, Capital, and Class Struggle around the Built Environment in Advanced Capitalist Societies." *Politics & Society* 6, no. 3 (1976): 265–95.

Heilmann, Sebastian. "From Local Experiments to National Policy: The Origins of China's Distinctive Policy Process." *China Journal* no. 59 (January 2008): 1–30.

"Policy Experimentation in China's Economic Rise." *Studies in Comparative International Development* 43, no. 1 (2008): 1–26.

"Regulatory Innovation by Leninist Means: Communist Party Supervision in China's Financial Industry." *China Quarterly* no. 181 (2005): 1–21.

Heilmann, Sebastian and Elizabeth Perry, eds. *Mao's Invisible Hand: The Political Foundations of Adaptive Governance in China*. Cambridge, MA: Harvard University Asia Center, 2011.

Herrigel, Gary. *Industrial Constructions: The Sources of German Industrial Power*. Cambridge: Cambridge University Press, 1996.

Ho, Peter. *Institutions in Transition: Land Ownership, Property Rights, and Social Conflict in China*. Oxford: Oxford University Press, 2005.

"Who Owns China's Land? Policies, Property Rights and Deliberate Institutional Ambiguity." *China Quarterly* no. 166 (2001): 394–421.

Ho, Samuel P. S. and George C. S. Lin. "Emerging Land Markets in Rural and Urban China: Policies and Practices." *China Quarterly* no. 175 (2003): 681–707.

Hoffman, Lisa M. *Patriotic Professionalism in Urban China: Fostering Talent*. Philadelphia: Temple University Press, 2010.

Holland, Alisha C. "The Distributive Politics of Enforcement." *American Journal of Political Science* 59, no. 2 (April 2015): 357–71.

Hsing, You-tien. *The Great Urban Transformation: Politics of Land and Property in China*. Oxford: Oxford University Press, 2010.

Hsing, You-tien. "Land and Territorial Politics in Urban China." *China Quarterly* no. 187 (2006): 575–91.

Huang, Philip C. C. "Chongqing: Equitable Development Driven by a 'Third Hand'?" *Modern China* 37, no. 6 (2011): 569–622.

Huang, Yasheng. *Capitalism with Chinese Characteristics: Entrepreneurship and the State*. Cambridge: Cambridge University Press, 2008.

Inflation and Investment Controls in China: The Political Economy of Central–Local Relations during the Reform Era. Cambridge: Cambridge University Press, 1996.

Huang, Youqin. "Low-Income Housing in Chinese Cities: Policies and Practices." *China Quarterly* no. 212 (2012): 941–64.

Hunter, Floyd. *Community Power Structure: A Study of Decision Makers*. Chapel Hill: University of North Carolina Press, 1953.

Hurst, William. *The Chinese Worker after Socialism*. Cambridge: Cambridge University Press, 2009.

Hurst, William, and Kevin J. O'Brien. "China's Contentious Pensioners." *China Quarterly* no. 170 (2002): 345–60.

Jin, You. "Pearl of the Liaodong Peninsula." *Straits Times* (Singapore), October 12, 1994, 14.

Johnson, Ian. "China Releases Plan to Incorporate Farmers into Cities." *New York Times*, March 17, 2014, at www.nytimes.com/2014/03/18/world/asia/china-releases-plan-to-integrate-farmers-in-cities.html?_r=0, accessed March 3, 2015.

"China's Great Uprooting: Moving 250 Million into Cities." *New York Times*, June 15, 2013, at www.nytimes.com/2013/06/16/world/asia/chinas-great-uprooting-moving-250-million-into-cities.html, accessed March 3, 2015.

Jones, E. L. *The European Miracle: Environments, Economies, and Geopolitics in the History of Europe and Asia*. Cambridge: Cambridge University Press, 1981.

Kelliher, Daniel R. *Peasant Power in China: The Era of Rural Reform, 1979–1989*. New Haven, CT: Yale University Press, 1992.

Kennedy, John James. "From the Tax-for-Fee Reform to the Abolition of Agricultural Taxes: The Impact on Township Governments in North-West China." *China Quarterly* no. 189 (2007): 43–59.

Kohli, Atul. *The State and Poverty in India: The Politics of Reform*. Cambridge: Cambridge University Press, 1987.

Lai, Renee. "City Aspires to Be Chinese Detroit." *South China Morning Post*, July 7, 1994, 7.

Lan, Deng, Qingyun Shen, and Lin Wang. "Housing Policy and Finance in China: A Literature Review." Washington, DC: U.S. Department of Housing and Urban Development, 2009.

Landry, Pierre F. *Decentralized Authoritarianism in China: The Communist Party's Control of Local Elites in the Post-Mao Era*. Cambridge: Cambridge University Press, 2008.

Landry, Pierre F. "The Political Management of Mayors in Post-Deng China." *Copenhagen Journal of Asian Studies* 17 (2003): 31–58.

Larsson, Tomas. *Land and Loyalty: Security and the Development of Property Rights in Thailand*. Ithaca, NY: Cornell University Press, 2012.

Lee, Ching Kwan. *Against the Law: Labor Protests in China's Rustbelt and Sunbelt*. Berkeley: University of California Press, 2007.

"Pathways of Labor Activism." In *Chinese Society: Change, Conflict, and Resistance*, ed. Elizabeth Perry and Mark Selden, 57–79. New York: Routledge, 3rd ed., 2010.

Levi, Margaret. *Of Rule and Revenue*. Berkeley: University of California Press, 1988.

Levine, Ross. "Law, Endowments and Property Rights." *Journal of Economic Perspectives* 19, no. 3 (2005): 61–88.

Levitsky, Steven, and María Victoria Murillo. "Variation in Institutional Strength." *Annual Review of Political Science* 12, no. 1 (2009): 115–33.

Levy, Jonah D. *The State after Statism: New State Activities in the Age of Liberalization*. Cambridge, MA: Harvard University Press, 2006.

Li, Guo, Scott Rozelle, and Loren Brandt. "Tenure, Land Rights, and Farmer Investment Incentives in China." *Agricultural Economics* 19, nos. 1–2 (September 1998): 63–71.

Li, Linda Chelan. *Rural Tax Reform in China: Policy Processes and Institutional Change*. London: Routledge, 2011.

Li, Xia. "The Changchun Economic and Technological Development Zone: Trying to Turn China's Northeast Around." *China Today* (December 1996): 25–27.

"Liaoning's Experience of Putting Counties under Jurisdiction of Cities." Xinhua, January 20, 1983. BBC Summary of World Broadcasts: The Far East, FE/7242/C/2, January 27, 1983.

Libecap, Gary D. *Contracting for Property Rights*. Cambridge: Cambridge University Press, 1989.

Lieberthal, Kenneth G. *Revolution and Tradition in Tientsin, 1949–1952*. Stanford, CA: Stanford University Press, 1980.

Lin, George C. S. *Developing China: Land, Politics and Social Conditions*. London: Routledge, 2009.

"Emerging Land Markets in Rural and Urban China: Policies and Practices." *China Quarterly* no. 175 (2003): 681–707.

"Reproducing Spaces of Chinese Urbanisation: New City-Based and Land-Centred Urban Transformation." *Urban Studies* 44, no. 9 (2007): 1827–55.

Lin, Justin Yifu. "Rural Reforms and Agricultural Growth in China." *American Economic Review* 82, no. 1 (1992): 34–51.

Lindblom, Charles E. *Politics and Markets: The World's Political Economic Systems*. New York: Basic Books, 1977.

Liu, Mingtai. "Changchun, a City of Many Wonders." *China Daily*, November 15, 2007.

Liu, Shouying and Ulich Schmitt. "China's Urbanization and Land: A Framework for Reform." In *China: Toward Efficient, Inclusive, and Sustainable Urbanization*, ed. World Bank and Development Research Center of the State Council of the PRC, 163–336. Washington, DC: World Bank Group, 2014.

Locke, Richard M. *Remaking the Italian Economy*. Ithaca, NY: Cornell University Press, 1995.

Logan, John R., and Harvey Luskin Molotch. *Urban Fortunes: The Political Economy of Place*. Berkeley: University of California Press, 1987.

Long, Norton E. "The Local Community as an Ecology of Games." *American Journal of Sociology* 64, no. 3 (1958): 251–61.

Looney, Kristen. "China's Campaign to Build a New Socialist Countryside: Village Modernization, Peasant Councils, and the Ganzhou Model of Rural Development." *China Quarterly*, no. 224 (December 2015).

Looney, Kristen E. "The Rural Developmental State: Modernization Campaigns and Peasant Politics in China, Taiwan and South Korea." PhD diss., Harvard University, 2012.

Lou, Jiwei. "The Reform of Intergovernmental Fiscal Relations in China: Lessons Learned." In Jiwei Lou and Shuilin Wang, *Public Finance in China: Reform and Growth for a Harmonious Society*, 155–69. Washington, DC: World Bank, 2008.

Lyons, Thomas P. *Economic Integration and Planning in Maoist China*. New York: Columbia University Press, 1987.

MacFarquhar, Roderick. *The Origins of the Cultural Revolution. 2. The Great Leap Forward 1958–1960*. New York: Columbia University Press, 1983.

Markus, Stanislav. "Secure Property as a Bottom-Up Process: Firms, Stakeholders, and Predators in Weak States." *World Politics* 64, no. 2 (2012): 242–77.

Marx, Karl. *Selected Writings*, ed. David McLellan. Oxford: Oxford University Press, 2nd ed., 2000.

Mavin, Duncan. "From Davos to Dalian." *Financial Post*, September 1, 2007, at www.financialpost.com/story.html?id=de8a188d-8f00-43ba-a3f4-e49083758336, accessed February 6, 2015.

"Mayor of Changchun Urges Protesters to Act 'Reasonably.'" BBC Summary of World Broadcasts, June 8, 1989.

Mertha, Andrew C. *China's Water Warriors: Citizen Action and Policy Change*. Ithaca, NY: Cornell University Press, 2008.

"From 'Rustless Screws' to 'Nail Houses': The Evolution of Property Rights in China." *Orbis* 53, no. 2 (2009): 233–49.

Mertha, Andrew. *The Politics of Piracy: Intellectual Property in Contemporary China*. Ithaca, NY: Cornell University Press, 2005.

Mitchell, Timothy. "The Work of Economics: How a Discipline Makes Its World." *European Journal of Sociology* 46, no. 2 (2005): 297–320.

Molotch, Harvey. "The City as a Growth Machine: Toward a Political Economy of Place." *American Journal of Sociology* 82, no. 2 (1976): 309–32.

Montinola, Gabriella, Yingyi Qian, and Barry R. Weingast. "Federalism, Chinese Style: The Political Basis for Economic Success in China." *World Politics* 48, no. 1 (October 1995): 50–81.

Moore, Barrington, Jr. *Social Origins of Dictatorship and Democracy: Lord and Peasant in the Making of the Modern World*. Boston: Beacon Press, 1966.

Morajee, Rachel. "No Dilly Dalian: Dalian." *Monocle* 4, no. 31 (March 2010): 95–99.

Naughton, Barry. "China's Economy: Complacency, Crisis and the Challenge of Reform." *Daedalus* 143, no. 2 (2014): 14–25.

The Chinese Economy: Transitions and Growth. Cambridge, MA: MIT Press, 2007.

Growing Out of the Plan: Chinese Economic Reform, 1978–1993. Cambridge: Cambridge University Press, 1995.

North, Douglass C. *Institutions, Institutional Change, and Economic Performance*. Cambridge: Cambridge University Press, 1990.

Structure and Change in Economic History. New York: Norton, 1981.

North, Douglass C., and Robert Paul Thomas. *The Rise of the Western World: A New Economic History.* Cambridge: University Press, 1973.

North, Douglass C., John Joseph Wallis, and Barry R. Weingast. *Violence and Social Orders: A Conceptual Framework for Interpreting Recorded Human History.* Cambridge: Cambridge University Press, 2009.

North, Douglass C., and Barry R. Weingast. "Constitutions and Commitment: The Evolution of Institutional Governing Public Choice in Seventeenth-Century England." *Journal of Economic History* 49, no. 4 (1989): 803–32.

O'Brien, Kevin J. "Rightful Resistance Revisited." *Journal of Peasant Studies* 40, no. 6 (2013): 1951–62.

ed. *Popular Protest in China.* Cambridge MA: Harvard University Press, 2008.

O'Brien, Kevin J., and Lianjiang Li. *Rightful Resistance in Rural China.* Cambridge: Cambridge University Press, 2006.

O'Clery, Conor. "Comrade Mayor Sporting Old-School Tie." *Irish Times,* November 10, 1997, 12.

Oi, Jean C. *Rural China Takes Off: Institutional Foundations of Economic Reform.* Berkeley: University of California Press, 1999.

Oi, Jean C., and Andrew G. Walder, eds. *Property Rights and Economic Reform in China.* Stanford, CA: Stanford University Press, 1999.

Ong, Lynette H. "Indebted Dragon: The Risky Strategy behind China's Construction Economy." *Foreign Affairs,* November 27, 2012, at www.foreignaffairs.com/articles/138449/lynette-h-ong/indebted-dragon, accessed January 27, 2015.

"State-Led Urbanization in China: Skyscrapers, Land Revenue and 'Concentrated Villages.'" *China Quarterly* no. 217 (2014): 162–79.

Ostrom, Elinor. *Governing the Commons: The Evolution of Institutions for Collective Action.* Cambridge: Cambridge University Press, 1990.

"Other Reports on Unemployment: Changchun Employment Conference." Jilin Radio. BBC Summary of World Broadcasts, November 7, 1980.

Paik, Wooyeal and Kihyun Lee. "I Want to Be Expropriated! The Politics of Xiaochanquanfang Land Development in Suburban China." *Journal of Contemporary China* 21, no. 74 (2012): 261–79.

Pearson, Margaret M. *China's New Business Elite: The Political Consequences of Economic Reform.* Berkeley: University of California Press, 1997.

Pei, Minxin. *China's Trapped Transition: The Limits of Developmental Autocracy.* Cambridge, MA: Harvard University Press, 2006.

Peterson, Paul E. *City Limits.* Chicago: University of Chicago Press, 1981.

Polanyi, Karl. *The Great Transformation.* Boston: Beacon Press, 1957.

Pomeranz, Kenneth. *The Great Divergence: China, Europe, and the Making of the Modern World Economy.* Princeton, NJ: Princeton University Press, 2000.

Pomfret, John. "One Corrupt City Reflects Scourge Plaguing China: Political System Infected, Some Say." *Washington Post,* March 6, 2002, A10.

Ramzy, Austin. "Leaders: Bo Xilai." *Time,* April 29, 2010, at http://content.time.com/time/specials/packages/article/0,28804,1984685_1984864_1985416,00.html, accessed February 12, 2015.

Rithmire, Meg E. "China's 'New Regionalism': Subnational Analysis in Chinese Political Economy." *World Politics* 66, no. 1 (2014): 165–94.

Rosenthal, Jean-Laurent and R. Bin Wong. *Before and beyond Divergence: The Politics of Economic Change in China and Europe*. Cambridge, MA: Harvard University Press, 2011.

Sargeson, Sally. "Villains, Victims and Aspiring Proprietors: Framing 'Land-Losing Villagers' in China's Strategies of Accumulation." *Journal of Contemporary China* 21, no. 77 (2012): 751–77.

Segal, Adam. *Digital Dragon: High-Technology Enterprises in China*. Ithaca, NY: Cornell University Press, 2003.

Shao, Qin. "Waving the Red Flag: Cultural Memory and Grassroots Protest in Housing Disputes in China." *Modern Chinese Literature and Culture* 22, no. 1 (Spring 2010): 197–232.

Shih, Victor C.. "Local Government Debt: Big Rock-Candy Mountain." *China Economic Quarterly*. Vol.14, no. 2 (June 2010): 26–36.

Factions and Finance in China: Elite Conflict and Inflation. Cambridge: Cambridge University Press, 2008.

Shirk, Susan L. *The Political Logic of Economic Reform in China*. Berkeley: University of California Press, 1993.

Shue, Vivienne. *Peasant China in Transition: The Dynamics of Development toward Socialism, 1949–1956*. Berkeley: University of California Press, 1980.

Snow, Edgar. *Red Star over China*. New York: Grove Press, 1961.

Snyder, Richard. *Politics after Neoliberalism: Reregulation in Mexico*. Cambridge: Cambridge University Press, 2001.

Sokoloff, Kenneth L., and Stanley L. Engerman. "History Lessons: Institutions, Factors Endowments, and Paths of Development in the New World." *Journal of Economic Perspectives* 14, no. 3 (2000): 217–32.

Solinger, Dorothy J. *China's Transition from Socialism: Statist Legacies and Market Reforms, 1980–1990*. Armonk, NY: M. E. Sharpe, 1993.

"Labour Market Reform and the Plight of the Laid-Off Proletariat." *China Quarterly* no. 170 (2003): 304–26.

Sorace, Christian. "China's Vision for Developing Sichuan's Post-Earthquake Countryside: Turning Unruly Peasants into Grateful Urban Citizens." *China Quarterly* no. 218 (2014): 404–27.

Soto, Hernando, in collaboration with the Instituto Libertad y Democracia. *The Other Path: The Invisible Revolution in the Third World*. New York: Harper & Row, 1989.

State-owned Assets Supervision and Administrative Commission of the State Council (SASAC). "List of Central SOEs," February 9, 2015, at www.sasac.gov.cn/n86114/n86137/c1725422/content.html, accessed March 6, 2015.

Steinfeld, Edward S. *Forging Reform in China: The Fate of State-Owned Industry*. Cambridge: Cambridge University Press, 1998.

Stone, Clarence N. *Regime Politics: Governing Atlanta, 1946–1988*. Lawrence: University Press of Kansas, 1989.

Sun, Yatsen. *Three Principles of the People*. Taipei: China Publishing Company, 1964.

Szelenyi, Ivan. "Third Ways." *Modern China* 37, no. 6 (2011): 672–83.

Tang, Wenfang and William L. Parish. *Chinese Urban Life under Reform: The Changing Social Contract*. Cambridge: Cambridge University Press, 2000.

Thompson, E. P. *Whigs and Hunters: The Origin of the Black Act*. New York: Pantheon Books, 1975.

Thun, Eric. *Changing Lanes in China: Foreign Direct Investment, Local Governments, and Auto Sector Development*. Cambridge: Cambridge University Press, 2006.

Tiebout, Charles M. "A Pure Theory of Local Expenditures." *Journal of Political Economy* 64, no. 5 (October 1956): 416–24.

Tsai, Kellee S. "Adaptive Informal Institutions and Endogenous Institutional Change in China." *World Politics* 59, no. 1 (2006): 116–41.

   Back-Alley Banking: Private Entrepreneurs in China. Ithaca, NY: Cornell University Press, 2002.

   Capitalism without Democracy: The Private Sector in Contemporary China. Ithaca, NY: Cornell University Press, 2007.

Tyler, Patrick E. "Changchun Journal: Motor City Keeps Communism in the Driver's Seat." *New York Times*, May 22, 1995, A4, at www.nytimes.com/1995/05/22/world/changchun-journal-motor-city-keeps-communism-in-the-driver-s-seat.html, accessed February 8, 2015.

Verdery, Katherine. *The Vanishing Hectare: Property and Value in Postsocialist Transylvania*. Ithaca, NY: Cornell University Press, 2003.

Verdery, Katherine and Caroline Humphrey, eds. *Property in Question: Value Transformation in the Global Economy*. Oxford: Berg, 2004.

Vogel, Ezra F. *Canton under Communism: Programs and Politics in a Provincial Capital, 1949–1968*. Cambridge, MA: Harvard University Press, 1969.

Wallace, Jeremy L. *Cities and Stability: Urbanization, Redistribution, and Regime Survival in China*. Oxford: Oxford University Press, 2014.

Wang, Hui et al. "Farmland Preservation and Land Development Rights Trading in Zhejiang, China." *Habitat International* 34, no. 4 (2010): 454–63.

   et al. "Rural Residential Properties in China: Land Use Patterns, Efficiency and Prospects for Reform." *Habitat International* 36, no. 2 (2012): 201–9.

Wang, Shaoguang and Angang Hu. *The Political Economy of Uneven Development: The Case of China*. Armonk, NY: M. E. Sharpe, 1999.

Wang, Ya Ping. "Recent Housing Reform Practice in Chinese Cities: Social and Spatial Implications." In *China's Housing Reform and Outcomes*, ed. Joyce Yanyun Man, 19–44. Cambridge, MA: Lincoln Institute for Land Policy, 2011.

Wank, David L. *Commodifying Communism: Business, Trust, and Politics in a Chinese City*. Cambridge: Cambridge University Press, 1999.

Weimer, David L., ed. *The Political Economy of Property Rights: Institutional Change and Credibility in the Reform of Centrally Planned Economies*. Cambridge: Cambridge University Press, 1997.

Weingast, Barry R. "The Economic Role of Political Institutions: Market-Preserving Federalism and Economic Development." *Journal of Law, Economics, & Organization* 11, no. 1 (1995): 1–31.

   Violence and Social Orders: A Conceptual Framework for Interpreting Recorded Human History. Cambridge: Cambridge University Press, 2009.

White, Tyrene. *China's Longest Campaign: Birth Planning in the People's Republic, 1949–2005*. Ithaca, NY: Cornell University Press, 2006.

Whiting, Susan H. "Fiscal Reform and Land Public Finance: Zouping County in National Context." In *China's Local Public Finance in Transition*, ed. Joyce Yanyun Man and Yu-Hung Hong, 125–44. Cambridge, MA: Lincoln Institute of Land Policy, 2011.

Wines, Michael. "A Village in Revolt Could Be a Harbinger for China." *New York Times*, December 26, 2011, at www.nytimes.com/2011/12/26/world/asia/in-china-the-wukan-revolt-could-be-a-harbinger.html?pagewanted=all&_r=0, accessed January 26, 2015.

    Power and Wealth in Rural China: The Political Economy of Institutional Change. Cambridge: Cambridge University Press, 2001.

Whiting, Susan. "Values in Land: Fiscal Pressures, Land Disputes and Justice Claims in Rural and Peri-Urban China." *Urban Studies* 48, no. 3 (March 2011): 569–87.

Wittfogel, Karl A. "The Marxist View of China (Part 1)." *China Quarterly* no. 11 (1962): 1–22.

    "The Marxist View of China (Part 2)." *China Quarterly* no. 12 (1962): 154–69.

Wittfogel, Karl August. *Oriental Despotism: A Comparative Study of Total Power*. New Haven, CT: Yale University Press, 1957.

Woetzel, Jonathan et al. "Harbin: Moving On from Central Planning." In *Preparing for China's Urban Billion*. McKinsey Global Institute, 2009, at www.mckinsey.com/mgi/publications/china_urban_billion/, accessed February 17, 2015.

Wong, Christine. "The Fiscal Stimulus Programme and Public Governance Issues in China." *OECD Journal on Budgeting* 11, no. 3 (2011): 1–22.

Wong, Christine P. "Paying for Urbanization in China: Challenges of Municipal Finance in the Twenty-First Century." In *Financing Metropolitan Governments in Developing Countries*, ed. Roy W. Bahl, Johannes F. Linn, and Deborah Wetzel, 273–308. Cambridge, MA: Lincoln Institute of Land Policy, 2013.

Wong, Christine P. W., Christopher Heady, and Wing T. Woo. *Fiscal Management and Economic Reform in the People's Republic of China*. Hong Kong: Oxford University Press, 1995.

World Bank and Development Research Center of the State Council of the PRC, ed. *Urban China: Toward Efficient, Inclusive, and Sustainable Urbanization*. Washington, DC: World Bank Group, 2014.

Wu, Fulong. "Place Promotion in Shanghai, PRC." *Cities* 17, no. 5 (2000): 349–61.

    "The (Post-) Socialist Entrepreneurial City as a State Project: Shanghai's Reglobalisation in Question." *Urban Studies* 40, no. 9 (2003): 1673–98.

Wu, Fulong, Jiang Xu, and Anthony Gar-On Yeh. *Urban Development in Post-Reform China: State, Market, and Space*. London: Routledge, 2007.

Wu, Weiping. "Fiscal Decentralization, Infrastructure Financing, and Regional Disparity." In *China's Public Finance in Transition*, ed. Joyce Yanyuan Man and Yu-Hung Hong, 41–56. Cambridge, MA: Lincoln Institute of Land Policy, 2011.

Yang, Dali L. *Calamity and Reform in China: State, Rural Society, and Institutional Change since the Great Leap Famine*. Stanford, CA: Stanford University Press, 1996.

Yang, Jisheng. *Tombstone: The Great Chinese Famine, 1958–1962*, ed. Edward Friedman, Guo Jian, and Stacy Mosher. New York: Farrar, Straus & Giroux, 2012.

Yew, Chiew Ping. "Pseudo-Urbanization? Competitive Government Behavior and Urban Sprawl in China." *Journal of Contemporary China* 21, no. 74 (2012): 281–98.

Yin, Le, and Alfred Muluan Wu. "Urbanization, Land Development, and Land Financing: Evidence from Chinese Cities." *Journal of Urban Affairs* 36, no. S1 (2014): 354–68.

Young, Susan. *Private Business and Economic Reform in China*. Armonk, NY: M. E. Sharpe, 1995.

Zhang, Loretta. "Evolution of the Real Estate Market in Southern China." A.B. thesis, Harvard University, 1993.

Zhang, Q. Forrest and John A. Donaldson. "From Peasants to Farmers: Peasant Differentiation, Labor Regimes, and Land-Rights Institutions in China's Agrarian Transition." *Politics & Society* 38, no. 4 (2010): 458–89.

Zhang, Qian Forrest. "Retreat from Equality or Advance Towards Efficiency? Land Markets and Inequality in Rural Zhejiang." *China Quarterly* no. 195 (2008): 535–57.

Zhang, Yue. *"The Fragmented City: Politics of Urban Preservation in Beijing, Paris, and Chicago."* PhD diss., Princeton University, 2008.

——— "Steering towards Growth: Symbolic Urban Preservation in Beijing, 1990–2005." *Town Planning Review* 79, no. 2–3 (2008): 187–208.

Zhao, Dingxin. *The Power of Tiananmen: State–Society Relations and the 1989 Beijing Student Movement*. Chicago: University of Chicago Press, 2001.

Zhao, Ziyang. *Prisoner of the State: The Secret Journal of Zhao Ziyang*, ed. Bao Pu, Renee Chiang, and Adi Ignatius. New York: Simon & Schuster, 2009.

Zhou, Kate Xiao. *How the Farmers Changed China: Power of the People*. Boulder, CO: Westview Press, 1996.

Zhu, Jiangnan. "The Shadow of the Skyscrapers: Real Estate Corruption in China." *Journal of Contemporary China* 21, no. 74 (2012): 243–60.

Zhu, Zheng and Bohong Zheng. "Study on Spatial Structure of Yangtze River Delta Urban Agglomeration and Its Effects on Urban and Rural Regions." *Journal of Urban Planning and Development* 138, no. 1 (2012): 78–89.

Zweig, David. *Freeing China's Farmers: Rural Restructuring in the Reform Era*. Armonk, NY: M. E. Sharpe, 1997.

CHINESE-LANGUAGE SOURCES

Bai Xiaodong (白晓东), ed. *Xin Zhongguo tudi guanli dashiji, 1949–2008* (Chronology of Land Management in New China, 1949–2008) (新中国土地管理大事记: 1949–2008). Beijing: Zhongguo dadi chubanshe, 2009.

Cai Xuefu (蔡学富), Wang Fang (王方), and Zheng Jiazhan (郑嘉战). "Chu yi jiang Dalian shi jianshe chengwei xiandaihua guoji xing chengshi de fazhan moshi" (Consider Building Dalian City's Form to Become a Modern International City) (初议将大连市建设成为现代化国际性城市的发展模式). *Chengshi guihua* (Urban Planning) (城市规;划) no. 4 (1992): 52–55.

Changchun jingji jishu kaifaqu zhi, 1992–2004 (Changchun Economic and Technology Development Zone Gazetteer, 1992–2004) (长春经济技术开发区志, 1992–2004). Changchun: Jilin renmin chubanshe, 2008.

Changchun keche chang zhi, 1954–1990 (Changchun Coach Company Gazetteer, 1954–1990) (长春客车厂志, 1954–1990). Changchun: Jilin renmin chubanshe, 1997.

Changchunshi tigaiwei (Changchun Municipal Restructuring Committee). (长春市体改委). "Woshi shichang tixi jianshe qude fengshuo chengguo" (Results of Building a Market System in Our City) (我市市场体系建设取得丰硕成果), 1993. In *Changchun nianjian, 1993* (Changchun Yearbook, 1993) (长春年检, 1993), 49–52.

Changchun qiche yanjiusuo zhi, 1950–1985 (Changchun Auto Research Institute Gazetteer, 1950–1985) (长春汽车研究所志, 1950–1985). Beijing: Changchun qiche yanjiusuo, 1987.

Changchun shi zhi: Gongshang xingzheng guanli zhi (Changchun Industrial and Commercial Management Gazetteer) (长春市志：工商行政管理志). Changchun: Changchun shi difangzhi bianzuan weiyuanhui, 2006.

Changchun shi zhi: Laodong zhi (Changchun Labor Gazetteer) (长春市志：劳动志). Changchun: Changchun shi difangzhi bianzuan weiyuanhui, 2006.

Changchun shi zhi: Tudi zhi (Changchun City Land Gazetteer) (长春市志：土地志). Changchun: Jilin renmin chubanshe, 1998.

Cheng Hu (程湖) and Zhang Lu (张璐), eds. *Zhongguo fangdichan redian datexie* (Collection of Special Writings on China's Real-Estate Craze) (中国房地产热点大特写). Beijing: Zhongguo shenji chubanshe, 1993.

Chengshi guihuaju (Urban Planning Bureau) and Ha'erbin shi chengshi guihua xuehui (Urban Planning Society of Harbin Municipality) (城市规;划局, 哈尔滨市城市规;划学会). *Ha'erbin yinxiang, 1950–2000*) (Glance Back at the Old City's Charm, 1950–2000) (哈尔滨印象 1950–2000). Beijing: Zhongguo jianzhu chubanshe, 2005.

Dalian Jinzhou xinqu fazhan baogao 2011 (Dalian Jinzhou New Area Development Report 2011) (大连金州新区发展报告 2011).

Dalian shi aiguo weisheng yundong zhi, 1988–1998 (Dalian City Patriotic Sanitation Movement Gazetteer, 1988–1998) (大连市爱国卫生运动志, 1988–1998). Dalian: Dalian shi aiguo weisheng yundong zhi bianweihui, 2001.

Dalian shi shizhi bangongwu (Dalian City Gazetteer Office) (大连市志办公屋), ed. *Dalian shi zhi: Tudi zhi* (Dalian City Land Gazetteer) (连市志：土地志). Dalian: Dalian chubanshe, 1998.

Dalian shi zhi: Chengshi jianshe zhi (Dalian City Construction Gazetteer) (大连市志：城市建设志). Beijing: Fangzhi chubanshe, 2004.

Dalian shi zhi: Huanjing baohu zhi (Dalian City Environmental Protection Gazetteer) (大连市志：环境保护志). Dalian: Dalian ligong daxue chubanshe, 2003.

Dalian shi zhi: Waijing waimao zhi (Dalian City Foreign Trade and Opening Gazetteer) (大连市志：外经外贸志). Beijing: Fangzhi chubanshe, 2004.

Dangdai Zhongguo de chengshi jianshe (Contemporary China's Urban Construction) (当代中国城市建设). Beijing: Zhongguo shehui kexue chubanshe, 1990.

Dichan jiang gei Dalian lai shenme? (What Will Real Estate Bring Dalian?) (地产将给大连来什么?). *Dalian ribao* (Dalian Daily) (大连日报), July 3, 1993.

Feng Ximing (馮錫銘). "Jianchi yi jingji wei zhongxin, qieshi jiaqiang dangde jianshe, ba shehuizhuyi xiandaihua shiye jixu tuixiang qianjin: 1990 nian 12 yue 23 ri zai Zhonggong Changchun shiwei qijie liuci quantishang de baogao (zhaiyao)" (Adhere to the Economy as the Center of Building to Strengthen the Party, Continue to Push Forward the Cause of Socialist Modernization: Speech to the Sixth Session of the Seventh Plenum of the Changchun CCP, December 23, 1990 [Excerpt]) (堅持以經濟為中心切實加強黨的建設把社會主義現代化事業繼續推向前進：1990 年12 月23 日在中共长春市委七届六次全体上的报告 [摘要]). In *Changchun nianjian, 1991*(Changchun Yearbook, 1991), 1–3. Changchun: Jilin renmin chubanshe, 1991.

Gaige kaifang shiqi de Dalian (Dalian in the Era of Reform and Opening) (改革开放以来的时期的大连). Beijing: Zhonggong dangshi chubanshe, 2004.

Gu Wanming (顧万明). "Yizhi chengshi bing: Ha'erbin chengshi gaizao lüeji" (Treating Urban Illness: Harbin City's Renovation Strategy) (医治城市病：哈尔滨城市改造略记). *Liaowang xinwen zhoukan* (Outlook News Weekly) (瞭望新聞周刊), no. 44 (1987): 21–22.

Ha'erbin shi chengshi guihuaju (Harbin Urban Planning Bureau) (哈尔滨市城市规;划局), "Ha'erbin shi Songbei xinqu zongti guihua fang'an, 2010–2020" (Harbin City Songbei New Area Master Plan Draft, 2010–2020) (哈尔滨市松北新区总体规;划方案, 2010–2010). In Yu Binyang, *Ha'erbin xin shiji chu chengshi guihua zuopin xuanji* (Selected Works of Harbin City Planning at the Beginning of the New Century) (哈尔滨新世纪初城市规;划作品选集), 144–46. Ha'erbin: Ha'erbin chubanshe, 2002.

Ha'erbin shi jingji fazhan diaocha weiyuanhui (Harbin Economic Development Investigation Committee) (哈尔滨市经济发展调查委员会). *Ha'erbin shi zhi: Chengshi guihua, tudi, shizheng gongyong jianshe* (Harbin City Gazetteer: Urban Planning, Land, and Municipal Utilities) (哈尔滨市志：城市规;划, 土地, 市政公用建设). Ha'erbin: Heilongjiang renmin chubanshe, 1998.

Ha'erbin shi zhi: Laodong, renshi, dang'an (Harbin Labor, Personnel, and Archives Gazetteer) (哈尔滨市志：劳动, 人事, 档案志). Ha'erbin: Heilongjiang renmin chubanshe, 1997.

Ha'erbin Yamachang yuanzhi fujin Yama bolan zhongxin, baohu jianzhu baoliu" (Harbin to Build Yama Exhibition Center on Site of Yamachang, Leaving Preserved Architecture) (哈尔滨亚麻厂原址附近亚麻博览中心, 保护建筑保留). *Dongbei wang* (Northeastern Net) (东北 网), March 14, 2009.

Han Shouqing (韩守庆), Li Chenggu (李诚固), and Zheng Wensheng(郑文升). "Changchun shi chengzhen tixi de kongjian guanzhi guihua yanjiu" (Study of the Spatial Governance Plan of Changchun) (长春市城镇体系的空间管制规;划研究). *Chengshi guihua* (Urban Planning) (城市规;划) no. 9 (2004): 81–84.

Hu Xin (胡欣). "Dalian shi shizhang Bo Xilai jiu chengshi guihua de benkan jizhe wen" (An Interview with Bo Xilai, the Mayor of Dalian, about City Planning) (大连市市长薄熙来就城市规;划的本刊记者问). *Renmin luntan* (People's Forum) (人民论坛), December 1999, 30–31.

Hua Lanhong (华揽洪). *Chongjian Zhongguo: Chengshi guihua sanshinian, 1949–1979* (Reconstructing China: Thirty Years of Urban Planning, 1949–1979) (重建中国：城市规;划三十年, 1949–1979). Beijing: Shenghuo dushu, xinzhi, Sanlian shudian, 2009.

Huang Xiaohu (黄小虎), ed. *Xinshiqi Zhongguo tudi guanli yanjiu* (A New Era in China Land Management Research) (新时期中国土地管理研究). 2 vols. Beijing: Dangdai Zhongguo chubanshe, 2006.

Hui Chen (惠臣) and Li Lin (李林). "Shenhua zhufang zhidu gaige tuijin zhufang fenpei huobihua" (Deepening Reforms in Housing Distribution and Commodification) (深化住房制度改革推进住房分配货币化). In *Changchun nianjian, 2002* (Changchun Yearbook, 2002) (长春年鉴, 2002), 13. Changchun: Changchun chubanshe, 2002.

"Kaizhan 'Dalian ren yu da kaifang' de taolun huodong" (Kickstarting the "Dalian People and the Grand Opening" Discussion Event) (开展'大连人与大开放' 的讨论活动). *Dalian ribao* (Dalian Daily) (大连日报), June 26, 1993.

Li Shu (李述). "Zhengfu gongzuo baogao" (Report on the Work of the Government) (政府工作报告). 2000. In *Changchun nianjian, 2001* (Changchun Yearbook, 2001) (长春年鉴, 2001), 4. Changchun: Changchun chubanshe, 2001.

Li Xueling (李雪灵), Wang Lijun (王利军), and Yao Yiwei (姚一玮). "Chengshi chuan-gye zhidu huanjing manyi de pingjia yanjiu: Yi Changchun shi wei lie" (Evaluation Research on the Satisfaction of Urban Entrepreneurs with the Institutional Environment: Changchun City as an Example) (城市创业制度环境满意的评价研究: 以长春市为列). *Chengshi fazhan yanjiu* (Urban Studies) (城市发展研究) no. 10 (2010): 1–4, 8.

Li Yuan (李元) [Vice Minister of Land Resources]. "Yi kexue fazhanguan wei tongling quanmian tuijin guotu ziyuan guanli yifa xingzheng tixi jianshe" (Use the Scientific Development Concept to Comprehensively Promote a Land Source Management System for Administrative Building) (以科学发展观为统领全面推进国土资源管理依法行政体系建设). January 10, 2006. In *Zhongguo guotu ziyuan nianjian, 2007* (China Land and Resources Yearbook, 2007) (中国国土资源年检, 2007), 62–67. Beijing: Zhongguo guotu ziyuan nianjian bianjibu, 2008.

Li Zhenquan (李振泉), Li Chenggu (李诚固), and Zhou Jianwu (周建武). "Shilun Changchun shi shangye diyu jiegou" (On the Structure of the Commercial District in Changchun) (試论长春市商业地域结构). *Dili kexue* (Scientia Geographica Sinica) (地理科学) no. 2 (1989): 133–41.

Liu Changde (刘长德), ed. *Chengshi jiaoxiang: Dalian chengshi linian yu shixian* (Urban Symphony: Dalian City Theory and Practice) (城市交响: 大连城市理念与实现). Beijing: Qinghua daxue chubanshe, 2003.

(刘长德), ed. *Dalian chengshi guihua 100 nian: 1899–1999* (One Hundred Years of Dalian City Planning: 1899–1999) (大连城市规;划100年: 1899–1999). Dalian: Dalian haishi daxue chubanshe, 1999.

Liu Shouying (刘守英). *Zhimian Zhongguo tudi wenti* (Land Issues and Transitional China) (直面中国土地问题). Beijing: Zhongguo fazhan chubanshe, 2014.

Liu Zhiming (刘志明). "Jiucheng gaizao guihua yu shixian: Changchun shi Quan'an guangchang jiu zhuzhaiqu gaizao gaikuang" (Planning and Implementation in Renovating the Old City: Renovation of Changchun City's Quan'an Square) (旧城改造规;划与实现: 长春市全安广场旧住宅区改造概况). *Zhuzhai keji* (Housing Science) (住宅科技) no. 10 (1983): 6–7, 26.

Lu Jun (麗军). "Ba liyong waizi gongzuo tigao dao yige xin shuiping" (Improve FDI Work to a New Certain Level) (把利用外资工作提高到一个新水平). *Dalian ribao* (Dalian Daily) (大连日报), March 8, 1992, 1.

Lu Shichao (卢十超), Qi Yong (戚勇), and Li Bingxin (李冰心). "Changchun shi cheng-shi jianshe yongdi jiegou yanbian ji qidongli fenxi" (Study on the Evolution and Driving Force of the Urban Construction Land Structure in Changchun City) (长春市城市建设用地结构演变及起动力分析). *Jilin jianzhu gongcheng xueyuan xuebao* (Journal of the Jilin Institute of Architecture and Civil Engineering) (吉林建筑工程学院学报) 27, no. 5 (October 2010): 45–48.

Lu Ying (卢颖). "Chengshihua zuizhong shenghuo anzhi wenti de kaolü" (Reflections on the Problem of Allocating Support to Peasants Rendered Landless during Urbanization) (城市化最终生活安置问题的思考). *Nongye jingji* (Agricultural Economics) no. 6 (2006): 56–57.

Ma Jiuqi (马九器). "Gansu Longnan shijian: Baoli xu qianze, siwei xu geming" (甘肃陇南事件:暴力须谴责, 思维需革命), *Nanfang baowang* (南方报网), November 19, 2008, at www.nfdaily.cn/opinion/opinionlist/content/2008-11/19/content_4714177.htm, accessed January 26, 2015.

Mi Fengjun (米凤君). "Mayor's Message." *Zhongwai fangdichan shibao* (China International Real-Estate Times) (中外房地产时报), no. 13 (1994): 8.

Ming Da (明达) and Tian Mu (田牧). "Liyong waizi kaifa fangdichan" (Use Foreign Capital to Develop Real Estate) (利用外资开发房地产). *Dalian ribao* (Dalian Daily) (大连日报), May 21, 1992, 1.

Mu Yinghua (穆英化). "Lüelun chengshi de xingzhi: Yi Changchun shi wei lie" (Brief Discussion on the Nature of the City: Changchun as an Example) (略论城市的性质：以长春市为列). *Dongbei shifan daxue keji xuebao (Ziran kexueban)* (Northeast Normal University Journal [Natural Science Edition]) (东北师范大学科技学报 [自然科学版]) no. 2 (1983): 73-76.

Pei Fuxiang (裴辅祥). "Panhuo qiye tudi zichan, cujin qiye shunli zhuanzhi" (Liquidate Land Assets, Promote a Smooth Restructuring of Enterprises) (盘活企业土地资产，促进企业顺利转制). In *Tudi de nahan* (Crying Out about Land) (土地的呐喊), ed. Pei Fuxiang (裴辅祥). Changchun: Jilin renmin chubanshe, 1996.

Qin Hui (秦晖). *Nongmin Zhongguo: Lishi fansi yu xianshi xuanze* (Peasant China: Historical Reflections and Practical Choices) (农民中国：历史反思与现实选择). Zhengzhou: Henan renmin chubanshe, 2003.

Su Wei (苏伟), Yang Fan (杨帆), and Liu Shiwen (刘士文). *Chongqing moshi* (The Chongqing Model) (重庆模式). Beijing: Zhongguo jingji chubanshe, 2010.

Wang Qichun (王祁春), Li Chenggu (李诚固), and Ding Wanjun (丁万军). "Changchun shi chengshi diyu jiegou tixi yanjiu" (Study on the Urban Area Structure of Changchun City) (长春市城市地域结构体系研究). *Dili kexue* (Scientia Geographica Sinica) (地理科学) 21, no. 1 (February 2001): 81-88.

Wang Yanju (王燕巨) and Yang Xiaoze (杨小泽). *Fangdi chanye jingying guanli shouce* (Real-Estate Industry Management and Operations Handbook) (房地产业经营管理手册). Shanghai: Shanghai renmin chubanshe, 1990.

Wang Yu (王钰). "Dalian shi tudi caizheng de jingji shehui yingxiang jiqi lixing lujing fenxi" (Multidimensional Analysis of the Economic and Social Influence and the Rational Path of Dalian Land Finance) (大连市土地财政的经济社会影响及其理性路径分析). *Dongbei caijing daxue* (Northeast Finance University) (东北财经大学) (November 2012).

Xiao Zongyi (萧宗谊) and Fu Handong (付汉东). "Dalian Shengli qiao bei xiaoqu lishi jianzhu de baohu yu zai kaifa" (Protecting and Reopening Dalian City's Shengli Bridge North Community's Historical Architecture) (大连胜利桥北小区历史建筑的保护与再开发). *Chengshi guihua* (Chengshi guihua) (Urban Planning) (城市规划), no. 4 (1990): 32-35.

Xiu Chengguo (修成国). "Chuangye jiannan baizhan duo: Dalian tudi guanli jishi" (Entrepreneurship is the More Difficult Battle: Notes on Dalian Land Management) (创业艰难百战多：大连土地管理记事). *Zhongguo tudi* (Chinese Land) (中国土地), no. 23 (2008): 60-61.

Xu Guijun (许桂君). "Yong jingying chengshi de linian gaohao dengshi lianghua gongcheng dazao pinpai jielu pinpai guangchang" (An Effective Street-Lighting Campaign to Renovate Famous Streets and Squares) (用经营城市的理念搞好灯饰亮化工程打造品牌街路品牌广场). In *21 shiji Ha'erbin chengshi guihua duice yanjiu*, ed. Yu Binyang, 157-63.

Yang Liu (杨柳). "Jingti tudi jiufen baolihua miaotou" (Guarding against a Trend of Land Dispute Violence) (警惕土地纠纷暴力化苗头). *Liaowang xinwen zhoukan* (Outlook News Weekly) (瞭望新闻周刊) no. 29 (July 2005): 32-33.

Yu Binyang (俞滨洋), ed. *21 shiji Ha'erbin chengshi guihua duice yanjiu* (Research on Harbin City Planning Measures for the Twenty-First Century) (21 世紀哈尔滨城市规;划对策研究). Ha'erbin: Ha'erbin chubanshe, 2002.

(俞滨洋), ed. *Ha'erbin xin shiji chu chengshi guihua zuopin xuanji* (Selected Works on Harbin City Planning at the Beginning of the New Century) (哈尔滨新世纪初城市规;划作品选集). Ha'erbin: Ha'erbin chubanshe, 2002.

Yu Chunlin (郁春林). "Changchun shi Taoyuan lu penghuqu gaijian guihua" (Renovation Plan for the Peach Blossom Road Slums in Changchun City) (长春市桃园路棚户区改建规;划). *Zhuzhai keji* (Housing Science) (住宅科技) no. 8 (1986): 29–31.

Yu Deman (于德满). "Jiakuai kaifaqu jianshe, tansuo chengshi jingying jingyan" (Boosting Construction of Development Zones as a Way of Running Cities) (加快开发区建设, 探索城市经营经验). *Chengshi fazhan yanjiu* (Urban Studies) (城市发展研究) no. S1 (2001): 23–26.

Yu Jianrong (于建嵘). "Dangqian Zhongguo quntixing shijian de zhuyao leixing jiqi jiben tezheng" (Major Types and Basic Characteristics of Mass Incidents in Today's China) (当前中国群体性事件的主要类型及其基本特征). *Zhongguo zhengfa daxue xuebao* (Journal of China University of Political Science and Law) (中国政法大学学报) no. 6 (2009): 114–20.

Yu Yongshun (于永顺), ed. *Zhongguo fangdi chanye yu jinrong fazhan wenti yanjiu* (Research on Problems Related to China's Real-Estate Industry and Financial Development) (中国房地产业与金融发展问题研究). Beijing: Jingji guanli chubanshe, 1995.

"Yuandan xianju" (New Year's Word) (元旦献句). *Dalian ribao* (Dalian Daily) (大连日报), January 1, 1993.

"Zai kaifang zhong zhao zhun Dalian de weizhi" (Searching for Dalian's Place Under Reform) (在开放中找准大连的位置). *Dalian ribao* (Dalian Daily) (大连日报), April 5, 1993.

Zeng Juxin (曾菊新) and Liang Bin (梁斌). "Zhongguo quyu jingji zengzhang bijiao yanjiu" (Comparative Research on Regional Economic Growth in China) (中国区域经济增长比较研究). *Jingji dili* (Economic Geography) (经济地理) no.1 (1994): 16–20.

Zhang Hongbo (张洪波) and Xu Zhenwen (許振文). "Changchun jingji jishu kaifaqu gongye buju yanjiu" (Research on the Industrial Layout in Changchun Economic and Technology Development Zone) (长春经济技术开发区工业布局研究). *Changchun shifan xueyuan xuebao* (Journal of Changchun Teachers' College) (长春师范学院学报) no. 2 (March 2000): 70–77.

Zhang Tianshou (张田收). "Fangdichan da remen" (The Big Start of Real Estate) (房地产大热门). *Dalian ribao* (Dalian Daily) (大连日报), January 1, 1993.

Zhang Yuanduan (张元端), ed. *Zhongguo fangdi chanye qushi* (Trends in Chinese Real Estate) (中国房地产业趋势). Ha'erbin: Ha'erbin chuanbo gongcheng xueyuan chubanshe, 1992.

Zhao Peixing (赵培星), ed. *Zhonggong Heilongjiang jian shi* (Brief History of the Heilongjiang CCP) (中共黑龙江简史). Beijing: Zhongyang wenxian chubanshe, 2003.

Zheng Guo (郑国). *Chengshi fazhan yu guihua* (Urban Development and Planning) (城市发展与规;划). Beijing: Zhongguo renmin daxue chubanshe, 2009.

Zheng Hongliang (郑洪亮). "Tudi guanli zhidu de zhongda tupo" (Major Breakthroughs in the Institutions of Land Management) (土地管理制度的重大突破). *Dalian ribao* (Dalian Daily) (大连日报), June 10, 1992, 3.

Zhongguo chengshi guihua xuehui (China Urban Planning Society) (中国城市规;划学会), ed. *Wushinian huimou: Xin Zhongguo de chengshi guihua* (Looking Back on Fifty Years: Urban Planning in New China) (五十年回眸：新中国的城市规;). Beijing: Shangwu yinshuguan, 1999.

STATISTICAL SOURCES

CEIC. China Premium Database.
China Data Online (China Data Center, University of Michigan).
EPS Net.com, China City Data.

Changchun nianjian, 1988 (Changchun Yearbook, 1988) (长春年鉴, 1988). Changchun: Jilin renmin chubanshe, 1988.
Changchun nianjian, 1989 (Changchun Yearbook, 1989) (长春年鉴, 1989). Changchun: Jilin renmin chubanshe, 1989.
Changchun nianjian, 1991 (Changchun Yearbook, 1991) (长春年鉴, 1991). Changchun: Jilin renmin chubanshe, 1991.
Changchun nianjian, 1993 (Changchun Yearbook, 1993) (长春年检, 1993). Changchun: Jilin renmin chubanshe, 1993.
Changchun nianjian, 1996 (Changchun Yearbook, 1996) (长春年鉴, 1996). Changchun: Jilin renmin chubanshe, 1996.
Changchun nianjian, 1999 (Changchun Yearbook, 1999) (长春年鉴, 1999). Changchun: Jilin renmin chubanshe, 1999.
Changchun nianjian, 2003 (Changchun Yearbook, 2003) (长春年鉴, 2003). Changchun: Jilin renmin chubanshe, 2003.
Changchun nianjian, 2011 (Changchun Yearbook, 2011) (长春年鉴, 2011). Changchun: Jilin renmin chubanshe, 2011.
Changchun tongji nianjian (Changchun Statistical Yearbook) (长春统计年鉴). Beijing: Zhongguo tongji chubanshe. Various years.
Dalian nianjian, 1987–1989 (Dalian Yearbook, 1987–1989) (大连年鉴, 1987–1989). Dalian: Dalian chubanshe, 1990.
Dalian shi nianjian, 2001 (Dalian City Yearbook, 2001) (大连市年鉴, 2001). Beijing: Zhongguo tongji nianjian, 2001.
Dalian tongji nianjian (Dalian Statistical Yearbook) (大连统计年鉴). Dalian: Dalian shi tongjiju. Various years
Dongbei jingjiqu tongji nianjian, 1987 (Northeast Economic Region Statistical Yearbook, 1987) (东北经济区统计年鉴, 1987). Beijing: Zhongguo tongji chubanshe, 1987.
"Guding touzi: Fangdichan" (Fixed Investment: Real Estate) (固定投资:房地产). National Bureau of Statistics (NBS), via CEIC.
Ha'erbin nianjian, 1987 (Harbin Yearbook, 1987) (哈尔滨年鉴, 1987). Ha'erbin: Heilongjiang renmin chubanshe, 1987.
Ha'erbin nianjian, 1988 (Harbin Yearbook, 1988) (哈尔滨年鉴, 1988). Ha'erbin: Heilongjiang renmin chubanshe, 1988.
Ha'erbin nianjian, 1989 (Harbin Yearbook, 1989) (哈尔滨年鉴, 1989). Ha'erbin: Heilongjiang renmin chubanshe, 1989.
Ha'erbin nianjian, 1990 (Harbin Yearbook, 1990) (哈尔滨年鉴, 1990). Ha'erbin: Heilongjiang renmin chubanshe, 1990.

Ha'erbin nianjian, 1992 (Harbin Yearbook, 1992) (哈尔滨年鉴, 1992). Ha'erbin: Ha'erbin nianjianshe, 1992.

Ha'erbin nianjian, 1995 (Harbin Yearbook, 1995) (哈尔滨年鉴, 1995). Ha'erbin: Ha'erbin nianjianshe, 1995.

Ha'erbin nianjian, 1998 (Harbin Yearbook, 1998) (哈尔滨年鉴, 1998). Ha'erbin: Ha'erbin nianjianshe, 1998.

Ha'erbin nianjian, 1999 (Harbin Yearbook, 1999) (哈尔滨年鉴, 1999). Ha'erbin: Ha'erbin nianjianshe, 1999.

Ha'erbin nianjian, 2000 (Harbin Yearbook, 2000) (哈尔滨年鉴, 2000). Ha'erbin: Ha'erbin nianjianshe, 2000.

Ha'erbin shi Daowaiqu shehui jingji fazhan tongji zonghe nianjian, 1978–1987 (Daowai District of Harbin City Social and Economic Development Comprehensive Statistical Yearbook, 1978–1987) (哈尔滨市道外区社会经济发展统计综合年鉴, 1978–1987). Harbin, 1988.

"Ha'erbin shi shangye wangdian jianshe guanli banfa" (Harbin City Measures on Construction Management of Commercial Space) (哈尔滨市商业网点建设管理办法). *Ha'erbin nianjian, 1990.*

Ha'erbin tongji nianjian, 2001 (Harbin Statistical Yearbook, 2001) (哈尔滨统计年鉴, 2001). Ha'erbin: Ha'erbin nianjianshe, 2001.

Ha'erbin tongji nianjian, 2010 (Harbin Statistical Yearbook, 2010) (哈尔滨统计年鉴, 2010). Beijing: Zhongguo tongji chubanshe, 2010.

Heilongjiang jingji tongji nianjian, 1991 (Heilongjiang Economic Statistical Yearbook, 1991) (黑龙江经济统计年鉴, 1991). Ha'erbin: Zhongguo tongji chubanshe, 1991.

Heilongjiang minying jingji nianjian, 2004 (Heilongjiang Province Private Enterprise Yearbook 2004) (黑龙江民营经济年鉴, 2004) Ha'erbin: Heilongjiang renmin chubanshe, 2004,

Jilin tongji nianjian, 1987 (Jilin Statistical Yearbook, 1987) (吉林统计年鉴, 1987). Beijing: Zhongguo tongji chubanshe, 1987.

Laodong gongzi tongji nianbao, 1982 (Labor and Wages Statistical Annual Report, 1982) (劳动工资统计年报, 1982). Ha'erbin: Heilongjiangsheng tongjiju, 1983.

Xin Zhongguo chengshi wushinian, 1949–1998 (Fifty Years of Cities in New China, 1949–1998) (新中国城市五十年, 1949–1998). Beijing: Xinhua chubanshe, 1999.

Zhongguo caizheng nianjian (China Finance Yearbook) (中国财政年鉴). Beijing: Zhongguo caizheng zazhishe. Various years.

Zhongguo chengshi tongji nianjian, 1985 (China Urban Statistical Yearbook, 1985) (中国城市统计年鉴, 1985). Beijing: Xin shijie chubanshe, 1985.

Zhongguo chengshi tongji nianjian, 1990 (China Urban Statistical Yearbook, 1990) (中国城市统计年鉴, 1990). Beijing: Zhongguo tongji chubanshe, 1990.

Zhongguo guding zichan touzi shudian, 1950–2000 (Statistics on Investment in Fixed Assets in China, 1950–2000) (中国固定资产投资数典, 1950–2000). Beijing: Zhongguo tongji chubanshe, 2002.

Zhongguo guotu ziyuan nianjian (China Land and Resources Yearbook) (中国国土资源年检). Beijing: Zhongguo guotu ziyuan nianjian bianjibu. Various years.

Zhongguo laodong tongji nianjian (China Labor Statistical Yearbook) (中国劳动统计年鉴) Beijing: Zhongguo tongji chubanshe. Various years.

ARCHIVES, DOCUMENTS, UNPUBLISHED REPORTS

Changchun City Document 45 (1988)

Changchun shi chengshi guihuaju (Changchun City Urban Planning Bureau) (长春市城市规;划局). "Changchun shi 1985 chengshi zongti guihua fang'an shuoming shu" (Changchun City 1985 Draft Master Draft Explanation Book) (长春市1985城市总体规;划方案说明书). 1986.

Changchun shi chengshi zongti guihua, 1996–2020: Shuoming shu (Changchun Urban Master Plan, 1996–2020: Explanatory Book) (长春市城市总体规;划, 1996–2010: 说明书). 1997.

"Daowaiqu weifang gaizao guihua" (Planning the Renovation of Slum Housing in Daowai) (道外区危房改造规;划). 2000.

Fang Cunzhong. "Liangge kaifaqu cunzai de wenti he jianyi" (Problems in Two Zones and Suggestions) (两个开发区存在的问题和建议). In *Ha'erbin kaifaqu wenxian, 1991–1994* (Documents on the Harbin Development Zone, 1991–1994) (哈尔滨开发区文献, 1991–1994), ed. Ha'erbin kaifaqu guanli weihui (Management Committee of the Harbin Development Zone) (哈尔滨开发区管理委会). HMA F129.935/1-53.

"Ha'erbin dangshi ziliao" (Harbin Party History Materials) (哈尔滨党史资料). Part 3. HMA, D235.351/01-3.

Ha'erbin jingji jishu kaifaqu guanli weiyuanhui (Harbin Economic and Technology Development Zone Management Committee) （哈尔滨经济技术开发区管理委员会）, Ha'erbin gao xin jishu chanye kaifaqu guanli weiyuanhui (Harbin High Technology Park Management Committee) (哈尔滨高新技术产业开发区管理委员会), and Ha'erbin shi chengshi guihua sheji yanjiuyuan (Harbin Urban Planning and Design Institute) （哈尔滨市城市规;划设计研究院）. "Ha'erbin kaifaqu xinqu zongti guihua zhuanti baogao" (Harbin Development Zone New Area Master Plan Report) (哈尔滨开发区新区总体规;划专题报告). December 2004.

"Ha'erbin jingji jishu kaifaqu zongti guihua" (Master Plan of Harbin Economic and Technology Development Zone) (哈尔滨经济技术开发区总体规;划). Ha'erbin: Ha'erbin shi chengshi guihua guanliju, 1984.

Ha'erbin shi chengshi guihuaju (Urban Planning Bureau of Harbin Municipality) (哈尔滨市城市规;划局) and Ha'erbin shi chengshi guihua sheji yanjiuyuan (Urban Planning and Design Research Institute of Harbin Municipality) (哈尔滨市城市规;划设计研究院). *Ha'erbin chengshi zongti guihua (2004–2020): Shuoming shu* (Master Plan of Harbin Municipality, 2004–2020: Manual) (哈尔滨城市总体规;划 [2004–2020]: 说明书). 2004.

Ha'erbin Yamachang Yama fenchen baozha shigu yu jingguo yu chuli" (The Aftermath and Treatment of the Harbin Yamachang Dust Explosion Accident) (哈尔滨亚麻厂亚麻粉尘爆炸事故与经过与处理).

Harbin City Management Department. "Harbin City 1985 Master Plan." 1984. Archives of the Ha'erbin shi chengshi guihua xuehui (Urban Planning Society of Harbin Municipality) (哈尔滨市城市规;划学会).

"Heilongjiangsheng: Chengzhen jumin jiating yici xing ziliao 1984" (Heilongjiang Province: Results from the Inaugural Urban Household Survey of 1984) (黑龙江省：城镇居民家庭一次性资料). HMA C832.35/03.

Heilongjiangsheng kexue xuehui lianhehui (Joint Science Society of Heilongjiang Province) (黑龙江省科学学会联合会), *Heilongjiangsheng: Sheng kexue xuehui lianhehui diwuci daibiaohui* (Heilongjiang Province: Fifth Provincial Joint Science Society Representative Meeting) (黑龙江省: 省科学学会联合会第五次代表会). (097). June 1989. HMA C262.1.

MBIC. "Guanyu xiafang hezuo jingying qiye (minban jiti) he geti gongshang yehu shenpi quanxian de tongzhi" (Notice on the Devolution of Authority Over Registration of Jointly Operated Enterprises and Private Industrial and Commercial Enterprises) (关于下放合作经营企业[民办集体]和个体工商业户审批全县的通知). In *Heilongjiang minying jingji nianjian, 2004*.

MBIC [1980] Document 95. "Guanyu shidang fazhan chengzhen geti gongshang yehu ruogan wenti de guiding" (Some Regulations on the Problems Related to the Appropriate Development of Urban Private Industrial and Commercial Enterprises) (关于适当发展城镇个体工商业户若干问题的规;定). In *Heilongjiang minying jingji nianjian, 2004*.

State Council Document [1992] 62. "Guoyuyuan guanyu fazhan fangdi chanye ruogan wenti de tongzhi" (State Council Communiqué Regarding Issues in Developing the Real-Estate Sector), November 4, 1992, at www.kj2100.com/Html/1992/11/04/201110334737.html, accessed January 28, 2015.

State Council Document [1998] 23. "Guowuyuan guanyu jinyibu shenhua chengzhen zhufang zhidu gaige jiakuai zhufang jianshe de tongzhi" (Notice on Further Deepening Reform in the Urban Housing System and Accelerating Housing Construction) (国务院关于进一步深化城镇住房制度改革加快住房建设的通知), at www.ggj.gov.cn/vfggw/qtfg/200806/t20080610_262964.htm, accessed February 9, 2015.

Wang Shouchuan (王守川). "Kaifaqu yu qiye yidi banqian gaizao yanjiu" (Research on Offsite Relocation of Enterprises in the Development Zone) (开发区与企业异地搬迁改造研究). In *Ha'erbin kaifaqu wenxian, 1991–1994* (Documents on the Harbin Development Zone, 1991–1994) (哈尔滨开发区文献, 1991–1994), ed. Ha'erbin kaifaqu guanli weihui (Management Committee of the Harbin Development Zone) (哈尔滨开发区管理委会). HMA F129.935/1-53.

Wen Shizhen (闻世震). "Zhenxing Liaoning laogongye jidi de silu yu shixian" (Thought and Practice on Revitalizing the Liaoning Industrial Base) (振兴辽宁老工业基地的思路与实现), 2004. Liaoning Provincial Archives.

Index

Printed in the USA
CPSIA information can be obtained
at www.ICGtesting.com
JSHW081301130923
48439JS00001B/25